Historical Association Studie

The Reformation in Ge

Historical Association Studies

General Editors: Muriel Chamberlain, H. T. Dickinson and Joe Smith

Published Titles

China in the Twentieth Century
(second edition)
Paul J. Bailey
*Postwar Japan: 1945 to the Present
Paul J. Bailey
The British Welfare State
John Brown
The Causes of the English Civil War
Norah Carlin
Decolonization: The Fall of the
European Empires (second edition)
M. E. Chamberlain
From Luddism to the First Reform
Bill: Reform in England 1810–1832
J. R. Dinwiddy
The Reformation in Germany
C. Scott Dixon
Radicalism in the English Revolution
1640–1660
F. D. Dow
British Politics Since 1945
(second edition)
David Dutton
The French Revolution
Alan Forrest
Britain and European Cooperation
since 1945

Sean Greenwood
Oliver Cromwell
Peter Gaunt
Occupied France: Collaboration and
Resistance 1940–1944
H. R. Kedward
The Vikings in Britain
Henry Loyn
Appeasement (second edition)
Keith Robbins
The Cold War (second edition)
Joe Smith
*Britain in the 1930s
Andrew Thorpe
The Normans in Britain
David Walker
Bismarck
Bruce Waller
The Russian Revolution 1917–1921
Beryl Williams
The Making of Modern South Africa
(third edition)
Nigel Worden
*Lloyd George
Chris Wrigley

*Out of print titles

The Historical Association, founded in 1906, brings together people who share an interest in, and love for, the past. It aims to further the study and teaching of history at all levels: teacher and student, amateur and professional. This is one of over 100 publications available at preferential rates to members. Membership also includes journals at generous discounts and gives access to courses, conferences, tours and regional and local activities. Full details are available from The Secretary, The Historical Association, 59a Kennington Park Road, London SE11 4JH, telephone: 020 7735 3901.

The Reformation in Germany

C. Scott Dixon

Blackwell
Publishers

Copyright © C. Scott Dixon 2002

The right of C. Scott Dixon to be identified as author of this work has been asserted in accordance with the Copyright, Designs and Patents Act 1988.

First published 2002

2 4 6 8 10 9 7 5 3 1

Blackwell Publishers Ltd
108 Cowley Road
Oxford OX4 1JF
UK

Blackwell Publishers Inc.
350 Main Street
Malden, Massachusetts 02148
USA

British Library Cataloguing in Publication Data

A CIP catalogue record for this book is available from the British Library.

Library of Congress Cataloging-in-Publication Data

Dixon, C. Scott
  The Reformation in Germany / C. Scott Dixon.
    p. cm. – (Historical Association studies)
  Includes bibliographical references and index.
    ISBN 0-631-20252-8 (alk. paper) – ISBN 0-631-20253-6 (pbk. : alk. paper)
    1. Reformation – Germany. 2. Germany – Church history – 16th
  century. I. Title. II. Series.
  BR305.3 .S38 2002
  274.3′06 – dc21

                                                              2001003372

ISBN 0631202528 (hbk) 0631202536 (pbk)

Typeset in 10.5 on 12 pt Times
by Best-set Typesetter Ltd., Hong Kong
Printed in Great Britain by Antony Rowe, Chippenham, Wilts

This book is printed on acid-free paper

Contents

Preface

'In accordance with our project,' wrote Martin Luther in his tract *To the Christian Nobility of the German Nation* (1520), 'I have put together a few paragraphs on the amelioration of the condition of Christendom. I intend the writing for the consideration of Christians belonging to the ruling classes in Germany. I hope that God will grant help to his Church through the laity, since the clergy, who should be the more appropriate persons, have grown quite indifferent.' With these words Luther made explicit a relationship which had characterized the Reformation from the very outset: the close association between the evangelical movement and the German laity. Luther spoke of the ruling classes – the princes, nobles and magistrates of the realm – and in the end the fate of the Reformation, as he recognized, would be in the hands of these members of the political elite. But in the beginning the movement provoked a very broad response; it was not just the ruling classes that were caught up in the Luther affair, but a vast multitude of urban and rural parishioners as well. The first supporters of the Reformation came from every walk of life, from wealthy merchants to impoverished peasants, city secretaries to soldiers, urban cobblers to imperial knights.

The aim of this short book is to analyse the nature of the relationship between the Reformation and the German people. As in most Reformation histories, the point of origin is the Luther affair (*causa Lutheri*), and more precisely the famous posting of the theses on the door of the Castle Church in Wittenberg; but once this familiar story has been told, the main focus of the narrative moves away from the religious dialogue to the spread, reception and impact of the evangelical movement in the German lands. In essence, this work sets out to examine how the Reformation movement was experienced by the ruling elite and the subject population in the communes and territories of the realm. How was the message broadcast to the faithful in the towns and the villages? How was evangelical theology understood by the laity? How did the parishioners, urban and rural alike, react to the movement? Questions of this kind necessarily force the historian to extend the range of analysis from the local or personal dimensions of history to the broader patterns of social, political and cultural development. Thus this work also examines the extent to which the Reformation effected a change in the constitution of the German lands in the sixteenth century. What was the impact of the movement on the political culture of the age? How was the complexion of the Holy Roman Empire affected by the onset of religious division? What was the legacy of confessional change in the social and cultural spheres? Throughout the text the narrative tries to maintain points of contact between the Reformation movement, broadly conceived, and the level at which it was experienced.

In many ways this book is a synthesis of recent work in the field. The concerns at the heart of it are a reflection of some general trends in the discipline. Of course, not all of the themes are new, as the concluding chapter on Reformation histories makes clear; but the narrative does rely on recent secondary works to tell its story, and wherever appropriate the most important insights and advances in modern Reformation scholarship have been drawn into the work. However, there is no explicit or extended dialogue with current trends in historiography. Readers interested in a survey of that kind may consult the study by Robert W. Scribner (*The German Reformation*, 1986), a work which identifies many of the themes that have informed the narrative of this book. Finally, due to limitations of space, it has not been possible to draw on the full range of related scholarship. I hope my colleagues will forgive me for relying so heavily on their work without always finding room for everything on the page.

Chronologies

Political Chronology of the Reformation in the Holy Roman Empire (1521–1555)

(These four chronologies were compiled by Mark Greengrass; taken from Mark Greengrass and C. Scott Dixon, *The Protestant Reformation: Religious Change and the People of Sixteenth Century Europe*. TLTP History Courseware Consortium, CD-ROM, Glasgow, 1999.)

Jan.– May 1521	Diet of Worms.
Nov. 1522– Feb. 1523	Diet of Nuremberg. The Estates were dominated by proposed legislation to regulate the Empire's economic life and institutions. Negotiations with the nuncio Francesco Chieregato, who sought the enforcement of the decision against Luther at the diet of Worms, were met by counter-demands from the Estates for a 'free Christian Council'. The recess of 9 February confirmed this demand.
1522–3	The 'Knights' War'. The free imperial knights, part of the independent Estates of the Empire, had already proved a disruptive (even bandit) element in the peace of the Empire in the 1510s. Led by Franz von Sickingen (1481–1523), an able mercenary captain, they formed a 'fraternal association' in Franconia and the Rhineland, and mobilized forces against the Bishops of Bamberg and Würzburg. They were particularly provoked by a law, part of the recess of the diet of Worms, which made it criminal for a nobleman to enter into a feud with another member of the Empire. The revolt certainly exploited elements of the instability caused by the religious crisis and von Sickin-

gen was supported by the Humanist noble Ulrich von Hutten. It did not take much effort, however, for the princely armies of the Swabian League to repress the revolt, razing the castles of those who had taken part.

1524–5	Great Peasants' War.

June–Aug. 1526 Diet of Speyer. It took place in the shadow of the creation of the defensive league at Torgau and the recent defeat of the Peasants' War. The emperor proposed to eradicate heresy and rebellion and enforce the edict of Worms against Luther. The princes feared for their privileges and, by the recess of 27 August, the diet declared that each Estate was to deal with religious problems on a territorial basis until the meeting of a general council or national assembly.

Mar.–Apr. 1529 (Second) diet of Speyer. Catholics predominated among the Estates. The imperial proposition demanded the revocation of the previous Speyer recess and the enforcement of the edict of Worms wherever possible. A majority of the Estates agreed and banned any further religious novelties. The recess of 22 April banned the introduction of Zwinglianism in the Empire and condemned to death anyone convicted of adult baptism. In territories where Luther's teaching had made inroads, the celebration of the Mass was to continue. This was declared unacceptable by a minority of Estates who produced a minority decision.

19 July 1529 The publication of the minority decision or protest (hence the term 'Protestants'), signed by a small number of princes and 14 cities of the Empire. It declared that a decision of a majority could not annul a unanimous decision (the recess of Speyer of 1526) and that decisions of conscience in religious matters were between an individual and God. The evangelical Estates of southern German cities, where Zwinglianism had gained adherents, found it impossible to join the protest.

Apr.–Sep. 1530 Diet of Augsburg. The diet was held in the presence of Emperor Charles V whose propositions announced his intention to abolish religious diversity in the Empire but guaranteeing everyone a fair hearing. His chancellor asked for written statements on the religious question. The Protestants responded with the Articles of Torgau, which dealt mainly with questions of ecclesiastical organization. Philipp Melanchthon, however, who attended the diet, decided to include a statement of doctrine among the documentation. On 11 May he sent it to Luther for his endorsement. It was presented under the signature of seven princes and two cities to the Estates on 25 June and became known as the Confession of Augsburg.

A further confession, known as the Tetrapolitana and composed by Wolfgang Capito and Martin Bucer, was also submitted. Both statements were rejected by the assembled Catholic theologians (in the Confutatio or 'Refutation' of the Augsburg Confession). The recess of the diet of Augsburg (22 September) required the enforcement of the edict of Worms throughout the Empire, the suppression of all heretical innovations and the compliance of Protestants to these terms by 15 April 1531. Failure to comply would result in the use of force and prosecution before the Imperial Chamber Court.

Feb. 1531   Emergence of the Schmalkaldic League of Protestant Estates of the Empire. In response to the recess at Augsburg, Landgrave Philipp of Hesse and Elector Johann of Saxony, the leaders of the Protestant princes in the Empire, convened a meeting at the town of Schmalkalden (Thuringia) in December 1530. The original members of the League included seven north German princes and the cities of Bremen and Magdeburg. The League later saw many new adherents and, in the end, only the city of Nuremberg and the principality of Brandenburg-Ansbach among the Protestant territorial entities of the Empire stood aloof from it. By its charter, any attack on one member was an attack on all and should be resisted by the full force of the League. Each member was assessed in order to provide a substantial military force of 10,000 infantry and 2,000 cavalry. The League adopted the Augsburg Confession as its religious statement and attempted to frustrate efforts to use the Imperial Chamber Court against it. It remained the major Protestant confessional bloc in the Empire until the outbreak of the Schmalkaldic War in 1546.

1532   'Peace' of Nuremberg offered by Emperor Charles to the princes of the Schmalkaldic League. Cases due to be heard by the Imperial Chamber Court were rescinded. No action would be taken against Protestant princes by the Emperor until a meeting of a general Church council.

1540–1   Colloquies of Hagenau (1540); Worms (1540–1); Regensburg (1541) failed to resolve religious differences in the Holy Roman Empire.

1546–7   The Schmalkaldic War, in which Emperor Charles secured the alliance of the Duke of Bavaria and the Protestant Duke Moritz of Saxony, promising him the electoral title. Although the Protestant League had superior numbers of troops, they had difficulties in co-ordinating and paying them. When Duke Moritz invaded Electoral Saxony, the Elector retreated to defend his territories, splitting the Protestant forces.

24 Apr. 1547   Elector Johann Friedrich of Saxony captured and defeated. His title and much of his territory passed to Moritz of Saxony by the Wittenberg capitulation of the following month. Philipp of Hesse also surrendered, leaving only Magdeburg and some other northern cities prepared to continue resistance.

1547–May 1548   The so-called 'armed diet' of Augsburg. Emperor Charles' reform of the Empire resisted as an infringement of its constitution.

15 May 1548   The 'Augsburg Interim' decreed by the Emperor at the close of the diet of Augsburg. It was designed as an interim compromise settlement of religious questions, imposed by the Emperor, which would stand until the conclusions of the Church council convened at Trent. The compromise concentrated on practical matters of religious worship and ritual, rather than doctrine. Concessions were made to Protestants over married priests and communion in two kinds to the laity. Images were to be retained but not venerated. Feast days in the Church calendar were retained. A clause on confession suggested some acceptance of justification theology. The Interim made no mention of ecclesiastical properties.

1548–1551   Various Protestant elements, led by the city of Magdeburg, rejected the Interim. Some Protestant pastors chose to resign their posts rather than operate under the compromise which it required of them. The pastors of the city of Magdeburg began a propaganda campaign against the Interim and refused to accept it within the walls of the city. This resulted in a prolonged siege and the Magdeburg Confession.

1552   Second Schmalkaldic War in which the Protestant princes, led by Duke Moritz of Saxony and enjoying the support of Henri II of France, resisted the Emperor. Invasion of the three bishoprics of Metz, Toul and Verdun by French forces, followed by a military stalemate.

1555   Peace of Augsburg.

The Indulgences Dispute, 1514–1518

9 Mar. 1514	Albrecht von Brandenburg elected Cardinal-Archbishop of Mainz.
31 Mar. 1515	Pope Leo X issued Albrecht with a Bull giving him authority to offer the indulgence (the proceeds of which would rebuild the basilica of St Peter's in Rome).
22 Jan. 1517	The Dominican Johann Tetzel entered the service of Albrecht as the agent for the indulgence in the province of Magdeburg.
24 Feb.	Luther criticized indulgences in a sermon.
Apr.	Tetzel in Jüterbog on the borders with electoral Saxony.
4 Sep.	Luther published his *Disputation against Scholastic Theology*.
31 Oct.	Luther invited a debate over indulgences in his 95 Theses and wrote to Cardinal-Archbishop Albrecht about the false notions which were being spread abroad about the benefits to be gained from purchasing an indulgence. He enclosed a copy of his theses.
Nov.	Publication of the 95 Theses without Luther's involvement or consent; the publication was a success and generated widespread popular comment.
13 Dec.	Albrecht reported that he had forwarded a copy of the 95 Theses to Rome with an accompanying denunciation of Luther.

Jan. 1518	Tetzel replied by defending 106 theses (prepared by Conrad Wimpina, professor of theology at the University of Frankfurt an der Oder) at a meeting of the Dominican Order of Saxony.
Feb.	Luther announced that he would publish a further explanation of his theses.
Mid-Mar.	Wittenberg students burned copies of the Tetzel/Wimpina theses. Luther preached and published his *Sermon on Indulgence and Grace.*
24 Mar.	Luther reported seeing a copy of Johannes Eck's attack on him in the treatise *Obelisci* ('Obelisks') in which Luther's theses were described as 'false', 'impudent' and 'Bohemian poison' (i.e. full of the heresy of Jan Hus). Luther responded shortly afterwards with his own *Asterisci* ('Asterisks').
Apr.	Tetzel published his extensive *Rebuttal of a Presumptuous Sermon Containing Twenty Erroneous Articles on Papal Indulgences . . .*
9 Apr.– 15 May	Luther attended a chapter meeting of the Augustinian order in Heidelberg and defended his theological stance; Tetzel issued a further set of 50 theses raising (and defending) papal authority.
May	Karlstadt issued 380 theses against Tetzel and Eck without Luther's prior knowledge. These defended the position that the judgement of an individual Christian in matters of faith (when based on scripture) should, if necessary, take precedence over all other forms of authority – a more extreme position than Luther himself was yet prepared to assume.
30 May	Luther dedicated his *Explanations of the Ninety-Five Theses* to Pope Leo X (published in August). He amplified his views of papal authority, distinguishing between the person of a pope and the office of the papacy. Individual popes were men who could err in matters of faith and morals. Only a universal council of the Church could declare a new article of faith. Accepted articles of faith were to be established on the basis of a consensus of authority established between holy scripture, the Church Fathers, and the canons and decrees of the papacy. He hoped for a just verdict from Pope Leo, whom (unlike some of his advisors and flatterers), he admired and

respected. Luther also wrote a letter to Johannes von Staupitz, vicar-general of the reformed Augustinian Order of Germany, asking him to present the case favourably and continue his support for him.

June   Luther published his *A Defence of the Sermon Concerning Indulgence and Grace.*

The Broadening Lutheran Conflict, 1518–1519

26 Apr. 1518	The Dominican Thomas de Vio (Cardinal Cajetan) nominated papal legate to the imperial diet at Augsburg.
c.May	At the order of Pope Leo, the summons of Luther to Rome was prepared by the legal officer of the papal curia, Jerome Ghinucci; a theological response to Luther was commissioned from the official papal theologian, Sylvester Prierias (Sylvester Mazzolini), entitled *Dialogue Concerning Papal Power against the Presumptuous Positions of Martin Luther*. The response concentrated on four premises relating to Church power and infallibility as the basis on which to reject substantial elements of Luther's 95 Theses.
c.June	Luther preached his sermon *On the Power of Excommunication* (published at the end of August).
July	The summons to Rome and Prierias' *Dialogue* were forwarded to Cajetan in Augsburg to be sent on to Luther in Wittenberg. Luther responded by asking for advice from Georg Spalatin, the private secretary of Friedrich the Wise.
5 Aug.	Emperor Maximilian denounced Luther as a heretic in a letter composed by Cajetan. He offered to enforce ecclesiastical sanctions against Luther.
8 Aug.	Luther petitioned Elector Friedrich (attending the diet of Augsburg) to see that his case was heard in Germany, rather than in Rome.
23 Aug.	Pope Leo directed Cajetan (in the papal letter *Postquam ad aures*) to demand a recantation from Luther and to organize his arrest and deliverance to Rome if he refused.

End Aug.   Luther issued a *Response* to Prierias' *Dialogue* which reinforced his position on authority in the Church.

Sep.   Elector Friedrich persuaded Cajetan to treat Luther in a gentle fashion and not to arrest him. Friedrich departed from Augsburg on 22 September and Luther left Wittenberg for his meeting with Cajetan on 26 September.

12–20 Oct.   Luther in Augsburg. According to Luther's brief account, Cajetan received him 'with kindness'. Although specifically enjoined not to enter into debate with Luther, Cajetan responded to Luther's request to be shown specifically where he was in error. He cited Thesis 58 (and presented it as in contradiction to a papal decree) and Thesis 7 (where Luther had asserted that the person about to receive the sacrament of penance should trust with certainty in the words of absolution), arguing that anyone about to receive the sacrament remained uncertain of obtaining grace. Luther replied to the former by saying that the papal decree was against 'the unanimous opinion of the whole Church' – i.e. the consensus of authorities in the Church. On the latter point, Luther replied with a summary of his understanding of how faith alone works to justify humankind: 'No disposition [on any individual's behalf] can make them worthy, no work can make them fit for the sacrament, but only faith. For only faith in the word of Christ justifies, makes alive, makes one worthy and prepares one. Anything else is an exercise in presumption or despair.' Cajetan accepted a written statement from Luther, who placed a legally registered document on the cathedral door in Augsburg before he left, resubmitting his case to Pope Leo, 'a badly-informed pope who needs to be better informed'.

23 Oct.   Returning through Nuremberg, Luther was shown a copy of the papal brief to Cajetan (*Postquam ad aures*) which, along with the effect of the encounter at Augsburg, made him more pessimistic about papal intentions. By the end of December, Luther began to voice his fears that the Antichrist might be at work amidst the Roman hierarchy.

25 Oct.   Cajetan issued a demand to Elector Friedrich the Wise to hand Luther over to Rome or to banish him from his territories.

9 Nov.   Pope Leo issued the bull *Cum postquam*, drafted by Cajetan, which reinforced Catholic teaching on indulgences.

Nov.	Friedrich the Wise forwarded the ultimatum of Cajetan to Luther for comments; Luther prepared an account of the meeting with Cajetan for publication (the *Acta Augustana*) and appealed to a legitimately convened universal council of the Church.
Early Dec.	Although Luther expected the worst, Friedrich the Wise refused Cajetan's ultimatum and declined to banish Luther from Saxony.
Dec.–Jan. 1519	Attempted mediation between the papacy and Elector Friedrich the Wise by Karl von Miltitz (*c*.1490–1529), a Saxon nobleman and papal chamberlain.
Jan. 1519	Emperor Maximilian I died; the papacy suspended further attempts to enforce the summons against Luther.
Mar.	Johann Eck issued a set of 13 Theses, revising those which he had issued against Karlstadt six months previously, and challenging Luther to a disputation at Leipzig.
May	Luther responded with a set of 13 counter-propositions, the last of which (Proposition 13) was expounded in published form before the Leipzig disputation. In it Luther maintained the view that only 'the most intemperate decrees of the Roman pontiffs issued these last 400 years prove that the Roman church is superior to all other; against these stand the accepted history of the last 1,500 years, the text of divine scripture and the decree of the council of Nicea, the holiest of all councils.' He stopped short of rejecting all papal authority but drew on his intensive recent study of canon law to reject the claim that the Bishop of Rome was head of the Church by divine right. Luther displayed a remarkable resilience, despite the continuing tension; 'I fear neither the pope nor the name of the pope, much less those little popes and puppets.'
24 June	Karlstadt, Luther and the Wittenberg delegates arrived in Leipzig for the disputation.
27 June	Debate between Eck and Karlstadt began.
28 June	Charles V elected Holy Roman Emperor in Frankfurt. The papacy continued to suspend further efforts to enforce the summons against Luther until the end of the year.
4–14 July	Eck and Luther debate. Eck revived the familiar accusation that Luther was a new Hus (and Wyclif). Luther replied by affirming that some of the articles of belief of Hus and the Bohemians were 'most Christian and evan-

gelical' and could not be condemned. This enabled Eck to challenge Luther to say whether a council of the Church (such as the Council of Constance (1414–18) which had condemned them both) could also err. Luther was forced to admit that he regarded scripture as the norm by which other authorities within the church should be judged.

July/Aug.   Accounts of the debate were published both by Melanchthon (on behalf of Luther and Karlstadt) and by Eck himself. Eck declared Luther a heretic and invited the Universities of Paris and Erfurt to judge the matter in his favour. Eck wrote 17 treatises against Luther over the next few months to publicize the dangers Luther represented.

30 Aug.   Luther condemned by the University of Cologne.

Early Oct.   Luther received a copy of Jan Hus' treatise on *The Church from Prague*. He declared that he found himself in agreement with Hus over a wider area than he had declared at Leipzig. 'Up to now I have unwittingly taught and held all the beliefs of Jan Hus. Johannes von Staupitz has equally taught them without being aware of it. In short, we are all Hussites without knowing it. Even Paul and Augustine are in reality Hussites.'

Oct.   Luther's sermon *On the Sacrament of Penance* – the first of three important statements of the impact of his thinking for the sacraments of the Church.

7 Nov.   Luther condemned by the University of Louvain.

9 Nov.   Luther's sermon *On the Sacrament of Baptism*.

Dec.   Luther's sermon *On the Blessed Sacrament of the Holy and True Body of Christ* – banned in ducal Saxony when it was published. The effects of the widening controversy were felt by Luther to be at once alarming and energizing; in January of the following year he wrote 'This tribulation does not frighten me at all, but it fills the sails of my heart with an incredible wind . . . We are completely unaccustomed to the Christian life. Therefore, let it be. The more powerfully they rise up, the more securely I laugh at them. I am resolved to fear nothing.'

Luther's Excommunication, 1520–1521

9 Jan. 1520   The case against Luther reopened at Rome.

early 1520   Expanded German version of Luther's sermon *On the Power of Excommunication* published – including warnings about the 'tyrants' who 'today' unjustly make use of the power of excommunication – Luther's willingness to write in German and reach a different lay audience became noticeable in 1520.

1 Feb.   Pope Leo appointed the first commission to investigate Luther's writings and prepare the case against him.

11 Feb.   Appointment of second commission to investigate Luther's writings.

Feb.   Luther read an edition of Lorenzo Valla's *Donation of Constantine*, which demonstrated that a key document in the papal claims to temporal power was a forgery. Valla was a noted Italian fifteenth-century Humanist whose philology (i.e. his textual criticism) had much impressed Erasmus. 'I am so tormented, I can hardly doubt that the pope is properly that Antichrist which by common consent the world anticipates.'

Mar.   Eck arrived in Rome and played a prominent part in the drafting of the papal bull of excommunication.

26 Mar.   Luther responded to the condemnations of errors in his works issued by the Universities of Louvain and Cologne.

Apr.   Appointment of a third commission (including Eck) in Rome to prepare the text of a bull against Luther.

May–June   Luther published his *Treatise on Good Works in German*. As against all the worthless good works of satisfaction and ceremonies, Luther argued that genuine good works were the commandments of God which can only be observed when the greatest travail of all (faith) is at work. The text was intended for ordinary laymen and was dedicated to the brother of Elector Friedrich, Duke Johann of Saxony: 'Would to God that . . . I had brought about the conversion of one lay person.'

May   Luther published his short manuals of evangelical faith for the laity in German: *A Short Form of the Ten Commandments, A Short Form of the Creed* and *A Short Form of the Lord's Prayers*. The first provided a succinct evocation of our human sinfulness. The second showed where the remedy was to be found. The third showed how to obtain it. The works went through numerous editions in 1520 alone and formed the basis for Lutheran liturgical developments later on.

20 May   The Roman curia sent an ultimatum to Elector Friedrich the Wise.

June   Luther published a treatise in German, entitled *The Papacy at Rome*. It further publicized his attack on the claim of the papacy to be the head of the Church by divine right.

15 June   The papal bull against Luther (*Exsurge Domine*) was promulgated. It threatened him with excommunication if he did not recant and seek pardon within 60 days of its publication in Saxony. The Church must 'rise up' to protect the vineyard of the Lord from the 'wild boar' which has invaded it. Two days later, Eck (promoted to papal nuncio) and Jerome Aleander were appointed to see to its distribution in Germany.

18 Aug.   Luther's *Address to the Christian Nobility* appeared. Luther's most popular treatise in 1520. He wrote it at the behest of the legal officers of the Elector and dedicated it to one of them, a close colleague and supporter, Nikolaus von Amsdorf. The citadel of ecclesiastical reformation was protected by three walls behind which the 'Romanists' and 'papists' had protected themselves. When they are attacked with force, they claim that spiritual power has precedence over the secular arm. When scripture is used against them, they say that only the pope

can interpret scripture. When they have been threatened with a council, they claim that only the pope could summon a council. If the 'papists' do not surrender these outer defences, they are the agents of Antichrist. A radical reformation was necessary, beginning with the worldly pretensions of the pope. The pope should not be the representative of the glorified Christ but of the crucified Christ, weeping and praying daily for the toils of Christendom. The practice of indulgences, which deceived and exploited poor, simple people, proved that the pope was the Antichrist. 'Hear this, pope, not most holy, but most sinful: God will destroy your see straight from heaven and plunge it into the depths of hell'.

Sep.   The papal bull published by Eck in Meissen and Brandenburg; Aleander published it in Cologne and Antwerp. The 60-day 'period of grace' given to Luther in the bull began. Luther's supporters published it in Saxony as a way of gaining support for Luther.

Aug.–Sep.   Luther wrote his treatise *A Prelude on the Babylonian Captivity of the Church*. The Church was subjected to the tyranny of the 'papists' and needed to be liberated.

The papacy was the equivalent of the kingdom of Babylon. The entire sacramental fabric of the Church is the instrument of its tyranny and its tyrants insisted that they were above criticism. 'Although they are wolves, they wish to be regarded as shepherds; although they are Antichrists, they wish to be honoured as Christ. For this liberty and awareness alone I cry out.' The treatise ended with a defiant ultimatum; 'Because few know this glory of baptism and joy of Christian liberty (nor can they know it owing to the tyranny of the pope), I hear and now liberate myself and redeem my conscience, and I charge the pope and all papists that, unless they lift their own laws and traditions and restore to the churches of Christ the liberty which is theirs and see that this liberty is taught, they are guilty of all the souls which perish in this miserable captivity and the papacy is indeed nothing but the kingdom of Babylon and the true Antichrist.'

Oct.   Bull received in Wittenberg; Elector Friedrich the Wise and Emperor Charles V confer in Cologne cathedral.

Nov.   Friedrich met the papal nuncios at Cologne and refused to surrender Luther.

Nov.	Luther's treatise on *The Freedom of a Christian* appeared in German and Luther appealed for the summoning of a general council of the Church.
10 Dec.	Luther burnt the bull *Exsurge Domine* and other works in Wittenberg.
27 Dec.	Luther published his treatise on *Why the Books of the Pope and His Disciples Were Burned* – in effect a 'counter-bull' in which Luther selected 30 texts from canon law ('the pope's own books') as damnable.
23 Jan. 1521	Luther's excommunication formally pronounced in Rome in the bull *Decet Romanum Pontificem*.
27 Jan.	Opening session of the imperial diet at Worms.
Feb.	Artist Lucas Cranach prepared the woodcuts for his *Passional of Christ and the Antichrist*, a sequence of 13 twin images, illustrating the contrast between Christ and the pope and based on Luther's *Why the Books of the Pope and His Disciples Were Burned*.
6 Mar.	Luther was summoned to appear at Worms by Emperor Charles V.
15 Apr.	The theological faculty of the University of Paris (the Sorbonne) condemned the writings of Luther.
16 Apr.	Luther arrived in Worms.
17–18 Apr.	Luther appeared before the diet and presented a speech.
24–25 Apr.	Negotiations between Luther and representatives of the diet.
26 Apr.	Luther left Worms.
4 May	Luther was 'kidnapped' by agents of Elector Friedrich the Wise and taken to the Wartburg Castle (near Eisenach), where he remained until 1 March 1522.
8 May	Emperor Charles V placed Luther under the ban of the Empire.
26 May	Emperor Charles V published the edict of Worms against Luther.
29 Sep.	Luther's supporters in the Augustinian cloister at Wittenberg decided to discontinue the traditional celebration of the Mass and Luther reinforced their decision with a treatise on *The Misuse of the Mass* which he

dedicated to them (published in November): 'how difficult it is to call back a conscience dulled by long acquain-
tance with impiety to the wholesome knowledge of piety.'

Nov.   Luther's treatise *On Monastic Vows* dedicated to his
              father.

1 Dec.   Pope Leo died in Rome.

25 Dec.   Karlstadt celebrated an 'evangelical' eucharist in place of
              the Mass in Wittenberg cathedral against the express wish
              of Elector Friedrich the Wise.

1

Germany on the Eve of Reformation

When the Habsburg Emperor Maximilian I died on 12 January 1519, rumours were rife that ships were moving down the Rhine with sacks of French gold tied to their hulls. Denied bills of exchange by the German bankers, agents of the French monarch were forced to such desperate measures in order to ensure that their king, Francis I, had enough ready wealth at his disposal to contest the pending imperial election. Opposing Francis I was Maximilian's grandson Charles, Duke of Burgundy and King of Spain, whose agents, while conceding that 'these devils of Frenchmen scatter gold in all directions,' had managed to win most of the seven electors over to the Habsburg candidate using similar methods of bribes and benefices (Knecht, 1994, p. 166). Other potentates had come forward, including Henry of England and Friedrich the Wise of Saxony, but ultimately the imperial election crystallized into a contest between the Valois king of France and the Habsburg heir Charles of Ghent. And it was an event of profound importance, for in essence it was a struggle between the two most powerful sovereigns in Europe for rule over one of the largest empires of the age. All of the major European sovereigns followed the election with great interest, including the Medici Pope Leo X, who, fearing the King of Spain more than the King of France, sided with Francis I. But an imperial election was not decided by foreign powers. The electors of the Holy Roman Empire would choose the next king, and in the end Charles was elected unanimously because it was thought that the Habsburg was the best choice for the German lands. The King of France, it was believed, would not respect the liberties of the Empire, and no internal candidate had enough personal might to command the realm. As the Archbishop of Mainz observed, the Empire was too weak and exhausted to preserve itself, and as no German prince had the power or the wealth to shoulder the burdens, it was necessary to elect a sovereign who was feared (Kohler, 1999, p. 68). For these reasons the electors that gathered on 28 June 1519 at Frankfurt am Main chose the Habsburg sovereign as the next King of the Romans and, in imitation of Charlemagne, crowned him in the city of Aachen in the following year.

On his election the Habsburg candidate became Emperor Charles V. As a ruler over a dominion, no other European sovereign of the age could claim to be his equal. 'Sire,' wrote his Grand Chancellor Mercurino Gattinara, 'God has been very merciful to you: he has raised you above all the Kings and princes of Christendom to a power such as no sovereign has enjoyed since your ancestor Charles the Great. He has set you on the way towards a world monarchy, towards the uniting of all Christendom under a single shepherd' (Brandi, 1965, p. 112). In part this was the rhetoric of Empire, and few spoke so eloquently on the theme as Gattinara; but for many of Europe's rulers it must have seemed a fairly realistic assessment. In 1506 Philip the Fair of Burgundy died, thus leaving the possessions of his Burgundian house to his son Charles. In addition to a claim to the duchy of Burgundy (in French hands since 1477), the holdings included Franche-Comté and the provinces which came to be known as the Netherlands (including the duchies of Luxembourg and Brabant, the counties of Flanders, Holland, Zeeland and Hainault, and a host of smaller lordships). Ten years later, on the death of his grandfather Ferdinand of Aragon, and with his mother Joanna of Castile unfit to rule, Charles inherited Castile and Aragon and thus the kingdom of Spain. Castile also secured him sovereignty over much of the New World, while the Aragonese empire brought with it Sardinia, Sicily, Naples and the Balearic islands. Finally, when his grandfather Maximilian I died in 1519, Charles added the Habsburg dynastic lands of Austria, a stretch of territory that ran into parts of southern Germany and the Tyrol. Moreover, once he had become the German king and future emperor, he could number the largest realm in Christendom among his already extensive domains.

In the year when Charles was elected (1519), the core area of the Empire comprised the German-speaking heartlands (roughly equivalent to modern-day Germany and Austria), but the realm also reached north-west to the Netherlands, further north to the regions of Holstein, Dithmarschen, Frisia and the Baltic lands of the Teutonic Order, east to Brandenburg, Pomerania, the kingdom of Bohemia (which encompassed Moravia, Silesia and Lusatia) and the Austrian lands (Austria, the Tyrol, Styria, Carinthia, Carniola), while to the south parts of northern Italy belonged to the Empire, as did the lands of modern Switzerland. Some of these frontier regions had very loose relations with the Empire. The states of northern Italy, the Kingdom of Bohemia and the Swiss lands were in effect independent powers, while imperial sovereignty was very weak in the Netherlands and the lands of the Teutonic Order. But it was a massive realm nonetheless, and the crowning glory for Charles of Ghent. A few weeks after the election Gattinara suggested that in future all official documentation should lead with the following formula: 'King of the Romans, elected Roman Emperor, semper augustus'.

By the late fifteenth century the Empire had effectively contracted to a core of German territories. The sources begin to speak of the Holy Roman Empire of the *German Nation*, even if the pluralized designation 'the German lands' was still common parlance. The ambiguity is understandable, for Germany was far from a unified country (Scott, 1998, pp. 337–66). Geography could not offer a precise definition. Well into the sixteenth century Alsatian Humanists continued to debate the contours of Germania, and neither the histories nor the atlases of the day could agree on the details. Even the cartographer Abraham Ortelius, a precise and exacting man, admitted that the dimensions escaped him. Nor was language much of a guide, even if the reference to the German tongue (*Gezünge*) was at times taken as synonymous with nation. The lands were divided by dialects, with some strands of High German and Low German mutually incomprehensible. Against this, as we will see, was a maturing sense of nationalism, part political and part historical in inspiration, but the most articulate notion of political identity was still tied to the doctrine of the *translatio imperii*, the belief – indeed, the foundation idea of Charlemagne's dominion – that the Empire had been created in order to protect and oversee the Christian commonwealth. Repeated attacks from the Hussites and the Turks in the fifteenth century strengthened the conviction that this was a specifically *German* duty, but it remained a very vague and abstract vision at a time when an inclusive sense of identity was evolving in other parts of Europe. Indeed, even in the Empire itself it was something of an unnatural notion, for the real thrust of state development and political solidarity was located at the territorial level. Yet the two ideas of Germany made up its national character, and its history was a dialogue between these two conceits.

Medieval emperors believed that they had been elected to rule alongside the papacy in preservation of the Christian faith. The ideal purpose of their rule was the religious and political unity of Christendom. With this idea guiding their actions, it is little wonder that many of them considered the interests and the integrity of the German lands as secondary to the idea of empire. History is replete with examples of kings who neglected Germany in order to pursue broader ambitions (Heer, 1995, pp. 94–175). A quick survey of some fifteenth-century monarchs will make the point: Sigismund, the last of the Luxemburgs, spent little more than two years of his twenty-seven-year reign in the German lands. He was consumed with foreign affairs, especially the politics of his kingdom of Hungary. Friedrich III, for many the founder of Habsburg world power, spent most of his time and energy consolidating his Austrian inheritance. During his reign there were two separate royal chanceries, one in Austria and one for the imperial lands. It was Friedrich who once scribbled in his notebook the cryptic monogram AEIOU for the Latin phrase *Austriae est imperare orbi universo* – 'all the world is subject to Austria.' Maximilian I, the grandfather of Charles V, patterned his rule on that of Charlemagne, and he still believed that the primary task of the emperor was to defend the Christian commonwealth. He never acquired a command of German, though he knew seven languages, and his main interest in the land was always financial: he needed money to pursue his imperial ambitions.

The German Estates, in contrast, especially the electors and the powerful secular princes, were more concerned with the preservation of peace and order than the foreign policy of their elected king. Moreover, by the late fifteenth century the imperial office was explicitly associated with the German Nation, and the Estates were naturally suspicious of any king who threatened the traditional liberties of the realm or used imperial resources for dynastic ends. The summit of this mistrust was reached during the reign of Charles V, when the Catholic emperor was accused of scheming to reduce the German princes to a state of slavery. In part it was a battle of conscience, for by this stage the Reformation had polarized the Empire. Yet it was also a question of German liberty, now categorically contrasted with imperial ambition. Indeed, it was the Catholic chancellor of Bavaria, Leonhard von Eck, who warned the princes that 'nothing less than a monarchy' was the ultimate aim of the emperor and his councillors. 'Therefore it is crucial for the German princes that they keep an eye on how things develop, lest one after the other are swallowed up, destroyed, and hunted down' (Schmidt, 1999, p. 85).

The political constitution of the Empire reflected the complex history of the realm. In essence it was a community of feudal ties (*Lehensverband*) and thus a matrix of dependency and obligation (though there were enclaves of communal rule in some of the towns and villages). At the peak of the feudal pyramid was the emperor, and all other powers in the realm derived their sovereignty from him. At certain levels, there was scope for common action – between princes, between cities, or between sympathetic parties at the imperial diets – but the sovereign powers rarely had the same political agenda in mind and contradictory tendencies were common. The crucial point of division remained the conflict of interests between the emperor and the German Estates (though relations were in constant flux and not all of the great dynasties were related to the emperors in the same way). By the late fifteenth century the tensions had become pronounced. 'The dualism of the Empire is reflected in the two issues which remained running sores throughout the century,' observes Tom Scott: 'on the one hand, the need for the kings to establish a dynastic power base (*Hausmacht*) strong enough to enable them to rule effectively as emperors; on the other, the concern of members of the *Reich* to establish public order and the rule of law within Germany' (Scott, 1998, p. 350). Over time, a political system had evolved which served to negotiate between the conflicting interests. Allusions to the various 'members' of the Empire were eventu-

ally superseded by more specific references to the imperial
Estates (*Reichsstände*), the earliest and most influential being
the electors entrusted with the duty of selecting the king and
watching over the security of the realm. When Charles V came
to power, the seven electors were the three spiritual princes of
Trier, Mainz and Cologne, along with the four secular rulers of
Bohemia, Ernestine Saxony, Brandenburg and the Palatinate.

By the late fifteenth century, following a period of reform initiated during the reign of Maximilian (1493–1519), the imperial
diet (*Reichstag*) had emerged as the principal forum for political affairs, though its powers were limited to the granting or
withholding of taxes and military aid. Membership was comprised of the leading estates of the realm. The electors, who generally exercised the most influence, were joined by the major
spiritual and secular sovereigns (the princes, dukes, margraves, landgraves, archbishops and bishops), the lesser prelates
(abbots, abbesses, provosts) and the lesser secular rulers (counts
and lords), and the free imperial cities (though the urban communes did not get a vote until the seventeenth century). At the
same time new legal institutions emerged, with the functions of
the imperial Chamber Court (*Reichskammergericht*), a forum
of justice independent of the emperor, confirmed at the diet of
Worms (1495). Further initiatives included the creation of imperial circles (*Kreise*), fairly precise regions that could serve as
intermediary levels of control between the Empire and the
Estates, and a regency council (*Reichsregiment*), which, though
very short-lived, was composed of a select committee of men
who would have powers of executive rule. Ultimately, all of
these measures, from the diets to the courts to the councils, had
the effect of limiting the powers of the emperor (or indeed any
of the great princes with visions of absolute rule) and ensured
that Germany remained a composite of territorial powers rather
than a monarchy under the sway of a single ruler.

Thus, well before the election of Charles V, significant powers
of rule were effectively in the hands of the territorial lords. The
medieval ideal of a *sacrum imperium* had not been abandoned,
especially by Charles V, but the realities of rule pressed hard on
public understanding of the realm. It is worth noting this fact,
that during the century of Reformation, despite the scale of the
Habsburg empire, the promises of imperial reform and the evo-

lution of the Estates, the leading nobles continued to dominate the German lands. By embracing an ideology of absolutism, 'the princes came to regard themselves as trustees and guardians of distinct, separate territories and no longer as the emperor's personal followers and liegemen' (Wilson, 1999, p. 38). In the end, real power lay in the rights and responsibilities granted to the princes by the emperors, and as such the matrix of power in Germany, to a great extent, had already been determined by former relations to imperial rule. The path to power had remained constant: in order to substantiate princely status, the candidate had to participate in imperial governance, and this meant sitting in councils and court, holding ceremonial offices, and honouring the Empire and its legal constitution. In return the candidate held an imperial fief, which could be a large principality, along with independent rights of rule, including powers of jurisdiction, defence, taxation and regalia. All of these rights and privileges comprised the princes' sovereignty (*Herrschaft*), the range of powers a prince might exercise. Over time, inevitably, the gradual accumulation of these endowments had given rise to extremely powerful lords. By the fifteenth century some of the princes in Germany were near equals of the emperor, similar in kind to the leading monarchs of the age. One century after the Reformation Veit Ludwig von Seckendorff made note of this in his work *The German Princely State* (1660), observing how the German principalities, while not kingdoms in the sense that France or Spain were kingdoms, were nevertheless expansive units of rule 'with all manner of languages and nations, various customs and characteristics, unruly subjects, powerful and hostile neighbours, and the other difficult and weighty conditions found in the great kingdoms of the world'. Fundamental to understanding the rise of the Reformation in Germany is the role played by these princely states, both in domestic terms, that is, with reference to the evolution of these lands into 'great kingdoms', and in the broader context of imperial relations.

The other important feature of the political landscape in the late medieval period was the rise of the urban commune. Germany was not just a land of princes and prelates, but a realm, as Aeneas Silvius Piccolomini observed in the mid-fifteenth century, of 'rich and populous cities'. This was true to a point.

There was a large number of German towns in the sixteenth century – perhaps as many as 3,000 in Germany proper, with eighty-eight in the Swiss lands and almost double that number in Habsburg Austria. But the vast majority of the urban communes were rather small, with less than 2,000 inhabitants gathered in a fairly congested space. Even the large cities such as Nuremberg, Augsburg and Cologne (with populations ranging between 20,000 and 30,000) were dwarfed when compared with the city-states of the Italian peninsula. Nevertheless, there is no doubt that urban culture had developed enormously throughout the medieval period. Towns and cities had won rights and privileges from their lords in return for a fee or a loan. Over the course of decades, the gradual accumulation of such benefits had given rise to a number of powerful civic centres (Isenmann, 1988, pp. 74–102, 131–98). The first such privilege to be granted was the right of trade (usually awarded because it benefited the local seigniorial economy), but the communes secured other rights and liberties as well, including the right to administer justice, the right to impose taxation, the right to form independent alliances, and the right to issue and enforce laws and statutes independent of the lord. City governments, made up of councils, courts and executive committees, could exercise almost unlimited sovereignty over the local population. From the preservation of the peace and the security of trade to the common defence, the application of laws and the maintenance of public order (*Polizey*) – the entire spectrum of local rule was, in many instances, in the hands of an urban elite. The emergence of the urban commune, the 'self-administrating and, for the most part, self-governing *res publica* or community', was a feature of central importance to the political culture in the German lands (Dilcher and Brady, 1997b, p. 220).

Of course, not all cities enjoyed the same range of powers. A distinction must be made between the territorial cities (*Landstädte*) and the free and imperial cities (*Frei- und Reichsstädte*). In both cases the relationship between the lord and the city defined the nature of the commune. In the territorial city, the sovereign powers of the lords were the most intense and the powers of the commune the weakest. This did not rule out a considerable degree of power. Some of the largest cities in the Empire (Prague, Munich, Vienna) were territorial cities, while a number of others, especially in the north, became virtual independent powers. Bremen was considered powerful enough to have received a summons to the *Reichstag*, an honour usually reserved for the imperial cities alone. But the vast majority of territorial towns and cities in the Empire were fairly weak dependent communities, serving a broader territorial unit and thus subject to the legal, political and economic manipulation of the local lord. By far the most influential communes in the Empire were the imperial cities, a species of urban settlement whose liberties and privileges inspired Niccolò Machiavelli to write in *The Prince* that the 'cities of Germany enjoy unrestricted freedom, they control only limited territory, and obey the emperor only when they want to'. Unlike the territorial city, the greatest of the imperial cities (which included, among others, Nuremberg, Ulm, Schwäbisch Hall, Augsburg and Rothenburg) did not have an intermediate overlord, but rather derived their rights and privileges directly from the emperor. In return for considerable wealth and a promise of allegiance, the German emperors had granted select urban communes a range of liberties. Nuremberg, perhaps the most influential city in the Empire, achieved its independence in this manner, first winning the favour of the emperor in its quarrel with the Hohenzollern castellans, and then progressively amassing a range of rights and prerogatives. Some communes had experienced a different path of evolution, in particular the free cities (*Freie Städte*), the most famous of which were the diocesan capitals along the Rhine (Cologne, Worms, Speyer, Strasbourg), which could claim a degree of independence from their overlords and were thus grouped among the imperial cities, even if this independence was not constitutionally recognized. Moreover, it must be stressed that the imperial cities differered greatly in size and status in the Empire, whatever their institutional or historical similarities. The great cities of Cologne and Nuremberg, for instance, had very little in common with the free city of Zell am Harmersbach, an urban commune with little more than 200 people within its walls.

Late medieval Germany was thus a landscape of disparate powers, from large princely territories to smaller duchies and imperial cities; but for the majority of men and women life was experienced within the confines of a rural parish. Most people, perhaps 85 per cent of the population, lived and worked on the land. Given the sheer number of territorial lords in the Empire, it is not feasible to describe the typical conditions of life in the rural context or the typical form of political culture. At best, it is possible to identify general trends (Rösener, 1996, pp. 63–83; Scott, 1996, pp. 1–31). First, a clear distinction emerged between the system of rule in place in the western part of Germany (a type of landlordship, *Grundherrschaft*) and those lands east of the River Elbe, where a much more extreme feudal relationship was common (*Gutsherrschaft*). On the eve of the Reformation the subject peasants in Prussia, Pomerania, Mecklenburg and Brandenburg were less free than the peasants in Switzerland, Swabia, Bavaria, or the territories of Franconia. In the west a gradual transformation had taken place. During the medieval period the manorial system had largely disappeared, having been replaced by a weak feudal matrix based on the payment of rents and dues instead of labour services. In addition, many of the tenants had been invested with hereditary rights over the lands they cultivated. By the fifteenth century, in certain regions, some peasant households enjoyed substantial freedoms and considerable wealth. Second, as a result of the changes in economic and political relations, the German lands, especially in the south-west, witnessed the rise of the village commune. The commune (*Gemeinde*) emerged as the political association at the local level, roughly (but not exactly) equivalent to the village itself. Over time, as the lords waned in strength or fell back on regular income from rents and dues, the communes assumed fairly independent powers of rule. Based on the principles of cooperation, peace and neighbourhood, the rural communes became quite powerful units of governance (Wunder, 1986, pp. 33–79). Indeed, in some areas, such as Switzerland, Graubünden, Vorarlberg and the Tyrol, peasant communes were represented at the territorial diets. But even in those regions where the peasants did not have a voice in territorial governance, the very fact of this alternative form of political culture had an effect on the nature of rule.

The social structure of the German lands evolved within this political framework, with each of the Estates, from princes to peasants to urban patricians, laying claim to distinct powers of rule. It could be an unstable mix, and social relations on the eve of the Reformation were in flux (Rabe, 1991, pp. 77–100). In general, the most comprehensive sovereign powers were those enjoyed by the nobles. Yet the nobility was far from a unified Estate. By the late fifteenth century the leading princes of the realm (electors, dukes and margraves) had emerged as major sovereigns ruling over major states, while the lesser nobility (the imperial knights) had suffered a loss of prestige. No longer central to military affairs or political developments, many of the lesser nobles reacted by turning against the princely state, while others entered into princely service. This was the age of feuding knights, noblemen caught between the economic and political changes of the day. Equally unsettling for the tradi-tional social hierarchy were the developments taking place in the larger urban communes. By the late medieval period, many of Germany's greatest cities were in the hands of a patrician elite, a closed caste of families with most of the wealth and almost total control of governance. As a ruling elite they were exclusive, and as an economic elite, as the Fuggers and the Welsers of Augsburg demonstrated, they could be without equal in the Empire. But this was the urban minority. The majority of people lived under the rule of this patriciate and worked within the town walls – from merchants to artisans, labourers and menial servants. Some were citizens of the city, permanent members of the community with inherited property and fixed employment; but many others were non-citizens, a tolerated underclass with basic civic rights and limited personal posses-sions. By the fifteenth century, as more and more people migrated from the countryside to the towns, the number of res-ident non-citizens was on the rise and the divisions between the rich and the poor, the powerful and the powerless, were becom-ing magnified. And the reason for the rise in the urban popula-tion was rooted in the changing conditions of rural life, for even the social structure of the agrarian setting was suffering strain. For while it is true, as we have seen, that in certain areas of Germany the peasantry lived under relatively favourable con-ditions, there was a general trend at work which drove many peasants off the land: the intensification of territorial rule. Faced with the demands of a developing monetary economy, noble landlords reacted by increasing the dues and fees required of their tenants. As they did this, they also restricted the use of the common lands, including the woods, waters and meadows essen-tial to the developing rural communes. In response, the peasants either moved to the towns and cities or petitioned their land-lords for a return to the ancient laws. And on occasion, more ominously, they would rise up in revolt.

Despite the tensions, the rural context remained the bedrock of the German economy; but it was a vast and multiform geography, and there was no uniform or consistent character to the agrarian setting. Aside from some regions of natural uniformity, such as the river valleys of the Rhine, the East Frisian marsh-lands, or the forest lands stretching from Thuringia to the Palatinate, the economic setting was just as elaborate as the social and political framework. The most a historian can do is identify some very general features. First, the agrarian economy on the eve of the Reformation was still recovering from setbacks suffered during the Middle Ages. The population was increasing, settlements were expanding, and land that had lain fallow and deserted after the Black Death was being reclaimed. This was an age of agricultural development, as the many books of husbandry testify. Second, the price of grain and manufactured goods rose steadily, while the average wage, measured relative to inflation, did not keep pace. People of this century thought they had less to spend on basic household needs than their ancestors (Lutz, 1983, p. 46). But it is difficult to speak of an average wage or a general economic shift that affected the whole of Germany. There were too many different regions with too many different strengths and weaknesses. Most areas were primarily agrarian and were based on the production of cereal crops, especially the lands to the south-west and the holdings east of the Elbe. But other areas, where the land was not suited to crops, had to rely almost exclusively on grazing or dairying. This was the case in the Swiss lands and the Rhaetian Free State, for instance (where English travellers noted how young herds-men, always in search of valuable fertilizer, carried around manure in their hoods). Great swaths of southern Germany, including Württemberg, Upper Swabia, Franconia and lower Bavaria, were areas of extensive viticulture, and in years when there was a bad yield the local economies suffered. Similarly, in the regions around Lake Constance and Upper Swabia, where the production of linen was paramount, flax was the dominant crop and whole communities relied on its yield. Nor should we forget that this was an age of developed mining and metal-working. The first industrial landscapes dependent upon the extraction of base metal ores emerged in the mining districts of Thuringia, Tyrol, Bohemia, Salzburg and Hesse (Scott, 1996, pp. 1–25). The number of examples could be multiplied, but the basic point has been made: the economic landscape of Germany was immensely varied and complex, and while rural agriculture remained paramount in importance, there were certain crops and industries that shaped the features of certain regions.

And yet for all the regional diversity (indeed, perhaps because of it) the German lands formed the basis of an intricate network of communication and exchange. At the local level, most of the trade was fairly limited, and to a certain extent the markets were self-sufficient. Germany was crowded with regional markets trading in the basic foodstuffs, grain above all, manufacturing crops and limited industrial goods. But there were much broader constellations as well, some running the length of the Empire (Kießling, 1996, pp. 145–79; Scott and Scribner, 1996, pp. 113–43). In most instances the nucleus of a region of trade was a large urban commune, a town so big that it was unable to provide for itself. To offer a few examples: in order to provide grain for the imperial city of Nuremberg, it was necessary to draw on supplies within a radius of 100 kilometres. To feed the people of Cologne, over 10,000 wagons rumbled through the city gates every year. Areas were shaped and animated by the economic gravity of towns. In the south, Nuremberg and Augsburg dominated, while Strasbourg and Cologne commanded the banks of the Rhine, Magdeburg sat in central Germany, and wealthy Hansa towns such as Bremen, Lübeck and Danzig flourished in the north.

In addition to the urban networks running through the German lands were the vast constellations of regional trade and industry. The main commodity of the age was grain, and by the sixteenth century extensive markets ran throughout Germany. There was a concentration of activity in the south-west, a line of exchange that joined Strasbourg and Basle with Frankfurt and Cologne, while to the north the Hanseatic cities engaged in the international market, shipping grain to Holland, Flanders, England and Normandy. Trade in wine reached similar dimensions. The Neckar district in the south encompassed an area reaching from Lake Constance north to the river Main and east to the borders of Bavaria. And yet this was a fairly modest range of commerce compared to the enormous distances covered by the Rhine trade, an enterprise which shipped cargo as far afield as Scotland, Norway, Sweden, England and Russia. Of course, Germany had the advantage of many navigable rivers joining the interior with ports of trade – most famous of all, perhaps, being the Rhine, a waterway that linked Freiburg, Basle, Strasbourg and Cologne, and reaching, through the Main, to the markets of Bamberg, Würzburg and Nuremberg. It also sat at the centre of the many land routes intersecting the Empire, from the Baltic to the Mediterranean, the Levant to the Atlantic. The realm was immense, and in general there was great variety in the German lands, regions as different in kind as foreign nations, but there was also a complex web of transport and communication which created something of a whole.

Another force drawing the land and its people together was the developing sense of German identity (Dickens, 1974, pp. 1–48). In part it was pure fabrication, the self-serving fictions of the princely courts. But there was a pronounced note of a more general German nationalism in the late medieval period, and it would prove crucial to the spread of the Reformation movement. In its origins it was aggressively xenophobic, directed at the Italians, the French, and above all the papacy, and it would draw on legal and political precedent for support. When Lupold of Bebenburg drafted his *Tractate on the Laws of the Kingdom and the Empire* (1341), for instance, he appealed to written law to demonstrate the independence of the Empire from the pope. In his *De Concordantia Catholica* (1433) Nicholas of Cusa wrote in similar terms, rejecting the pope's claims to sovereignty and declaring that the emperor had been appointed by God to preserve the faith. The earliest expressions of German nationalism approached the theme from this perspective. The essential aim was to demonstrate that the German lands at the heart of the Empire had a common foundation and their own sovereign destiny. As notions of identity developed, the sentiment found voice in a wide variety of ways, including the run of prophecies common to the medieval age and the corpus of grievance literature assembled in the fifteenth century. *The Book of One Hundred Chapters* (*c.*1500), for example, referred to the Germans as the chosen people and the German language as mankind's tongue before Babel. A number of prominent scholars wrote works in this vein, including Jacob Wimpfeling, whose

Germany; *In Honour of the City of Strasbourg* (1501) was a paean to German culture, and Johannes Trithemius, the author of the *Illustrious Men of Germany* (1495), a biographical collection of pious and learned figures. But perhaps the most powerful voice was that of the Humanist Conrad Celtis, the poet laureate, who spent much of his working life gathering and editing texts of German history, including the *Germania* of Tacitus, rediscovered in 1455 and soon to become the foundation text of the nationalist movement. Celtis believed that the German Nation would not fulfil its true potential until it sloughed off the 'yoke of slavery' imposed by 'foreign barbarian kings' and united in common purpose. 'Behold the frontiers of Germany,' were his words during a public address in Ingolstadt, 'gather together her torn and shattered lands!' (Dickens, 1974, p. 35).

As the nation evolved, a new sense of secular identity and spirit of mind evolved, a type of intellectual awakening often associated with the Renaissance. And while there is no doubt that the cultural revolution in Italy found its supporters in the north as well, the German movement was more than just the imitation of Italian civilization. A distinct type of intellectual culture had evolved north of the Alps, and it would be this fateful combination of spiritualism, Humanism and scholasticism that created the conditions for the Reformation. This is not to suggest, however, that German culture was essentially different from the rest of Europe or that it was immune to broader influences. Rudolf Agricola believed that his countrymen were the equals of any scholars in Europe, and he measured their worth in terms familiar to the values of the Renaissance. 'I have the brightest hope,' he wrote, 'that we one day shall wrest from haughty Italy the reputation for classical expression which it has nearly monopolised, so to speak, and lay claim to it ourselves, and free ourselves from the reproach of ignorance and being called unlearned and inarticulate barbarians; and that our Germany will be so cultured and literate that Latium will not know Latin any better' (Spitz, 1996, p. 210).

By the start of the sixteenth century the intellectual culture of the German lands had reached a high level of sophistication. The Empire was home to numerous universities, sixteen in all, with the medieval foundations in Prague, Vienna, Heidelberg,

Erfurt and Cologne joined by more recent creations in Tübingen, Basle, Freiburg, Frankfurt an der Oder and Wittenberg.
Inside the universities the faculties were coming to terms with
the new trends of thought challenging the intellectual order.
Many schools of theology were divided between an older
approach, the *via antiqua*, a system derived in great part from
the work of the great medieval thinkers, and the modern way,
the *via moderna*, a philosophical approach which tended to
question the traditional assumptions and place its trust in empir-
ical knowledge and personal experience. Meanwhile, in the arts
faculties, the pursuit of the liberal arts (*studia humanitatis*) was
transforming the themes and objects of serious inquiry. The
movement sharpened the skills of the German scholars, for it
was emphatically philological and literary in nature, and it
demanded technical improvement; yet it had a wider application, and it had an impact on more than just the halls of higher
learning. It worked a transformation in other areas of culture as
well, including the realm of public governance, with its impact
on the rules of diplomacy and the reform of law, and the more
private spheres of life, where issues of conduct and discipline
were paramount. Indeed, in the German lands, the effects of the
intellectual movements of this age were felt most strongly in
the settings where the conditions of life were most vital and
complex: the urban communes, for instance, imperial cities like
Nuremberg, where Willibald Pirckheimer balanced his work as
a translator of Greek texts with his duties as councillor, diplomat and military leader. By the eve of the Reformation, these
German cities were at the heart of an intellectual culture as
advanced as any in Europe. It is no acccident that the first extant
representation of the earth in the form of a globe was designed
and executed in Pirckheimer's city of Nuremberg, or that the
first edition of the century's most important work of science, the
De revolutionibus (1543) of Nicolaus Copernicus, was first published within its walls. Nor should we forget that the printing-
press, perhaps the most important invention of the age, was first
put to use in the fifteenth century in the German city of Mainz.

 The evolution of intellectual culture also gave rise to a
heightened critical awareness. The late fifteenth century was
marked by a growing sense of unease and uncertainty in the
German lands. Critics of the secular realm claimed that
Germany had never been in a worse condition, pointing to the

widespread practice of usury and the growth of monopolies, the lack of morals and religion infecting the social order, and the rampant corruption crippling the state. A note of distress was sounded. In the predictions and prognostications of the age the authors continually made reference to the poor state of affairs and the need for public reform and renewal. One of the most influential publications in this vein was Joseph Grünpeck's *Speculum* (1508), a work which borrowed from traditions of medieval prophecy while directing its comments at contemporary affairs. For Grünpeck, it was clear that there was 'a pitiful disintegration of Christendom, destruction of good customs and laws, misery of all estates, raging of plagues, inconstancy in all things, dreadful events befalling everyone' (Strauss, 1995, p. 12). Some authors followed in kind, supporting their predictions of floods, feuds, social unrest and political revolution by drawing on the works of medieval astrologers such as Johann Lichtenberger and Regiomontanus. Other authors resurrected the legends associated with the advent of a conquering hero, tales of a reforming emperor in the mould of Friedrich Barbarossa, who would wake from a sleep of centuries and reform Church and State. Still other authors added to the literature of grievance by drafting manifestos and proposals for imperial renewal. The most influential tract written in this vein was probably the *Reformatio Sigismundi* (1438), a work which combined a sharp critical awareness with a traditional sense of prophetic foreboding. The tract claimed that God had withdrawn his grace and the Empire was gripped by corruption and decay. The only remedy was thorough reform, first of the Church and indeed the spiritual life *tout court*, and then of the secular estate, for the relations of power in the Empire had left it paralysed. 'What can a king do nowadays?' reads the *Reformatio*. 'He cannot stop wars; no one obeys him; the imperial cities, seeing that there is no sovereign in the land, do as they please. Thus, the empire falls sick . . .' (Strauss, 1971, p. 18).

Even more critical than the dissatisfaction with the state of secular society was the sense of grievance directed against the Church. The Empire had a long and unique history of uneasy relations with Rome, for unlike the situation in other lands of Europe, the papacy had not made substantial concessions in order to appease the secular powers of Germany. The result, as everyone seemed to realize, was that no other land was as richly exploited by the papacy as the German Nation. And when this realization was combined with the unhappy memories of the numerous conflicts between the emperors and the powerful popes of the medieval period, it is not difficult to understand why the Church became a natural target for criticism. Moreover, by the fifteenth century the reform proposals of the medieval era had assumed a much more nationalistic tenor (Dickens, 1974, pp. 1–48). The ideas first voiced by the Franciscan spiritualists remained alive, just as the proposals of the conciliarists surfaced on occasion, but by the fifteenth century most critics believed that the imperial Church (*Reichskirche*) was unique in its corruption and would require a remedy unique in its approach. The earliest proposals still thought in fairly general terms, and for men such as Lupold of Bebenburg, Nicholas of Cusa and Gregor Heimburg the constant refrain was greater distance from Rome. With time, however, the critics recognized the extent of the problems and a number of substantial reform manifestos emerged as a result. The *Reformatio Sigismundi*, for instance, listed the failings of the Church, beginning with a traditional attack against the greed of the papacy, and moved on to a much more detailed criticism of the quality of the Church and its servants. But the most striking testimony to the state of antagonism were the successive *Grievances of the German Nation (Gravamina nationis Germanicae)*, the long lists of criticisms written by the Estates and directed against Rome. Dating from the early fifteenth century, the grievances detailed the perceived failings of the Church and the 'oppressive burdens and abuses imposed on and committed against the Empire by the Holy See in Rome' (Strauss, 1971, p. 52).

In the final decades of the fifteenth century the state of the Church had become a matter of great urgency. Moreover, it was clear that the issues would only multiply if the Church did not accept the need for reform. By the time the Estates gathered at the imperial diet in Worms in 1521, the catalogue of grievances numbered 102, ranging from complaints about the 'unqualified, unlearned, and unfit persons' taking up benefices to the legal and fiscal misdealings of the papacy. But the diet of Worms would not be remembered for the criticisms directed against the Church by the German Nation. History would remember Worms for the criticisms voiced by a professor of theology from the University of Wittenberg. For at the diet the newly elected king Charles V would not only meet the German Estates for the first time, he would also encounter – for the first and only time – the most powerful German voice of the age, the Saxon theologian Martin Luther.

2

Religious Culture and the Reformation

The Reformation in Germany has always been strongly associated with the personal history of Martin Luther. For centuries scholars wrote accounts of the movement almost exclusively from the perspective of the Wittenberg reformer. Luther's crusade against Rome became a myth of origin for the rise of Protestantism, just as his theological insights gave meaning and purpose to the historical event. 'To caricature the common description,' reads a well-known survey of Reformation scholarship, 'Luther generally appears as a great sage, a kind of spiritual colossus, who attains his Reformation breakthrough, draws the broad consequences, and then drags his people with him as he strides through history handing out his truths right and left' (Moeller, 1972, p. 13). In recent times scholars have moved away from this approach. In place of an almost exclusive focus on the ideas of Luther and his Wittenberg supporters, historians have started to emphasize a broader range of critical voices. No one has ever doubted that Huldrych Zwingli, Jean Calvin and Thomas Müntzer represented alternative visions of religious reform, but now lesser figures have stepped out of the source materials as well. At the same time there is a general conviction that the Reformation cannot be explained with reference to religious factors alone. These days few historians would take issue with the suggestion that the movement was, to a substantial degree, the creation of social and cultural forces of the day, many of which had no direct or necessary association with religious issues. There is thus an elaborate context for understanding the event, and it would be a distortion to reduce the variety of the past in order to preserve the integrity of a sacred myth or vision.

Nevertheless, even with these caveats in mind, it still remains true to say that without recognizing the unique and profound importance of Martin Luther, it is impossible to understand the German Reformation. Perhaps there would have been a reform movement regardless, different in kind and certainly different in its course. But the historical reality is that the initiative fell to Luther once he had challenged the Church of Rome. Luther, not Zwingli or Karlstadt or any other like-minded theologian, emerged as the central figure of the reform movement in the German lands. History records that the controversy over indulgences provided the catalyst for a religious revolution. And there have been few occasions in the past when such a profound coincidence of historical circumstance met with such depth of personal insight and conviction. As Martin Brecht has remarked: 'Here [Luther's] life, his thought, and his work received a center around which they were oriented, one which resulted in a thorough reformation of theology, piety, and the church's structure and practice, indeed a reformation of the secular order itself, and one through which western Christianity was drastically changed' (Brecht, 1993, p. 176).

The Luther Affair

On 22 January 1517 Johann Tetzel became the general sub-commissary for the sale of indulgences in the province of Magdeburg and spent most of that year in northern Germany preaching the plenary indulgence proclaimed by Pope Leo X. Years later the reformer Friedrich Myconius would describe Tetzel's indulgence-peddling in his *Historia Reformationis* in very critical terms: 'The claims of this shameful monk were unbelievable,' wrote Myconius. 'Thus he said that if someone had slept with Christ's dear mother, the pope had power . . . to forgive as long as money was put into the indulgence coffer . . . He claimed that in the very moment the coin rang in the coffer, the soul rose up to heaven' (Johnston and Scribner, 1993, p. 12). As grim as this may have sounded to some ears, Tetzel was not acting against the theological orthodoxy of his day. Nor was he violating traditional religious practice. Criticisms had long been ranged against both the indulgence trade and the claims made by its preachers. Well before Tetzel picked up on the verse about the coin in the coffer the Paris theologians had raised objections to it. But indulgence-peddling remained a staple component of worship in Christian Europe. The plenary indulgence of Leo X, while unique in that most of its proceeds were earmarked for the rebuilding of St Peter's Basilica in Rome, could call on over two centuries of church history in its defence. Tetzel himself was working in accordance with the instructions issued by the Archbishop of Mainz, Albrecht of Brandenburg. Indeed, Archbishop Albrecht had a personal interest in the campaign, for in order to acquire the archdiocese of Mainz, the largest in Christendom, Albrecht, who was already the Archbishop of Magdeburg and administrator of Halberstadt, had been obliged to get a dispensation from the pope. And in order to pay for it, he worked out an arrangement with Leo X: Albrecht allowed for the sale of the plenary indulgence in his church provinces and agreed to grant half of the proceeds to Rome. This is the background to Tetzel's appointment and the scale of indulgence-peddling in northern Germany, and it helps to explain why Myconius witnessed a procession of the papal Bull so resplendent 'even God himself could not have been welcomed and received more beautifully.'

Despite the scale of the campaign and the authority behind it, the sale of plenary indulgences was not permitted in the electorate of Saxony. Tetzel could not take the campaign directly into the lands of Friedrich the Wise; the best he could do was skirt along the ill-defined borders in towns such as Jüterbog, and it was there that a number of parishioners from Wittenberg travelled to hear him preach. Eventually word of this reached Martin Luther and the news prompted him to act. Luther had already expressed his doubts about the indulgence trade in lectures and sermons. On this occasion, however, with firsthand reports from Jüterbog reaching him in the confessional, he resolved to write a letter to Albrecht, Archbishop of Mainz. Luther expressed his concern about the indulgence trade, and along with the letter he included a list of ninety-five theses written in Latin as a critique of current practice. Luther's intention, as he made clear in the letter, was to bring the abuse of the trade to the attention of the archbishop. His fundamental concern was the spiritual welfare of his parishioners. 'These unfortunate souls,' he wrote, 'seemingly believe that they are assured of salvation as soon as they purchase letters of indulgence' (Johnston and Scribner, 1993, p. 12). Luther thus wrote as both a theologian and a pastor caring for souls. The Archbishop of Mainz, however, did not reply. The letter did not reach him until November, at which time he was residing in Aschaffenburg, and once he was aware of the contents he had both the letter and the theses forwarded to Rome.

The origins of the Reformation are often traced to this initiative; indeed, there is even a famous gesture associated with the day, for this is when tradition has dated the posting of the theses at the door of the Castle Church of Wittenberg (31 October 1517). Some historians now question whether the posting ever took place, but there is no doubt that the controversy set in motion by the theses was the point of origin for the Reformation movement. The theses, once translated by supporters and sent to press, appeared in cities as far afield as Leipzig, Basle and Nuremberg. Within a few months Luther's objections to the indulgence trade had passed through a number of famous hands, including those of Erasmus of Rotterdam and Emperor Maximilian I. Moreover, a number of prominent figures, theologians and Humanists alike, now spoke out publicly in support of the Wittenberg professor. Inevitably the theses also attracted the attention of the papal authorities, especially as Albrecht of Mainz had forwarded his copy of Luther's letter to the curia, and their reaction was far less favourable. One of the first to speak up was Tetzel himself, who countered with a set of theses in support of the indulgence trade and pressed for harsh action against Luther. Even more fateful, however, was the intervention of the professor of theology at Ingolstadt, Johannes Eck. In 1518 Eck prepared a rebuttal of the ninety-five theses entitled *Obelisks*, a work which branded Luther a heretic and charged him with being a rebellious Bohemian and despiser of the pope. Luther, in an effort to defend himself and heal the breach with Eck, wrote *Asterisks* (1518) in reply, but even at this stage it was obvious that there were fundamental points of disagreement between Luther and the papal theologians. Later that year Luther would dedicate a published edition of his explanation of the ninety-five theses to Pope Leo X, but his relationship with the Roman Catholic Church was coming under strain.

In the same year Luther and Eck were exchanging religious views, the Estates of the Empire gathered at Augsburg for an imperial diet. Progress was slow, as the Venetian ambassador remarked, for the Germans continued to defend territorial interests at the expense of imperial politics. And once again the Estates used the diet as a forum for the grievances of the German Nation. By the summer of 1518, however, there was an added ingredient to traditional anti-papal antagonism – the Luther affair (*causa Lutheri*). Since the posting of the theses the themes of the debate had broadened. In addition to his criticism of the indulgence trade, Luther had also publicized his views about scholastic philosophy and preached against the ban. Papal theologians denounced him as a heretic, and the result, as expected, was a summons to appear in Rome (which Luther received on 7 August 1518). Sylvester Mazzolini, called Prierias, master of the sacred palace, had written a synthesis of basic objections to the ninety-five theses. For Prierias, the Church had a centre, the pope, and all who questioned papal pronounce-ments were necessarily heretics. Luther did not spend much time answering the *ex cathedra* condemnation of Prierias, but he did make it clear that he valued the authority of scripture above the testimony of tradition and canon law.

The growing divide became even more apparent when Luther met with the papal legate, Cardinal Cajetan, at Augsburg in October 1518. Cajetan's mission was to ensure that Luther revoked his errors, returned to the Catholic fold, and withdrew from similar speculation in the future. But things did not go as planned. As Luther declared after the event, 'I could not bring myself to say those six letters, REVOCO [I recant]!' (Oberman, 1993, p. 196). To Cajetan's insistence that he cede to the author-ity of the Church, Luther answered with appeals to further debate and demonstrations of proof. It was now even more apparent to him that both Christian tradition and ecclesiastical law could be ambiguous. Cajetan, mindful of his commission, did not enter a debate and forwarded Luther's answer to Rome. Moreover, in keeping with the close communication that had preceded the meeting, he also sent a letter to the Elector of Saxony. 'I exhort and beg Your Highness,' wrote Cajetan, 'to consider Your honor and Your conscience and either to have the monk Martin sent to Rome or to chase him from Your lands.

Your Highness should not let one little friar [*unum fraterculum*] bring such ignominy over You and Your house' (Oberman, 1993, p. 16). But Luther returned to Wittenberg unscathed, and Friedrich the Wise did not withdraw his protection of the university's most famous professor. In the months that followed the meeting in Augsburg Luther continued to teach, preach (up to two sermons a day), dispatch his pastoral duties and prepare his works for publication.

After Augsburg, it was impossible for Luther to return to his former life as a relatively unknown preacher and theologian. The controversy had raised too many crucial issues – and touched too many nerves – to fade away unresolved. If anything, the meeting did little more than confirm the papal theologians in their belief that Luther was an implacable heretic. At the same time Luther began to move farther and farther away from Rome, and once again the reformer's spiritual development became an issue of public concern in a meeting with the papal authorities. In the summer of 1519 Luther, along with his colleague Andreas Karlstadt and a small army of supporters, arrived in the city of Leipzig in order to participate in a debate with Johannes Eck. Karlstadt had provided the original motive in his attack against *Obelisks* and Eck welcomed the chance to meet the Wittenberg reformers in a public forum. In short order a point of contention revealed the distance between them – the question of papal primacy. By drawing on scripture, the Church fathers and canon law, Eck put forward the argument that Christ had established papal primacy over the Church. Luther did not agree with this. For him, Christ was the head of the Church and there was no special sacral dignity in the papal office. Moreover, the only true test of Christian truth was scripture, not the work of the scholastics or the fineries of canon law. As Luther remarked in a letter to Willibald Pirckheimer: 'The matter turns, as you see, on the sacred *canones*, i.e. the profane perversions of the sacred books' (Grane, 1994, p. 50). Other themes would surface, including indulgences and Purgatory, but it was this contest about papal authority that defined the debate. The discussion of papal primacy also allowed Eck to introduce into the exchange the ideas of Jan Huss, the Bohemian heretic who had gone to the stake a century before for professing similar things. By the end of the debate, due in part to Eck's ability to steer the discussion, Luther had publicly denied claims of papal primacy and sided with a condemned heretic. Leipzig ended with nothing resolved. A settlement looked less likely than ever, and meaningful dialogue soon gave way to censure and abuse.

Away from the halls and forums of public debate, Luther continued to develop his ideas. At the centre of it all was the reformer's reinterpretation of the relationship between man and the divine – complex in its theological apparatus, but in essence a turn away from the externals of the faith to a total reliance on the grace of God. It was this insight that ultimately inspired a fundamental programme of reform. As Brecht has remarked, 'Luther had been able to transform the new experience of justification by faith alone into a thoroughgoing alternative conception which extended across the entire breadth of religious and ecclesiastical life . . .' (Brecht, 1993, p. 387). The culmination of this period of activity was the appearance of three extremely influential publications in quick succession. *To the Christian Nobility of the German Nation* (1520) was a tract written explicitly for the nobility of the realm rather than the higher clergy. Conceived in German, rather than the Latin prose common to the genre, Luther outlined a series of proposals aimed at ending the exploitation of the German Church by Rome. It was, as Johannes Lang commented, little less than a trumpet of war, for it not only criticized the failings of the Roman Church (though it did this at every opportunity); the pamphlet was also a sophisticated programme of ecclesiastical reform which looked to the secular authorities rather than the Church for support. A few months later Luther followed this with the publication of *The Babylonian Captivity of the Church*, a work more expressly theological in tone (and written in Latin) which rejected the traditional understanding of the sacraments and accused the papacy of holding the true faith in thrall. The final tract in this series was *The Freedom of a Christian*, the last time Luther ever approached the papacy with the suggestion of reconciliation. In truth it was a very mild attempt at compromise, and its lasting importance lies rather in its exposition of the ideas of justification through faith alone and the priesthood of all believers. With these three publications, Luther had provided his supporters with the essentials of the evangelical faith. The basic framework for the Reformation movement in Germany was in place.

Among the defenders of the Catholic Church, the initial reaction to the Luther affair was characterized by a general concern with issues of order and authority rather than precise statements of theological orthodoxy. When the theologians first came forward, they did so for a variety of reasons: Eck condemned the attack against canon law and the authorities of the visible Church; Konrad Wimpina entered the lists in defence of the sacramental system; Prierias simply restated papal claims to authority. But all of the controversialists recognized in their various ways that Luther was challenging the basic authority of the Catholic Church. If he were not silenced, as Tetzel observed, his views 'will encourage many people to despise the might and authority of his Papal Holiness and of the holy Roman See. They will neglect the work of sacramental satisfaction. They will never now believe the preachers and doctors. Everyone will interpret Scripture as takes his fancy. And all sacred Christendom must come into great spiritual danger when each individual believes what pleases him most' (Bagchi, 1991, pp. 33–4). The issue of authority became even more explicit after the meeting in Leipzig when Luther began to question the traditional defence of the divine right of the papacy. Instead of turning to canon law and the works of the scholastic theologians, Luther looked almost exclusively to scripture. In doing so, he challenged papal claims to interpretative sovereignty, for truth was not the accumulated product of Church tradition or theological endeavour but the simple and absolute testimony of scripture. Ultimately Luther would question the authority of the councils as well. In doing this, he moved beyond the anti-papalism and the conciliarism of the previous century to a position that challenged all instances of church authority (Brockmann, 1998, pp. 63 ff.). In the eyes of the papal theologians, this was yet more evidence that Luther wished to undermine all order and authority in the Christian world. 'He sets himself up as a judge,' wrote Hieronymus Emser, 'but he allows no one to judge him. Canon law and the decretals he calls "cold". Even deified Fathers he calls mere men (and, of course, he won't accept the traditions of men)' (Bagchi, 1991, p. 90). These charges became even more pronounced after the publication of *To the Christian Nobility of the German Nation*, a work which took the debate to the public sphere. The Catholic controversialists now accused Luther of working to undermine all political order and all rule of law in the realm. To deny the authority of the papacy is to deny the authority of the emperor, ran the argument, and ultimately it would lead to the ruin of the Christian commonwealth.

One of the reasons why the indulgence controversy ultimately escalated into a crisis was the lack of dialogue between the papal theologians and the Wittenberg reformer. In part this was to be expected, as the Catholic Church did not engage in debate with suspected heretics. At the beginning, the authorities simply expected Luther to admit his errors and recant. Once he had refused, the only recourse was condemnation. Indeed, the papal nuncio Girolamo Aleander spoke for many when he suggested that any further dialogue with Luther would just fuel the cause. 'The cause of the revolution in Germany is something other than the sacraments,' he wrote. 'Besides, *rationes* and *disputationes* achieve nothing' (Bagchi, 1991, p. 220). Religious truth could not be revealed in a dialogue with a heretic. Later in the century, once the Reformation movement had become a political force, Catholic thinkers continued to shy away from open debate with the evangelicals. When the issue of a Church council first surfaced, many of the papal theologians would not countenance the idea as it was, by implication, conceding ground to a heretical movement. The Catholic Church had pronounced; further deliberation was unnecessary.

But the conflict ran deeper than this, for even on those few occasions when Luther and the Catholic authorities did engage in dialogue it was quickly apparent that they spoke in a very different theological language. When discussing the authority of scripture, for instance, Luther came to speak of Holy Writ as the only necessary source for the believer, a *depositum* of religious truth. The Catholics, in contrast, drew on other sources of religious understanding for help in interpretation, including custom, tradition, the scholastic commentaries, the decrees of ecumenical councils, the Church Fathers and community consensus (McGrath, 1993, pp. 140–74). Luther thought the papal interpreters were manipulating the Word 'like a nose of wax'; the Romanists held that Luther's approach was too subjective to allow for an authoritative interpretation. Thus even at this basic level, where issues of authority, testimony and the measure of truth were paramount, there was no ground for dialogue or understanding. 'It is the great paradox – and irony – of the sixteenth century,' writes Gillian Evans, 'that, at a time when the subtlety of the question of evidence was becoming more apparent than ever before, both sides in the debates should need, for polemical reasons, to oversimplify, to assert sometimes rather crude dogmatic statements about the grounds on which they were prepared to consider a truth authoritative' (Evans, 1992, p. 112). The Reformation would evolve out of this mutual, and deliberate, incomprehension.

The Luther affair was certainly not the first time that criticism of this kind had been directed at the scholastic theologians. Humanists and theologians had been trading barbs for decades, and for many of Luther's earliest supporters the controversy was viewed as yet another episode in this long-running feud. One of the reasons for the rapid spread and success of the evangelical movement, as has been noted, was the support created by this 'constructive misunderstanding' (Moeller, 1972, p. 29). The scholastics defended a restrictive approach to the interpretation of scripture; a proper reading required specialized theological training and the mind of a dialectician. Scripture, the scholastics argued, must not fall prey to the intellectual customs of the day, and this was precisely the threat posed by the Humanists with their reliance on grammar and philology and their veneration of the pagan authors. The Humanists, for their part, maintained that the scholastics had become slaves to convoluted logic and obscure commentaries. They passed their days in word games and senseless speculation and were thus held at a distance from the truths of the Gospel. By the early sixteenth century, the debate had taken root in the universities of northern Germany. Humanists at the university of Leipzig, for instance, started to challenge the primacy of the theologians, and similar episodes occurred in Heidelberg and Erfurt. In this climate, local scholars could look to the international stage for guidance and inspiration. Erasmus waged a public feud with the Louvain theologians, Maarten van Dorp and Jacques Masson, on the proper methods of biblical interpretation, while the conflict between the Hebraist Johann Reuchlin and the Cologne Dominicans became the most famous academic *cause célèbre* in Germany at the time. Many people would associate Luther's struggle with the issues raised during the Reuchlin dispute, in particular, the rights of a Humanist scholar to interpret scripture and the methods that might be used. As Heinrich Cornelius Agrippa remarked, the 'scholastic theologians of our day form a solid phalanx to fight language studies and persecute them as if they were the causes of all schisms and heresies' (Rummel, 1995, p. 128). The Reformation entailed much more than the issues at stake in this debate, as the Humanist community would soon recognize, but the 'constructive misunderstanding' was fundamental to the fortunes of Luther's protest.

In the years that passed from the posting of the theses to the meeting in Leipzig and the publication of the papal Bull of excommunication, the Luther affair had evolved from a regional dispute about indulgences to an event of national significance. The issues raised in the public debates and the published dialogues were discussed throughout the Empire, from the imperial court to the local inns. As early as 1518 the Nuremberg legal advisor Christoph Scheurl referred to Luther as the most famous man in Germany (Moeller, 1988, p. 77). Within two years of his appearance on the public stage, Luther had become a figurehead for the German peoples and his movement a public cause. Among the Humanists, Willibald Pirckheimer, Ulrich Zasius, Johannes Oecolampadius, Crotus Rubianus and Wolfgang Capito expressed their support in print and letters. Within a few years of his appearance in Augsburg, Luther had received letters of encouragement from cities as distant as Nuremberg, Prague, Augsburg, Basle, Heidelberg, Paris and Rome. His Latin works, published by the Froben press in Basle, were shipped to France, Spain, England, Italy and the Netherlands. 'All Switzerland, Constance, Augsburg and a good part of Italy depend on Luther,' exclaimed Zasius in a letter to Konrad Mutianus (Fife, 1957, p. 463). Of course, this was an exaggeration, but Luther was fast becoming a celebrity, and no one realized this better than his papal adversaries. Johannes Cochlaeus, whose *Commentaries on the Life and Writings of Martin Luther* (1549) was the most influential Catholic biography of the age, wrote of how the reformer 'soon gained the greatest favour for himself, not just among the simple people, who easily believe and freely open their wide-spread, itchy ears to every novelty; but also among many grave, learned men, who believing in his words through genuine simplicity, thought that the monk sought nothing else, other than defence of the truth against the seekers of indulgences'.

Word of Luther's quarrel with Rome spread throughout the Empire so quickly and so thoroughly that historians have referred to the Reformation as the first substantial 'media event' in history (Hamm, 1996b, pp. 137–66). In the beginning, traditional face-to-face encounters did much to create public awareness, not only through Luther's lectures and sermons at Wittenberg but his famous appearances at Heidelberg, Augsburg, Leipzig and Worms. Yet even more crucial for the lifeblood of the movement was the network of communication and the various forms of media employed in aid of the faith. As we shall see, the Reformation was in large part a creation of the printing trade. Without the abundant publications – the books, the pamphlets, the broadsheets and the woodcuts – the reach and momentum of the Reformation would not have been possible. More than any other historical constituent at the time, the fact that the reforming message was so closely associated with new forms of media explains how the Luther affair turned into such a powerful movement. There was no precedence for this in history; never before had there been such a flood of ideas and opinions in the public sphere. And more to the point, never before had there been such a broad base of contending beliefs. Now it was not just theologians speculating about the essentials of the faith, but lawyers, councillors, innkeepers and errant noblemen. The German Nation was in the grip of the movement. This is something else Cochlaeus took note of in his *Commentaries*, though in a wary and disapproving tone.

There is no doubt that the Luther affair owed much of its early momentum to the fact that it was perceived as a national event. For many people it was yet another contest between the German Nation and Rome. The *Reformatio Sigismundi* (1438) had already held Rome to account for the poor state of the Church in the German lands, speaking of the greed and the corruption of the papal courts. Similarly, the continued grievances of the Estates complained bitterly about the financial burdens imposed on the Empire by the papacy – including the peddling of indulgences. In some ways Luther was simply appropriated as a figurehead or a spokesman of national interests. Many early depictions of the reformer portrayed him as a champion of German honour against the trickery of Rome, the most explicit being Hans Holbein's *Luther as the German Hercules* (1523) which imagined the reformer as the classical hero Hercules, replete with lion's pelt and club, with the pope and a host of scholastic thinkers prostrate at his feet.

Perhaps the best example of the fusion of the Luther affair with national interests was the support offered to the early movement by Ulrich von Hutten, imperial knight and man of letters. Hutten had long been writing against the papacy and the clergy of Rome, once claiming that the pope had a plan to usurp the power of the emperor and enslave the German people. Later works would be directed to the same end, including his influential edition of Valla's treatise on the Donation of Constantine and the *Letters of Obscure Men* (written with Crotus Rubeanus), the infamous satire directed at the scholastic opponents of Reuchlin. Little wonder that Hutten emerged as a supporter of Luther in his contest with Rome, going so far as to declare that the liberation of the Germans was in the reformer's hands. In part this was misappropriation, for Luther was less concerned with the interests of the German Nation than the truths of scripture. But in part it was an association embraced by the reformer, a deliberate attempt to turn his private struggle into a public contest (Schmidt, 1999, pp. 55–70). Certainly Luther conceived his work *To the Christian Nobility of the German Nation* (1520) with the defence of German liberties in mind, and a close tie with national identity would abide as defining feature of the movement for most of the century.

Once the imperial election had been secured by the Habsburg candidate, the papal approach to the Luther affair began to change. The brief spate of hearings between Luther and the papal theologians came to an end. No longer needing to cultivate the favour of the Saxon elector, Rome was free to move against Luther. The result was *Exsurge Domine* (15 June 1520), the first papal Bull of excommunication. Luther's works were condemned, he was forbidden to preach and he was summoned to appear in Rome sixty days after receiving notice. By this stage, however, Luther had reconciled himself to the notion of separation, and as long as he enjoyed the support of the elector he was determined to defy papal censure. His reaction to the Bull was to burn it, along with some works of canon law, in a bonfire near the gates of Wittenberg. Still hoping for a settlement of the conflict, the elector requested of Charles V that Luther be given a hearing at the diet of Worms. The emperor agreed and plans were thus in place for Luther's famous appearance on the imperial stage. Public support for the Wittenberg reformer was now at its peak. As he travelled to the diet, passing through villages and towns and giving sermons along the way, he was received as a hero. When he arrived in Worms he was quickly surrounded by well-wishers and partisans. Aleander claimed that nine-tenths of the German peoples were on his side; while the remainder, if not too concerned with the reformer, were at the very least enemies of Rome (Schorn-Schütte, 1996, p. 34). Once before the authorities, however, Luther was treated as a suspect heretic, and it was quickly made clear to him that he was not called to Worms in order to engage in debate but rather to revoke his former statements and submit to the will of the Church. With his publications piled before him, he was asked two basic questions: Did he recognize the books as his own? Was he ready to recant what had been written in these books? Given a day to consider his answer, Luther's response on 18 April 1521 has become one of the defining moments of European history:

'Unless I am convinced by the testimony of the Holy Scriptures or by evident reason – for I can believe neither pope nor councils alone, as it is clear that they have erred repeatedly and contradicted themselves – I consider myself convicted by the testimony of the Holy Scripture, which is my basis; my conscience is captive to the Word of God. Thus I cannot and will not recant, because acting against one's conscience is neither safe nor sound. God help me. Amen.' (Oberman, 1993, p. 39)

Luther left Worms eight days after this famous scene. On his way home he was the subject of a friendly kidnapping by officials of the Saxon elector. He was taken to the Wartburg, where he remained in hiding for the rest of the year. The Emperor Charles V remained at the diet long enough to see through the Edict of Worms (26 May 1521), an imperial endorsement of the Bull which declared Luther an 'obstinate schismatic and manifest heretic' and placed him under the ban of the Empire. In many ways, this was the final act in the reformer's personal struggle against the papacy. The Luther affair would now become the Reformation movement.

The German Church

'The hour will come for all faithful Christians to witness the promulgation of the rightful order,' warned the author of the

Reformatio Sigismundi (Strauss, 1971, p. 6). No doubt this struck a chord with its readers, but in the German lands the difficulty lay in determining just who was responsible for establishing the rightful order in religious affairs. The German Church was different in kind from other Churches in Europe, for it was not subject to the designs of a single monarch. Like the political setting, the ecclesiastical setting lacked a strong royal hand. Granted, the papal crises had yielded some concessions, including the reform measures which followed in the wake of the councils in Constance and Basle; but the German kings had never been able to turn these gains to lasting advantage in the same way as the monarchs of France or England. The imperial Church remained in the hands of the aristocracy and its constitution was a reflection of this fact. Germany was the land of the great prince-bishoprics, large territorial states which combined the powers of secular and spiritual rule. At the summit were the three Rhenish electoral archbishoprics (Cologne, Mainz, Trier) due to their role in imperial politics, but many other prelates exercised secular powers of rule, and it was inevitable that the German bishops would find it difficult to defend the interests of the Church while they were engaged on so many fronts. The ecclesiastical authority of the Prince-Archbishop of Trier, for instance, extended into lands subject to the Counts of Nassau, the Electors Palatine, the Dukes of Lorraine and Luxembourg, and the Prince-Archbishop of Cologne. Nor was it exclusively the higher clergy who were caught up in the machinations of secular affairs. The network of aristocratic patronage reached from the bishops, chapters and archdeaconries to the regional foundations and the parishes. In 1458 Pope Pius II confirmed the ancient tradition of the Einsiedeln monastery that 'no monks shall be received except from noble families, provided that there are enough monks in the monastery' (Du Boulay, 1983, p. 189). A few years later Erasmus would raise doubts as to whether Christ himself could penetrate the network of patronage in the German lands.

That the Church was not in an ideal state to reform itself becomes even more apparent when we take into account the power enjoyed by the secular rulers. In few other lands in Europe were the regional lords so directly involved in the running of Church affairs (Schulze, 1991). In some cases, as in Austria, Saxony and Brandenburg, the territorial sovereigns had been able to facilitate their hold over the Church by way of a special agreement with the papacy, but in most instances it was simply the result of force of rule. In both the electoral Palatinate and Württemberg, for example, the gradual usurpation of ecclesiastical authority meant that the princes effectively dominated the territorial Church. Similarly, as early as the mid-fourteenth century the Duke of Bavaria could boast that the pope was powerless in his territories. This was testimony to a certain degree of cohesion at the territorial level, but this was also precisely the reason why the imperial Church remained so impotent and diffuse, as the author of the *Reformatio Sigismundi* recognized: 'It is plain that the Holy Father, the pope, and all our princes have abandoned the task set them by God' (Strauss, 1971, p. 6). There could be no general reform of an institution that lay in the hands of so many contending sovereign interests.

But the problems gripped more than just the rule of the Church. In the German Nation, Catholicism of the medieval period was suffering from a lack of theological clarity. Schools of scholastic thought had multiplied throughout the Middle Ages, especially in the face of the crises of the fifteenth century, with the result that there was considerable complexity and confusion on the eve of the Reformation (McGrath, 1993, pp. 9–28). This doctrinal plurality weakened the integrity of the Church, and it would prove instrumental in the rise of the reform movements. When the Luther affair surfaced, no single Catholic voice could be raised in defence. Within the universities two antagonistic trends of scholastic thought (the modern way, *via moderna*, and the ancient way, the *via antiqua*) quarrelled over the true understanding of the faith, while the Humanists, many of whom were recent additions to the faculties, challenged both the methods and the agenda of the theological schools. Numerous universities in the Empire experienced intellectual crosscurrents of this kind, including the university of Erfurt, where Luther matriculated in 1501. But it would be wrong to suggest that the German setting was unique in this respect. As the Paris theologian Jean Gerson remarked, all of Christendom was embroiled in 'violent controversy' over the most basic questions of the faith. Indeed, there was still no definitive understanding about the scheme of salvation (Pelikan, 1984, pp. 10–58; Ozment, 1980, pp. 22–42). Theologians could not agree on the extent to which God was constrained by his own will and justice

– a complex theme, but the issues of satisfaction, reprobation and predestination hung on the debate. Nor was there an unchallenged dogma on issues such as the communication of grace (in particular the role of Mary as mediatrix), the nature and function of the sacraments, or the essential features of the 'holy, catholic, and apostolic church'. With so many questions begging and so many essential issues unresolved, it is not surprising that the question of doctrinal authority was at the top of the agenda. In a work entitled *In Defense of Apostolic Obedience* the German theologian Gabriel Biel spoke for many by simply asserting that 'the truth that holy mother church defines or accepts as catholic is to be believed with the same veneration as if it were expressed in Holy Writ' (Pelikan, 1984, p. 125). But appeals to authority of this kind had been weakened by the sheer plurality of Catholic opinion, and it would not be long before the Roman Church was forced to defend its complex corpus of thought against unadorned citations of scripture.

On a less abstract plane, at the level where the Church and its ministers played a role in daily religious life, the failings and disorder of the medieval German Church were often the subject of public complaint. From popular works of literature such as Sebastian Brant's *Ship of Fools* (1494) to the reproaches of the Hussite communities and the opprobrium in political tracts like the repeated *Grievances of the German Nation*, there was a growing sense that the Church and its clergy were falling short of expectations. Of course, this critical mood was not unique to the Empire; all of Europe was commenting on the failings of the Church. And yet in Germany, where the climate of anticlericalism was infused with nationalism, the criticisms were especially detailed and relentless. The institutional Church was assailed on two fronts. On one level the grievances spelled out the perceived abuses of Rome, while on another level they pointed to the failings and deficiencies of the national Church. When the German Estates submitted the list of grievances at the diet of Worms (1521), for instance, the draft touched on issues ranging from the fiscal and jurisdictional abuses of the papacy to the poor standard of the 'motley persons' placed in the parishes and the misuse of indulgences and relics.

In part, criticism of this kind was sheer hyperbole, and we should not forget that the German Estates had a political agenda in mind when they submitted *gravimina* to the Emperor. Nor should we overlook the many reform initiatives introduced in medieval Germany, both in the various dioceses and territories (the diocese of Mainz was particularly active and influential) and in the Church as a whole. But public opinion spoke incessantly, and with increasing intensity, of the need for a reform of the Church. And with good cause, for there was no lack of evidence to bear out the accusations. Despite the repeated remonstrations of the Estates, huge sums of money continued to flow to Rome. Foreigners and powerful prince-bishops continued to amass numerous benefices, while native clergymen, high and low alike, took advantage of the system. It was not unusual for parish clergymen to hold more than one benefice at a time and exploit their powers and immunities at the local level. Often they were not even resident, having left their parishes in the hands of ill-trained and inexperienced vicars. The author of the *Reformatio Sigismundi* had no doubt about the damage caused by clergymen of this kind: 'We all know what pain and harm have been occasioned by the practice of beneficing unlearned, unqualified priests. Such men cannot preach the Gospel, nor can they administer the sacraments. We call such men "blind guides." Follow them and you fall into a ditch' (Strauss, 1971, p. 12).

Nevertheless, even when faced with the failings of the institution and its servants, no one within the fold ever seriously considered separating from the Roman Catholic Church. In medieval Germany, as in the rest of Europe, the only means of salvation were those provided by the Church Universal. Christians in the Empire realized that any religious beliefs not sanctioned by the Church of Rome were, to use a popular medieval metaphor, outside the walls of the faith. Only heretics thought otherwise. Thus the Church in Germany provided its faithful with the same social and spiritual unity as in the rest of Europe (Swanson, 1995, pp. 10–41). In order to become a member of the Christian community, each parishioner had to be baptized into the Church. Equally, in order to receive the grace of God during the course of a lifetime, each parishioner had to pay witness to a prescribed and ritualized plan of salvation. Theologians imagined the Catholic community as a unified whole, a single Church of believers which found the same purpose and meaning in its relationship to the divine. All members of the Church therefore had to observe the official declarations of belief. In practice, this meant that the parishioners had to be familiar with the vague definitions of the faith as captured in the creeds. It also required that they pay witness to the essential teachings of the Deca-logue. Beyond this, the average parishioner probably knew little more than what was related through litany, ceremony and obser-vance as defined by the Church authorities. After the Fourth Lateran Council (1215) all orthodox members of the Roman Church, whether they understood it or not, believed in the doctrine of the Trinity, the mystery of transubstantiation, and the essential importance of baptism and confession. And to bear witness to these convictions, all Christians were required to attend confession and communion on an annual basis, just as they were to avail themselves (where appropriate) of all seven sacraments in the trust of the priesthood. Until the Reforma-tion shattered the unity of this vision, these features of the Catholic faith drew all aspects of religious life into their orbit.

As an example of the relationship between sacramental ritual and the attainment of God's grace in medieval Catholicism, we might look at confession and penance. In the general scheme of things, the following process was thought to take place: mankind fell prey to sin, the sinner then went to confession, the priest granted absolution, fixed a penance (or work of satisfaction), and with the penance the sins were forgiven and the believer returned to a state of grace (Cameron, 1991, pp. 79–93; Bossy, 1987, pp. 35–56). Through penance the sinner would be trans-formed by God's grace, infused into the soul to facilitate redemption, and this would in turn promote acts of love and good works, which would then earn the sinner merit or worthi-ness before God. 'God's forgiveness of sins and justification of man is made possible by the granting of grace to man and by his subsequent good works and freedom from acts of mortal sin; these aspects of his nature then also become the condition of his sanctification after death' (Hamm, 1999b, p. 68). Most medieval theologians would have accepted this general descrip-tion of the pastoral process. Given the plurality of opinions, however, they might not have agreed over how much mankind could contribute to the process or indeed whether the sinner could accomplish anything at all without divine grace. Some thinkers within the *via moderna* school, for instance, imagined the cycle of salvation in terms of a covenant between God and man. The will of God, rather than any eternal necessity, bound his activity within the rules of the covenant, and God would respond reliably to the conditions he had set. If the believer fulfilled certain demands (or, as the theologians summarized it, committed to 'doing what lies within you') he or she would acquire semi-merit (*meritum de congruo*). Through the covenant, the sinner is then rewarded with 'uncreated grace' which in turn produced good works. The combination of God's grace and the believer's own good works thus result in the sinner's acceptation. But all schools, even the strict Augustinians, thought in terms of the cycle of salvation and the central importance of the Church and the sacrament of penance to the process of redemption. Ultimately, grace was acquired through penitential exercises, through good works.

It is important to remember the centrality of the doctrine of salvation to the religious culture of the age, for it is easy to assume that the advent of the Reformation movement is proof enough that traditional religion had lost its hold over the faithful. For centuries historians portrayed the evangelical movement as the healthy outgrowth of a religion that had begun to rot root and branch. But in fact the medieval religious world was not necessarily in decay. On the contrary, in one famous estimation there had never been a time in the history of Christianity more receptive to the official teaching of the Catholic Church or more devoted to the theory and the habitus of salvation (Moeller, 1972b, pp. 13–42). And not only the higher clergy were proof of this assessment; the parishioners themselves readily embraced what the Church had to offer. 'Ecclesiastical and religious life was intimately and inseparably fused with secular life, and the willingness, indeed the longing, to sanctify one's secular existence within the framework of ecclesiastical discipline and the aid of the treasury of grace made available by the church were at no time more widespread than in the late fifteenth century' (Moeller, 1972b, pp. 16–17). Granted, there was a climate of discontent and grievance, as we have seen, and there is no doubt that the Church was failing the faithful on many levels, but this did not stop the parishioners from seeking their salvation within the traditional framework of belief and observance. A brief survey of religious culture bears this out. The number of Mass endowments in Germany increased steadily throughout the fifteenth century. No other period in history witnessed so many feast days, processions and pilgrimages. Sites of assumed miracles multiplied, relic collections grew in scale, and the number of local saints increased rapidly. In general, people became more aware of the possibilities of their religion. In pictures and texts the details of the faith became more personalized and tangible. It is no accident that the religious art of this era was so preoccupied with the particulars of Christ's Passion. The Dutch historian Johan Huizinga once argued that medieval religion had become too opulent and sensual for the spiritual message it wished to relate (Huizinga, 1996, pp. 173 ff.). This may be true, yet the fact remains that no other age was more anxious to get as close to the divine.

A famous example of this spiritual appetite is provided by the imperial city of Nuremberg, whose healthy religious life was praised by Johannes Cochlaeus in his *Brevis Germaniae descriptio* (1512). On the eve of the Reformation Nuremberg was home to over 400 clergymen, many of whom served in the commune as Mass priests. In Saint Sebald's, one of the main city churches, there were four daily Masses, numerous feasts throughout the year, and an annual litany of public ceremonies involving both the clergy and the leading citizens of the city. (Indeed, the city councillors remained at the forefront of the Corpus Christi procession until 1523.) Nor was there any lack of a general piety on show. Preaching posts had been established by the council with the expressed purpose of holding public sermons on Sundays and Fridays. We can assume that they were in office to meet a need. In the Easter holiday the rush to the sacrament was so great the council had to arrange for crowd control. The city churches were adorned in art and imagery made possible by private donations, from the triptychs and paintings to the numerous relics assembled by the leading patricians of the city (Schlemmer, 1975, pp. 1–27). The point is this: in Nuremberg, as elsewhere in Germany, the Reformation was not successful because it came along in time to fill a spiritual void. On the contrary, religious life in the medieval age was extremely vibrant, and one of the prerequisites of the evangelical movement was 'the extreme acceleration of medieval ecclesiastical religiosity' (Moeller, 1972b, p. 30). This is an important point to keep in mind, for it obliges us to acknowledge that Reformation theology did not make an impact because it filled an absence. Reformation theology found a following because it was embraced as an alternative.

Medieval religious culture in Germany was thus a synthesis of abstract theory and ritual praxis. Theology provided the faithful with a language and a logic of meaning, while the daily patterns of religious experience (the rites, the liturgies, the customs of worship) provided the parishioners with a sense of cosmic order and a matrix for participation. For the majority of people, the most effective way to articulate the relationship between the sacred and the profane was to trust in the traditional points of contact between the two worlds. This was provided at two basic levels of experience: first, as we have seen, within the cycle of a single life, the Church offered ritual order and displays of sacramental power which helped to demonstrate the relationship between God and man. Second, within the broader horizon of the Church and its people, it provided a complex and an unceasing litany of ritual ordering – from the feasts to annual processions such as Corpus Christi to the rogation days. Taken together, all of these rites, symbols and observances made up what has been termed 'the economy of salvation'. Its final purpose, and indeed the final purpose of all piety, was to harness the sacral in order to benefit the profane (Scribner, 1987, pp. 1–16). To offer an example, this was the logic behind the intense reliance on the sacraments and the sacramentals in medieval religion. Both involved rituals and sacred objects, and both served as conduits to the divine – though in different measures. Sacraments were guarantors of divine favour *ex opere operato*, that is, they worked automatically and independently of earthly conditions, and central sacraments such as baptism and the eucharist were viewed as vital and indisputable proofs of God's favour. Sacramentals, in contrast, were not considered automatically efficacious by the churchmen; but few parishioners kept the distinctions in mind and as a consequence medieval religion was saturated with sacramental objects of worship (consecrated water, palms and salt, for instance, or indeed any object that may have been blessed by a clergyman, from a hearth to a candle to a church bell). The final purpose was the utilization of the supernatural. And in both their roles as manifestations of the divine and points of contact, by way of ritual action, with the sacral realm, sacraments and sacramentals were not unique. The entire economy of salvation was in place to facilitate this type of religious imagination.

From the survey above we might summarize the state of the medieval Church in Germany as follows: there was abundant criticism of the institution and its clergy, and to a large extent it was justified. The Church was lacking in leadership, especially at the national level. The clergy did take advantage of the system and, at times, neglect the welfare of their flocks. Moreover, medieval religion had become a very complex and contradictory system of belief. In the schools of theology the professors quarrelled over fine distinctions, some of which ultimately touched on the essentials of the faith, while in the parishes, especially in the urban parishes, popular piety had become more and more elaborate as the rituals and objects of worship multiplied beyond the comprehension of the faith. And yet, despite the declared weaknesses of the institution and its servants, the Roman Catholic doctrine of salvation remained central to Christian belief in the medieval age. Few people seriously suggested that salvation was possible without the Church as a shepherd and an intermediary. And fewer still thought to look for religious truth by stepping outside of the faith. On the contrary, there is evidence to suggest that religious culture had rarely been more attached to the Church than in the fifteenth century. Never before had the parishioners been more anxious about salvation or so engaged in discovering the truths of the faith. Perhaps it was this turn towards the heart of religion, rather than a turn away, which explains the resonance of the evangelical movement.

Reformation Thought

Many religious thinkers in Germany on the eve of the Reformation were beset with the need to reduce the faith to its essentials – perhaps with good cause. The reformers would later claim that medieval Catholicism had become a burden on the consciences of the faithful, that there were too many specious expectations (as they saw it) and not enough simple trust in the Word of God (Ozment, 1975, pp. 22 ff.) This was exaggeration, and there was method in it; but clearly, despite the means available for acquiring grace and salvation, it remained a religion infused with a strong sense of anxiety and doubt. Medieval Christians made repeated and graphic allusions to the fragility of life, the power of sin, the proximity of death, the feared destruction of order and the judgement of God. In reaction they sought out the grace and mercy of the divine, that they might be prepared for the hour of death and pardoned before the seat of judgement. All of this led to a heightened concern with grace and salvation. By the late medieval period there was a concentration of the theological imagination, a reduction of the complex field of worship to a 'reduced set of core principles identified as *the* road map for the pilgrimage in this world and as the guaranteed route to salvation in the next' (Hamm, 1999b, p. 317). Theologians began to summarize the essential features of the faith, emphasizing the importance of scripture and the centrality of Christ to salvation. Johann von Staupitz, for example, a thinker who had a profound effect on Luther, prefigured the evangelical stress on grace (*sola gratia*) by placing such stress in the mercy, suffering and Passion of Christ. A similar vision inspired the reform of the monastic communities, where the highest ideal of the Christian man became a life spent in imitation of Christ (*imitatio Christi*). Authors and artists published texts and painted images relating the new sense of piety to a growing audience. The general trend was a paring down, an effort to bring things into focus, with the centring of piety around the themes associated with Christ the redeemer (Passion, mercy, trust) rather than exclusively with Christ the judge. Even the pious fascination with the cult of saints and the intensification of devotion to Mary gravitated around these themes (grace, clemency, Passion, forgiveness) – with the final goal, if by way of advocacy, being a closer relationship with Christ. It did not yet result in a complete transformation of the faith, for medieval Catholicism was always firmly rooted in the cycle of salvation and obedience to the law; but by the fifteenth century there were clear signs that the faithful were striving to reduce religion to its essence. The legacy of this was twofold: 'an intense concentration on regularization, obedience to the law, the quest for virtue, and the sanctification of one's life on the one side; on the other, an increasingly focused emphasis on mercy, intercession, and grace that sought to relieve the burden of the conscience, and to fortify the soul' (Hamm, 1999b, p. 353).

When the Reformation movement emerged in the early decades of the sixteenth century it was guided by a similar spirit, and it was in large part inspired by the same questions that had animated the religious imagination of the late medieval period. The same concerns were at the heart of the inquiry. What were the essentials of the Christian faith? What was the path to salvation? How can the believer find a gracious God? This last question preyed on the mind of Martin Luther, and it was his attempt to answer it that gave rise to the Reformation in Germany. Of course, other figures contributed to the movement as well, and there is no doubt that reformers of the stature of Huldrych Zwingli and Jean Calvin (to name but two of the most prominent) were religious thinkers of profound originality. But it remains true to say that Reformation theology ultimately finds its origins in the thought of Martin Luther (Brecht, 1993, pp. 99–117). He was not just a theologian of genius; he was himself a prime example, at the extreme, of the religious mentality of the age. While a monk in the Augustinian order, Luther grew increasingly convinced of his inadequacy before God. 'Although I lived a blameless life as a monk,' he wrote years later in an autobiographical fragment (1545), 'I felt that I was a sinner with an uneasy conscience before God. I could also not believe that I had pleased him with my works. Far from loving that righteous God who punished sinners, I actually hated him' (McGrath, 1993, p. 95). The pregnant phrase here was 'the righteous God'. In the medieval Church, as we have seen, the righteousness of God was understood in a covenantal sense. If certain preconditions were met, the sinner would be justified before God. The sinner was judged according to merit, and merit was something that could be achieved through active faith. Eventually Luther began to doubt that sinful man could ever meet the expectations of God. And it was his questioning of whether sinful man was able to meet God's preconditions that would lead him down the road to his theological revolution. What follows below is a sketch of some of the basic themes of Reformation thought. Most begin with Luther, but as we shall see, there were other trajectories to Reformation theology as well.

In answering the question 'How may I find a gracious God?' Luther was addressing the issue of redemption. In medieval theology, a very elaborate arsenal of concepts and themes had grown up around this problem; but for many people the term 'justification' was the primary reference used to articulate the Christian experience of redemption. The term came to mean 'being in a right relationship with God' and it was usually conjured in any discussion of what a sinner had to do in order to be saved. Luther's theological breakthrough, and thus the point of departure for the Reformation movement, came when he rejected the medieval Catholic understanding of justification. Luther later suggested that it came to him when he fell upon the passage in Romans 1:17: 'For therein is the righteousness of God revealed from faith to faith: as it is written, The just shall live by faith.' In its mature form, this insight is referred to as justification by faith alone. It is a complex doctrine, but in essence Luther was suggesting that there is nothing a sinner can do of his own efforts to be righteous in the sight of God. Righteousness is given to the sinner as a gift by God – he meets the conditions – and the believer can do nothing other than have complete faith in the promises of Christ – not just faith in the promises, but faith in the integrity of those promises and faith in the trust that God will honour them. Faith thus unites the Christian with Christ. As Luther put it in *The Liberty of a Christian* (1520), 'Christ is full of grace, life and salvation. The human soul is full of sin, death and damnation. Now let faith come between them. Sin, death and damnation will then be Christ's; and grace, life and salvation will be the believer's' (McGrath, 1993, p. 99). In this view, Christ does everything necessary for salvation; it is his righteousness that meets the conditions. The believer is passive, trusting in the promises of Christ and a righteous God. Only in this way can the sinner stand in a right relationship with the divine.

All of Reformation theology found its meaning in the evangelical doctrine of justification. If there was one principle of the faith that remained inviolate throughout the century, it was the idea that the acceptance of God, and thus the bestowal of divine grace on sinful man, was not subject to causes or conditions. This insight represented a radical break with the Catholic past, for it spoke of an outright promise of unconditional salvation. No reasons or provisions had to be met, as was taught in the medieval Catholic Church. There was no system of worship, no cycle of redemption by means of which God's grace was acquired. Justification, in Luther's famous words, was through faith alone, *sola fide*, for the sinner had been given the promise of unconditional salvation through the redemptive work of Christ. In the Reformation understanding of justification, 'there can be no valid cause for man to be justified before God; not even God himself stands in such a causal relation to man and his actions. The acceptance of God, his bestowal of grace on his creature, is not subject to reasons or conditions' (Hamm, 1999b, p. 69). According to the reformers, nothing could remedy the deficiencies of Fallen Man. Radical sin was the basic nature of the whole man, and thus it was not possible to purify the soul of sin as had been presumed in the medieval cycle of worship. In evangelical theology, there was no longer a process of renewal or an infusion of God's grace. Righteousness was perceived as a state beyond ourselves (*extra nos*), essentially a new relationship with God (who sees mankind in light of Christ's righteousness) rather than a new quality inherent in man. That is why faith was so important for the Reformation doctrine of justification, 'for faith is the means whereby man is led from his moral subjective existence into the final validity of the righteousness of Christ, in which he is preserved for salvation – outside himself, where God looks graciously on him' (Hamm, 1999b, p. 79). Faith replaces active works and thus the entire medieval cycle of salvation becomes superfluous – an idea with obvious implications for the integrity of the Catholic community. A culture of worship based on the idea of participation was no longer viable, for there was no work to do or condition to meet that could earn or merit salvation. The idea of the Church as the sole repository of God's grace was abandoned. The believer no longer had to rely on the visible Church, its institutions or its ministers to stand in a right relationship with God. The entire economy of salvation in the Catholic system of belief was undermined.

At the root of this insight, and indeed at the heart of all Reformation thought, was an explicit reliance on scripture. For all of the evangelical thinkers, the Bible was the ultimate authority in matters relating to the faith. On the surface, very little about this notion was revolutionary. The Roman Church also based its authority on the testimony of scripture, and in general medieval theology (a few disembodied quotations notwithstanding) spoke of the Word of God as the final ruling in all religious matters. But there was a difference between the two conceptions. In Catholicism there were other sources of religious truth as well, primarily the unwritten traditions of belief, the appeal to the historical continuum, and the vague but commanding idea of a general consensus preserved by the Church (*consensus ecclesiae*). Moreover, final approval was in the hands of the papacy (or, to some minds, the hands of a council). The reformers, in contrast, maintained that scripture was the only source of authority for the true Church (scripture alone, *sola scriptura*). All certain knowledge of the faith could be derived from the Word of God; there was no need for *summae* or glossaries or centuries of unspoken tradition. This principle surfaced very early on in the conflict between Luther and Cochlaeus, and it was as much a question of hermeneutics as it was an article of faith. As David Bagchi has observed, 'what distinguished Luther's approach to theology from his opponents' was his reductionism, his adoption of a methodological razor that prevented the multiplication of authoritative theological sources beyond necessity' (Bagchi, 1991, p. 80). This did not necessarily mean that Luther and his followers appealed to scripture alone and no other source. Other authorities might be enlisted if they paid witness to the essential meaning of Holy Writ (and the essential meaning, always, confirmed Luther's doctrine of justification). But it did mean that the vast field of corresponding authorities sustaining the medieval Catholic Church was made redundant.

At the same time as the reformers appealed to God's Word to the exclusion of other authorities, they were quick to dismiss the pretensions of Rome as the premier interpreter of scripture. 'Their claim that only the pope may interpret scripture is an outrageous fancied fable,' wrote Luther in *To the Christian Nobility of the German Nation* (1520). To a certain extent, the reformers were simply confirming the advances made by the Humanist agenda, with its stress on ancient languages, its tools of exegesis and its appeal to the sources. By the time of the Luther affair it was now common knowledge that advances in textual criticism and philology had revealed the errors of the medieval interpreters. In the face of Lorenzo Valla's exposure of the Donation of Constantine as a fake, for instance, the Church's claim to sovereignty (and infallibility) in such matters had been fatally weakened. And yet the Reformation principle of *sola scriptura* went far beyond the criticisms of the Humanists. The reformers rejected the way that the medieval Church had interpreted and defined scripture. Instead, they spoke of God's Word as clear and total, with no need of an external gloss. And as the evangelicals associated their religion so closely with the Word of God, this worked to undermine the standing of the papacy while it invested the Reformation community with the stamp of divine approval. 'The difference between us and the papists,' observed Jean Calvin, 'is that they believe that the church cannot be the pillar of the truth unless she presides over the Word of God. We, on the other hand, assert that it is *because* she reverently subjects herself to the Word of God that the truth is preserved by her, and passed on to others by her hands' (McGrath, 1993, p. 143). In reality, the difference was not so great as Calvin implied, for in the end the Protestants also accepted parts of the Catholic tradition when they drew up syntheses of their religion. So too did the Protestants place restrictions on both the interpretation of Holy Writ and the people who were allowed to decipher the meaning of the Bible in the name of the congregation. But in the beginning, as evangelical theology started to slip free of Catholic thought, the reliance on scripture was a vital characteristic of the faith.

Reducing religion to the biblical essentials meant that all aspects of the Christian inheritance fell under scrutiny, including the sacraments. In the medieval Catholic Church the seven sacraments were the constituent elements in the system of salvation. Medieval theologians referred to the sacraments as 'sensible signs' of God's grace, manifest symbols of salvation, and they also spoke of them as signifying the gratuitous action of God and thus working in some way as channels of divine grace (Pelikan, 1984, pp. 50–9). But the reformers rejected this understanding. Within the context of Reformation theology, there was no place for a ritual which claimed to confer grace (especially one made efficacious through human action). Salvation was achieved through faith in the Word of God alone. Moreover, according to the evangelical reading of scripture, there was no biblical testimony to support the Catholic doctrine of the role and function of the sacraments. Nor was there any warrant for the traditional seven (baptism, the eucharist, penance, confirmation, holy orders, extreme unction and marriage), as Luther announced in his tract *The Babylonian Captivity of the Church*

(1520). Instead, maintaining that a true sacrament was a promise of God to which a sign was attached, Reformation theology reduced the sacraments to two – baptism and the eucharist. As the *Confession of Augsburg* put it, sacraments served 'not only as marks of profession amongst men, but still more as signs and testimonies of the will of God towards us, set forth for the purpose of arousing faith in such as use them' (Reardon, 1995, p. 72). Baptism and the eucharist qualified under this rubric; the remaining five, largely due to a lack of scriptural evidence, did not.

But the proper definition of the sacraments was certainly not straightforward for the reformers, even if they had little difficulty rejecting the medieval doctrines. This theme would divide them among themselves. Luther and Zwingli, for instance, had different ideas. In his understanding of the sacraments, Luther was closer in sentiment to the Catholic tradition than Zwingli. For Luther, the sacraments were inseparably linked with the Word of God, and as a consequence he spoke of the sacraments 'nourishing' faith or demonstrating the power and proximity of Christ. Zwingli, in contrast, kept Word and sacrament separate. For him, they were closer in kind to oaths or public demonstrations of the faith in the presence of the worshipping community. Zwingli thought of the sacraments as representing the faith by way of analogy. Luther, in contrast, thought of the sacraments in more literal terms.

Ultimately, the distance between Luther and Zwingli in their respective interpretations of the sacraments would come to the fore in the debate over the eucharist. This issue, more than any other in the century of Reformation, would create divisions within Protestantism. In essentials, there was widespread agreement, especially when the basic evangelical teaching was juxtaposed against Catholic doctrine. All of the reformers rejected the claim that the Mass was a sacrifice offered up by the priest for the living and the dead. According to the Protestants, there was no scriptural warrant for the idea that the clergyman was making a sacrifice. More to the point, to suggest that a priest could effect a sacrifice at his own bidding was blasphemy, for it was an offence to the sovereignty of God and Christ's unique offering on the cross. Following from this, it was idolatry to worship the eucharistic elements or claim to manipulate their sacral powers, just as it was wrong to deny the wine to the laity for the same reason. The evangelical communion was celebrated in two kinds (*sub utraque*), with both the bread and the wine given to the celebrants. And finally, all of the reformers rejected the medieval Catholic doctrine of transubstantiation (the theory in support of the idea that the elements of the eucharist were miraculously transformed into the blood and body of Christ at the moment of consecration).

Beyond these main points, however, there were many differences of opinion, and by far the most important for the fate of the movement was the controversy between Luther and Zwingli over the Real Presence (Steinmetz, 1986, pp. 72–84). It was a complex theme, far too complex to treat in any detail here. But in essence it was a conflict about the meaning of Christ's words in Mathew 26:26: *hoc est corpus meum* – 'this is my body'. Luther understood it in a more literal sense than Zwingli. Without endorsing the Catholic doctrine of transubstantiation, he did maintain that the body of Christ was 'truly and substantially' present in the sacrament. Zwingli, in contrast, thought of the phrase 'this is my body' as a figure of speech and rejected the suggestion (Lutheran and Catholic alike) that Christ was actually present in the elements. For Zwingli, the communion was an act of remembrance, an attempt to 'render present' Christ's act of sacrifice. As he described it, 'the Lord's Supper, if it is not a sacrifice for the soul, is a remembrance and a renewal of that which once happened, which is valid for all eternity, and which is dear enough to render satisfaction to God's justice for our sins' (Locher, 1981, p. 223). This debate would last through the century and beyond, and it would be the main theological reason why the two movements, Lutheranism and Zwinglianism, went their separate ways.

This evangelical understanding of the sacraments, and the reinterpretation of the Mass in particular, dramatically rewrote the purpose and function of the clergyman. Up to that point in Christian history, the priesthood had been set apart from the rest of society. Ordination conferred a privileged sacerdotal status and thus implied a special relationship with the divine, and this unique standing had its parallels in the social sphere (in distinct clerical dress, for instance, ritual celibacy and legal immunities). Moreover, the priesthood acted as points of contact between the profane world and the divine. The ritual of the Mass was the most emphatic testimony of this. With the Reformation, however, and the doctrine of justification through faith alone, the works righteousness of traditional religion was rejected. Salvation was the gift of God, not the work of man or a priest acting as an intercessor. The institutional Church, as a consequence, lost much of its urgency. And more to the point, the status of the clergyman underwent a fundamental reinterpretation.

The most forceful affirmation of the new understanding of the clerical estate appeared in *To the Christian Nobility of the German Nation* (1520), when Luther detailed his idea of the priesthood of all believers. Deliberately written with the princes and nobles in mind, the tract accused the Roman Church of having betrayed the faithful by elevating the spiritual above the secular sphere. In doing this, Luther charged, the clergy had made themselves masters of the faith and excluded the laity from Church affairs. In truth, he continued, this was pure deception, for scripture makes no fundamental distinction between the secular and spiritual estates. We are all consecrated priests through baptism, all equal heirs of the Gospel, and no one could presume a higher status before God. The only difference is that of office, for some people serve as clergymen at the behest of the Christian community while others follow different pursuits. 'And so it follows,' concluded Luther, 'that there is no true fundamental difference between lay persons and priests, between princes and bishops, between those living in monasteries and those living in the world. The only difference has nothing to do with status, but with the function and work they perform' (McGrath, 1993, p. 206). All of the main reformers agreed in principle with this distinction, though urban figures such as Huldrych Zwingli, Martin Bucer and Jean Calvin developed more elaborate Church ministries than Luther. Calvin, in particular, worked out a fairly complex network of Church officials with a range of titles. In the essentials, however, there was agreement, and with the priesthood of all believers the medieval Catholic clerical estate was dealt a deadly blow. From this point forward, the laity had the right to intervene in religious affairs. There was no need to make a distinction between secular and spiritual pursuits, and certainly no warrant for the conceit that the clerical life (a life of good works or ascetic seclusion) was more pleasing to God. The clergyman became a functionary, a servant of the commune, placed in office in recognition of his special gifts.

What then of the Protestant Church? A religion so impatient to distance itself from its medieval inheritance would necessarily need time to develop a comprehensive structure. This is even more evident when we remember that for the first generation of reformers the problem of ecclesiology was secondary to other concerns. When the first evangelical communities evolved in the German lands there was no dominant archetype to follow, and as a result the first churches (or communities of worship) assumed a number of different forms. According to one recent analysis, at least seven varieties took shape at some stage during the first century of reform (Scribner, 1993, pp. 5–32). At the most basic there was the *local church*, an idea of religious change which situated the Reformation at the level of the worshipping community. In such a model, the universal church was replaced by, *mutatis mutandis*, the church of Wittenberg, the church of Erfurt, the church of Nuremberg. Closely related to this vision was the notion of the *lay church* or the communal church. Often associated with the Peasants' War or the radical fringe, the lay church was in truth faithfully abstracted from Luther's notions of the priesthood of all believers and early ideas on the religious autonomy of the commune (the south German theologians, following Zwingli, contributed more to this tradition than Luther). As Protestantism quickly became politicized, however, this model lost its foothold in the Empire. The same is true of the *voluntary church*, a vision of reform which thought in terms of the elect community free of traditional church structures, and the *revolutionary church*, a much more radical reading of scripture and its sources so violently articulated during the Peasants' War of 1525. The revolutionary church projected a notion of *reformatio* which, though drenched in religious language, looked to overturn the socio-political order. Similar to this was the idea of the *purified church*, born of the conviction (held by the followers of Andreas Karlstadt and Thomas Müntzer) that the Reformation had not yet been completed. This voice of unease would shadow the movement throughout the century.

In the end, the models of church rule with the best chance of success were those in league with the existing systems of governance. The *bibliocratic church*, with its emphasis on scripture and its mission to construct the kingdom of God in this world, looked to the secular authorities to root local polity in biblical norms. Jean Calvin's Geneva was perhaps the final realization of this vision, but even the mild-mannered urban reformations were bibliocratic to a degree. The most successful variety of reform took shape as the *Marsilian church*, a church controlled by the secular powers. The name derives from Marsilius of Padua, whose medieval treatise *Defensor Pacis* (1324) spoke in defence of princely control of the Church and presaged Luther's ideas of the relations between the secular and the spiritual realms. As the movement matured, the Protestant Church in Germany would develop the ecclesio-political principles expressed in *Defensor Pacis* and thus became, to a degree, and to some extent against the intentions of the first-generation reformers themselves, a Marsilian phenomenon. At the end of the century, the Empire was home to numerous Protestant Churches defined according to princely declarations of the faith, structured according to the boundaries of the state and integrated into the secular systems of rule. The Protestant Church in the German lands became an appendage of the evolving state, and ultimately the local congregations would be absorbed by the territorial Church. But the success of this paradigm should not eclipse the initial variety.

As an independent theme in evangelical discourse, the issue of Church governance did not really surface until mid-century, after the failure of the theological colloquies made it clear that the dialogue between Catholics and Lutherans had reached an impasse. Of course, the reformers had spoken of the true Church before then, but with very little reference to particulars. In essence the first uncontested principle of ecclesiology to emerge was the conviction that the true Church was emphatically *not* the Church of Rome. Reluctant to separate at first, by 1519 Luther was referring to the pope as the Antichrist. The following year he broke with the papacy. In his own words: 'Farewell, unhappy, hopeless, blasphemous Rome!' But this left Luther and his followers in a difficult situation, for now they were caught between the institutional legacy of the Roman Catholic Church, which they rejected (whole or in part), and the views of the radical reformers, who held that the true Church was purely spiritual in nature. In negotiating this dilemma,

Luther took the middle ground: he confirmed the importance of the visible church to the Christian faith, for that is where the Word of God was preached and the sacraments administered; but he also spoke of the true Church in a spiritual sense as the community of true believers. 'Therefore he who wants to find Christ,' he wrote, 'must first find the church . . . the church is not wood and stone but the assembly of people who believe in Christ. With this church one should be connected and see how the people believe, live, and teach. They certainly have Christ in their midst, for outside the Christian church there is no truth, no Christ, no salvation' (Lohse, 1986, p. 180).

Most of the other leading reformers spoke in similar terms, referring to the Church as the assembly of believing Christians or the site where the Word of God was preached and the sacraments adminstered to the faithful. But there were other emphases, especially in the southern Empire where the context of development was so different. Zwingli agreed with Luther that the Church was the communion of true believers known only to God; but he also added the attribute of discipline as one of the defining marks of the Church. Martin Bucer embraced this notion, including discipline as a key feature of the Church in his work *On True Care of Souls* (1538). But the reformer who dealt most comprehensively with the theme of the earthly Church was Jean Calvin, whose *Institutes of the Christian Religion* (1536), especially in its later editions, was a studied attempt to abstract from the New Testament 'the order by which the Lord willed his Church to be governed' (McGrath, 1993, p. 195). For Calvin, proper Church governance was an essential mark (*nota*) of the true Christian Church, no less important than the preaching of the Word or the administration of the sacraments. In his *Ecclesiastical Ordinances of the Church of Geneva* (1541) he spelled out a system of Church rule which placed responsibility in the hands of the four main officers of the Church (pastors, doctors, elders, deacons) working within the organs of ecclesiastical governance (consistory, synods) (Bouwsma, 1988, pp. 25, 214–29). By the time Calvin assumed leadership over the Genevan church, the Reformation had taken root in many parts of the Empire. It was no longer a struggle for survival; the Protestant faith was now developing its own sophisticated systems of Church rule. And with this sense of security and permanence in the background, they strongly rejected the ecclesiological traditions of Rome and the close association between secular and spiritual power that had been a mark (in their eyes) of the medieval Church. By the second generation of reformers, there was little left of the Roman Catholic inheritance that had not been condemned.

However, it was one thing to reject the medieval Catholic tradition; it was quite another to construct a viable Church in its place. In order for the faith to survive, the reformers had to form an association with the systems of rule, and for all of the main Protestant theologians, the relationship between Church and State became a complex theme. Caught between the promises of scripture and the limitations of an earthly realm, the reformers had to effect a balance between Christian freedom and the lot of Fallen Man. To add to this, the issue was complicated by developments in the political sphere. As the radical tradition threatened to unseat all forms of rule and order in the realm, many of the Catholic princes, Duke Georg of Saxony prominent among them, promised to root out the evangelical faith. Expediency thus inspired Luther to turn his thoughts to this theme, and from the very beginning he had made no secret of his belief that the secular arm had the right to supervise religious reform. With the publication of his tract *On Secular Authority* (1523), he provided the conceptual framework for his views. Luther rejected the medieval distinction between the spiritual and the secular realms. Instead, as we have seen, he developed the idea of the priesthood of all believers, affirming that all Christians occupied a single plane. But this did not remove the necessity to protect and preserve the Church, and in order to establish a system of ecclesiastical rule Luther developed his doctrine of the Two Kingdoms.

At the heart of this idea was the assumption that there were two types of governance, spiritual and worldly, both of which were necessary and both of which had been ordained by God. The spiritual government was the rule of God's Word over the faithful. With this form of rule there was no need for laws or moral imperatives, for the true believer was under the guidance of the spirit and had no need of coercive government. However, since 'there are few true believers and fewer still who live a Christian life,' it was also necessary to establish a worldly government, a system of secular rule preserved by kings, princes and magistrates placed in office to maintain peace and suppress sin. No less than the spiritual kingdom, secular governance was a divine ordinance, and Luther made it clear that the authorities had the right to use the sword in order to preserve order. But they had no power to meddle in matters that touched on the spirit. This was Luther's main concern, that the State did not interefere in matters belonging to the Church. 'Therefore care must be taken to keep these two governments distinct' reads a passage in *On Secular Authority*, 'and both must be allowed to continue [their work], the one to make [people] just, the other to create outward peace and prevent evil-doing. Neither is enough for the world without the other' (Höpfl, 1991, p. 12).

Beyond Wittenberg, where relations between Church and State might be different in kind, alternative models of political thought developed – though it should be said that most of the major reformers shared the same basic principles as Luther. (Only the radical tradition withdrew completely from the secular world, imagining the community as 'an assembly of the righteous' which, by its very nature, could not compromise with the state.) Common to all of the prominent thinkers was the belief that secular rule was a necessity brought about as a result of sin. Those people put into office to exercise authority had a divine commission to rule, and to rule with force; but they had no right to pass judgement on the Word of God (and thus to meddle in spiritual affairs). Not all of the reformers were as concerned as Luther with maintaining the division between the secular and the spiritual spheres. Zwingli, for instance, encouraged a strong association between the evolving Church and the Zurich city council. In part it was a natural extension of his theology, for Zwingli's understanding of justification always had a worldly dimension; but in part it was simply the product of historical circumstance, for the Reformation in the city of Zurich necessarily required a close dialogue with the political authorities. A similar situation faced the other urban reformers, including Martin Bucer and Johannes Oecolampadius, and they developed similar ideas as a result. And with Calvin the collaboration between the secular and the spiritual realms was even more complex. Like Luther, the Genevan reformer sought to preserve distinct powers for the clergy (in particular, powers of discipline) and he did not advocate any intrusion of the worldly authorities in matters that touched on the spirit. But he gave full support to the idea that it was a Christian duty to obey secular authority (in most cases), and he went so far as to invest the Genevan officials with powers that had long been the pre-serve of the Church. In his view, the state was essential in order 'to foster and maintain the external worship of God, to defend sound doctrine and the condition of the church, to adapt our conduct to human society, to form our manners to civil justice, to reconcile us to one another, to cherish peace and common tranquility' (McGrath, 1993, pp. 215–16).

In truth, by the final decades of the sixteenth century there was very little common tranquillity in the Protestant Church of the German lands. Different contexts of development and dif-ferent theological trajectories led to serious conflicts between the Lutheran and Reformed communities. Many of the initial points of division between Luther and Zwingli were never resolved, and as the confessions grew in detail and complexity the likelihood of agreement was soon eclipsed by an arsenal of dogma and polemic (Preuss, 1970). The Word had not gathered the faithful together, as Luther had prophesied. And yet this should not obscure the more substantial fact that Reformation theology, in the general sense, did represent a radical break with the Roman Catholic tradition. When we examine the essentials of Reformation ideas against the beliefs of medieval Roman Catholicism, a fundamental coherence and corpus of beliefs are clearly in evidence (Hamm, 1995, pp. 71–102). In place of the cycle of salvation so central to medieval religion, with its rituals and its conditions and its gradualism, the Protestant creed spoke of faith alone. No need for complex hierarchies or a priesthood with claims to sacerdotal powers. In place of the religious culture of works righteousness and the many gradual steps to salvation, the Protestant religion spoke of passive faith and the helplessness of man before a punishing and merciful God. In place of the many traditions and interpreters of the medieval Roman Church, the reformers claimed that the Word of God alone was the arbiter of the faith. Scripture, not the Church, rules over the soul of Fallen Man. Trust in Christ and his Word alone, counselled the evangelical clergy, and do not place hope in an earthly institution or the works of man. The consequences of this approach were manifold – from the new understanding of sin to the priesthood of all believers to the revaluation of the sacraments. Protestant theologians would quarrel over the fine distinctions of this theological revolution, but in the beginning the points of departure had been held in common. Only later would the faith become the preserve of the theologians, and that is when many of the common features of Reformation thought faded from view.

3

The Reformation in the Parishes

From the very outset of the Reformation the essential aim was to deliver scripture into the hands of the faithful. In the beginning, the reformers spoke in terms of a general evangelical movement under the guidance of God's Word rather than distinct Lutheran or Zwinglian programmes of reform. Some leading figures, Huldrych Zwingli and Andreas Karlstadt among them, imagined a Christian community where the average layman could 'study God's Word and treat of it to those who are round him' without waiting for the imprimatur of the Church (Rupp, 1963, p. 123). For the age, this was a radical suggestion, and it soon proved one of the most potent principles of evangelical theology. The Word of God, spread in sermons, texts, images and pamphlets, was now made accessible to the parishioners, while questions fundamental to the faith, questions that had previously been reserved for the clerical elite, were discussed openly and debated in public. This was not just a new approach to old themes of Christian thought; it was a completely new understanding of the relationship between scripture and the religious conscience. The implications were profound. 'Few people realised that the real division lay between two opposed ways of thinking,' observed the historian Joseph Lortz. 'On the one side were the tradition and the organism of the Church, on the other, subjectivism – an essentially unfettered attitude of mind' (Lortz, 1960, vol. 2, p. 62).

The Reformation was, in its essence, a complete revaluation of the religious order, and the guiding spirits of the early movement relied almost exclusively on personal readings of Holy Writ. Tradition was likened to trickery and deception, while the reformers assured the faithful that any Christian who read the words of the holy Gospel in true faith, love and confidence in God, simply following the text, would understand everything necessary for salvation. The authority of the Church was no longer absolute, scripture was absolute, and the only true judge of faith was the individual conscience. For many, this was a liberating vision. But as the reformers soon realized, it was also a formula for confusion. For it was impossible to predict how the individual conscience, once free of traditional restraints, would come to understand scripture, just as it was senseless to speak of absolutes when the Word of God was in the embrace of such an 'unfettered attitude of mind'.

Spreading the Word

For most parishioners, the first substantial encounter with evangelical ideas probably took place in the parish church. This was not an age of mass literacy, and comparatively few people had the facility or the opportunity to work through a published text. Moreover, the ideas at the heart of the movement were fairly complex, and most parishioners probably required a sermon or reading from the pulpit in order to learn the essentials of the faith. Reformation ideas were spread in this way, and as a consequence there was scope for individual interpretation as each preacher emphasized certain aspects or themes. But this does not necessarily mean that the character of the movement varied in its essentials from parish to parish. According to the historian Bernd Moeller, the preaching movement in the towns was marked by a fairly consistent corpus of 'uniform teachings and maxims, uniform condemnations and recommendations' derived from the teachings of Martin Luther (Moeller, 1999, p. 52). The preachers shared the same sense of urgency, for instance, the same conviction that the Catholic Church had betrayed the faithful. The pope was projected as the Antichrist, just as Luther had written, and there could be no reconciliation. In its place the preachers spoke of a Church and a faith grounded in the insights developed by the Wittenberg reformer. Scripture was the only guide, and it was no longer held captive in the prison created by the medieval Church but rather revealed to all. As Paul Speratus declared, even the 'least polished, least accomplished peasant' could learn and understand (Moeller and Stackmann, 1996, p. 315). Christ's message of salvation was meant for everyone, from the lowest member of the social hierarchy to the most distinguished. The early evangelical sermons also spoke of Luther's doctrine of justification through faith alone. It emerged, for example, in the pithy formula of Sebastian Meyer, who summed it up by saying that whoever has faith shall be forgiven. Gone was the need for good works, an idea which no doubt shocked and confused many of the gathered faithful. To soften the blow, some reformers emphasized that good works were still a component of the faith – not, however, because they contributed to salvation, but rather because they were evidence of true faith and Christian love. 'For without works [of love],' Jakob Otter wrote, 'faith is dead' (Moeller and Stackmann, 1996, p. 325). But there could be no disguising the fact that the religion preached by the evangelical clergymen was a radical departure from the religion of old. From the notion of the Antichrist to the understanding of the sacraments, supporters of the early Reformation were using the pulpit to spread the central beliefs of the evangelical faith as it was first popularized by Luther.

Of course, not all of the preachers identified with Luther or understood the faith in terms of 'uniform teachings and maxims'. In the early 1520s the meaning of Reformation was still very much in the air. Even in Luther's land of Saxony and Thuringia, reform-friendly clergy did not always agree among themselves. In Zwickau, for instance, Friedrich Myconius, Gaspar Güttel and Nicolaus Hausmann lectured from the works of Luther and rejected Catholic teaching. But Johann Sylvius Egranus, who also preached against indulgences, the wealth of the papacy, and traditional rites and ceremonies, avoided association with Wittenberg. 'We should not be divided into sects,' he wrote, 'so that we say "I am a Martinian, I am an Eckite, I am an Emserite, I am a Philippist, I am a Karlstadter, I am a Leipziger, I am a papist" and whatever more sects there may be. I will follow Saint Paul and say that I am of Jesus Christ. I preach the gospel . . . In sum, I am a follower of the Gospel and a Christian' (Karant-Nunn, 1988, p. 84). For men like Egranus, the essence of the movement was the preaching of scripture rather than the ideas of a particular school or a leading theologian. A similar cast of mind marked the movement in the southern Empire, especially in the districts influenced by the spread of the Swiss Reformation. Zwingli held preaching to be no less fundamental to salvation than Luther, for if the faithful did not hear the Gospel preached to them 'clearly and purely', the Christian conscience could never be truly free. That is the main reason why Zwingli turned to the secular authorities at the very beginning of the movement, that the people might hear the words of scripture preached on a regular basis (Hamm, 1988, p. 18). In lieu of the fact that the vast majority of parishioners were illiterate, the reformers relied upon sermons and lectures to get the message across. Little wonder historians have thought of the early Reformation as a preaching revival (Scribner, 1986, p. 20).

For the illiterate, so reliant on the spoken word, the only other means of mass communication was the printed image, the woodcut or pamphlet illustration. The early reformers used this medium to great effect, often aided by the many artists and authors who emerged as supporters of the movement. Images, unlike the written word, had no formal narrative structure. It was difficult to limit interpretation in the same manner as printed text. Nor was there the need to associate images with authorship. Most of the early evangelical woodcut illustrations relied on traditional artistic strategies (satire, analogue, allegory, allusion, metaphor, tropology) and a basic understanding of scripture to relate the message rather than the words of a leading reformer.

In Hans Sebald Beham's *Allegory of the Monastic Orders* the image works at a number of different levels. On the one hand it seems to be something of an anticlerical jab at the monastic lifestyle, with a monk literally torn between a life of luxury and earthly pleasures (symbolized by the three female figures of Pride, Lust and Avarice) and the poverty and piety that inhere in his vows (symbolized by the peasant woman and the Bible that he refuses to ingest). On the other hand the image works as a commentary on the social character of the evangelical movement, for it is the peasant who is the advocate of God's Word in this image and thus the layman who must literally force the Word of God down the throat of the clergyman (Scribner, 1994, pp. 42–4) Beham's more elaborate *Christ in the Sheep Shed* also relied on allegory, though with reference to a specific biblical citation, on this occasion John 10:1 ('Verily, verily, I say

Figure 3.1   Hans Sebald Beham, *An Allegory of the Monastic Orders*, 1521.

Figure 3.2   Hans Sebald Beham, *Christ in the Sheep Shed*, 1524.

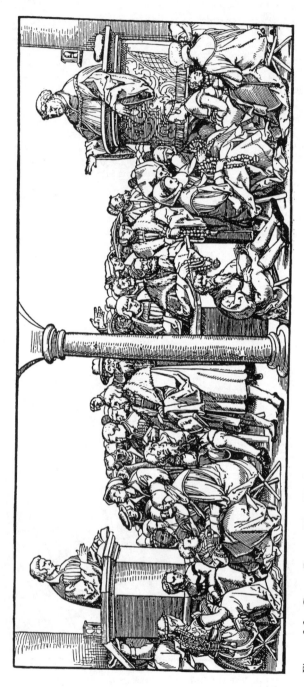

Figure 3.3 Georg Pencz, *Two Kinds of Sermons*, c.1529.

unto you, He that entereth not by the door into the sheepfold, but climbeth up some other way, the same is a thief and a robber'). Meaning could also be construed from the placement of images. Christ stands in the doorway, the sure way to salvation, while the true believers gather before him. Meanwhile the sheep shed, which stands for the Church, is besieged by Catholic clergy, the thieves and robbers of the biblical passage. At the base of the image a collection of verses by the Nuremberg poet Hans Sachs added meaning to the image. Georg Pencz's *Two Kinds of Sermons* effects a similar balance. Once again Hans Sachs provided verse for the woodcut, but the basic meaning of the illustration did not require too much elaboration. On the left is an evangelical preacher reading from scripture. This is clearly meant to suggest that this is a faith reliant on the Word of God. As the text relates, the Gospel consoles the believers and assures them that Christ alone is their mediator and advocate. On the right is the 'popish preacher', as Sachs terms him, rather more rotund and luxurious than the evangelical man, surrounded by people mired in 'pious exercises' (the rosary beads testify to this) and therefore oblivious of the pure truths of scripture. A more subtle approach is taken in *The Houses of the Wise and the Ignorant*. Christ appears above the evangelical House of the Wise at the left with the promise of peace. To the right, the Catholic House of the Ignorant is rent in two by the Antichrist, its foundations already weakened by the 'Word of God' flowing at its base. *The Houses of the Wise and the Ignorant* expected a basic knowledge of scripture (Matthew 7:24–27) from its audience, but the image itself did not need much elaboration to get the point across.

Despite the limitations of the medium, the illustrated woodcuts were able to relate fairly sophisticated theological themes. All four illustrations above manage to convey the centrality of God's Word to the faith, even if different strategies were used. The *Allegory of the Monastic Orders* allows for different readings, but there is little doubt that the artist wanted to emphasize the centrality of scripture to the movement. The artist of *The Houses of the Wise and the Ignorant* adopted a more direct approach, setting the Old and the New Testament in place as the pillars of the evangelical Church. In this image, scripture is quite literally the foundation of the faith. Meanwhile the Catholic Church, to the right, splits in two as the seven-headed

Figure 3.4 Erhard Schoen, *The Houses of the Wise and the Ignorant*, 1524.

beast of the Apocalypse rises from the depths. The two pillars of this Church, the weighty tomes of Duns Scotus and Thomas Aquinas, prove ineffective. *Christ in the Sheep Shed* also related key evangelical insights. To the left, an angel tries to redirect the attention of the Catholic faithful away from works to the Word. To the right stands Christ in the doorway, there to remind the viewer that there is only one route to salvation, for only those with faith in Christ, as the text relates, 'will surely be redeemed'. In general, even if the viewer had no understanding of evangelical theology or its main tenets, the Reformation woodcut could serve as a tool of indoctrination. Artists drew on biblical metaphors to relate basic themes, while more transparent images, such as the paschal lamb as the symbol of the risen Christ or the dove as the symbol of the Holy Spirit, could fix the meaning of the print (Scribner, 1994, pp. 190–228). Of course, pictures and icons had long played a role in Christian worship, but never before had religious imagery been used to relate such a complex theological message on such a wide scale.

Preaching was clearly fundamental for the spread of the faith, as was imagery and illustration, and yet the Reformation would not have developed into a coherent movement without the printed word. More than any other medium or vehicle of expression, the book, and in particular the published pamphlet, helped to fashion a Reformation public of common belief and purpose. Printing, a German invention, had been evolving for over half a century, and as such the reformers had the advantage of a cultural matrix already in place when they began to broadcast their message. But it was a mutually beneficial relationship, for on the eve of reform the book trade, despite its relative youth, was starting to reach its natural limitations. Books were expensive objects – large leather-bound quarto and folio volumes written, for the most part, in Latin for a learned audience. The buying public made up a very small proportion of the population; it did not really extend beyond the educated elite. With the Reformation, however, the printing industry was completely transformed (Wittmann, 1999, pp. 48–81). The majority of publications were now written in the vernacular, thus increasing the possible readership many times, while the books themselves were reduced in cost. No longer the expensive Latin tomes of late medieval scholasticism nor the weighty volumes of prolix humanists, the works published in association with the early Reformation were overwhelmingly smaller in scale and much cheaper in price. Printing became a very lucrative business – in no small part, as Eberlin von Günzberg noted, because the trade was exploiting the movement (Wittmann, 1999, p. 56). Centres sprang up throughout the German lands, from Strasbourg and Basle in the south to Augsburg, Nuremberg, Leipzig, Frankfurt and Wittenberg further to the north. In short order a clear association developed between the printing trade and the evangelical movement, a marriage of technology and ideas that turned a religious debate into a social movement.

However the early Reformation was understood, the printed word offered a forum for the variety of opinions. All types of publications emerged, from complex Latin diatribes to single-leaf illustrated satires. But without doubt the main heralds of evangelical ideas were the pamphlets (*Flugschriften*), the small, cheap, lightweight, ephemeral booklets that poured from the German presses. As they were an invention of the age, pamphlets had no history; they did not belong to any literary tradition, and this enabled the reformers to use them freely for the expression of religious ideas. Authors could present their views in the form of a dialogue, an exchange of religious opinions, with peasants, shoemakers, students, artisans, noblemen and clergymen assuming different parts in a set-piece play on a page. There were no restrictions on the figures or the roles they might create. Nor was there a limitation on the things they might think or say. Peasants might better bishops in public debate, weavers might lead an agnostic clergyman back to the true faith. Words could also break the constraints of traditional discourse and give added life to ideas. Pamphlet literature was animated throughout with unconventional dialogue and a wide range of outlandish terms – the crude, the vulgar and the carnival (Matheson, 1998). And there was also scope for extremes, such as the abuse heaped on the papacy and the clergy or the base antitheses used by the reformers to illustrate the divide between the faith of the reformers and the faith of the pope. Pamphlets were ideal for short, sharp polemic of this kind, a point understood by most of the early evangelical authors. Later in the century the genre would, on occasion, lapse into propaganda and sheer invective, and ultimately it would succumb to the rules of lettered culture and lose much of its initial urgency and invention. But in the beginning, when the Reformation was first taking root, the medium was as essential as the ideas themselves.

No other reformer in the German lands used the printed word to better effect than Martin Luther. He was not only the best-read author of his generation, but one of the most prolific writers of the century. His works brought him lasting celebrity. Luther himself was surprised by the reception of his early work and its resonance. As he observed in a letter to Christoph Scheurl, had he known his fame would gather so quickly, he would have formulated some of the theses differently (Moeller, 1988, p. 69). Yet Luther did nothing to discourage his rise to literary fame. By the year 1519, at least forty-five separate works were on the market, either written by Luther or directly associated with his actions (reports of the Leipzig disputation, for instance). On his death, there were approximately 700 works in his name circulating throughout the German lands in over 4,000 editions. He was prolific; his mind was never at rest. In the year 1520, for instance, Luther published three of his most important Reformation tracts within the space of five months and thereby provided the literate community with a summary of his main beliefs. Ultimately all of Luther's central ideas, from his theories of justification to his notions of the Antichrist to his open letters to city councils, found their way into print. He was one of the first literary celebrities the world has ever known, and he was himself, like the Reformation movement he inspired, a creation of the press.

For those followers of Luther who came to his defence, print proved just as effective. Within the first few years of his emergence as a public figure his supporters were hard at work spreading his ideas throughout the Empire. Indeed, as Adam von Schaumberg observed, even if he had died at Worms his name and his beliefs would have lived on. 'But God be praised,' Schaumberg remarked, 'Doctor Martin lives still; though had he been taken from us, there is no doubt that he has already left so many writings and so many followers that divine justice and godly truth, by way of God's help, would once again have arisen' (Hohenberger, 1996, p. 200.). Luther had become the author (in the Latin sense of *auctor*, inventor or progenitor) of a literary movement. His ideas stimulated reflection and conjecture and occasioned an unprecedented mood of engagement. But more than this, Luther's religious insights created the very themes of printed dialogue. The doctrine of justification through faith alone, for instance, despite its complexity and forensic peculiarity, was soon taken up by reform-friendly pamphleteers and discussed in print. Urbanus Rhegius managed to write a summary of the Wittenberg theology as early as 1521, centred on the idea of justification through faith alone. 'Thus speaks Luther,' wrote Rhegius, 'and it is the truth: the first and highest of all most noble work is faith in Christ' (Hohenberger, 1996, pp. 206–7). Michael Stifel, an Augustinian monk in Esslingen, wrote in a similar fashion, offering the reader a versified synthesis of Luther's thought on justification. Numerous other works followed suit, some paraphrasing Luther, some offering inspired summaries, some simply relating his words by way of a personalized narrative. One work will stand for many others: A pamphlet published in 1522 mentions Luther by name, defends his notions of justification in the same breath as its defence of the Gospel, and in the course of the dialogue makes reference to seven of his works, including *The Freedom of a Christian Man* and *The Babylonian Captivity* (Hohenberger, 1996, p. 222). In a work of this kind Luther's name was evoked not just to lend authority to an argument, but as a final reference to the revealed truth.

But not all evangelical authors set out to synthesize the ideas of the main reformers in this way. Other themes surfaced, other notions of what was fundamental to the meaning of Reformation. Paramount was the appeal to scripture, the perceived need to return to the Word of God. When the movement first emerged, the principle of scripture alone was viewed as an essential (perhaps *the* essential) feature of the new faith. Pamphleteers turned the doctrine against the Catholic authorities, for it enabled them to challenge centuries of history and tradition by appealing to a higher authority. The authors of the first generation thus went to great lengths, as Heinrich von Kettenbach did, to contrast the 'human fables, papal bulls, spiritless laws, and Imperial mandates' at the heart of the Roman Church with the 'clear and pure' Word of God which informed the evangelical faith. 'The laity set aside Scripture and the Word of God and they heed their clergy, right or wrong,' wrote Kettenbach while describing the errors of the Catholic faith. 'If the clergy in their seductive way were to tell the laity that the devil or an ass is God, they would believe that too' (Ozment, 1993, p. 49). But as the evangelical authors stressed again and again, the new faith was distinguished precisely by its trust in scripture. And it was more than just learned rhetoric. On those few occasions when the laity took up pen and paper to give voice to their religious views, the reliance on scriptural testimony was foremost. As an example we might look to the work of the Eisenberg tax-collector's wife Ursula Weyda, who challenged the understanding of a Catholic clergyman in a pamphlet entitled *Against the Unchristian, Slanderous Work of the Abbot of Pegau* (1524). 'You stupid, ignorant abbot,' she raged: 'you know as much about scriptures as a sow about harvesting a field of beets! . . . You know less about scripture than a cow about dancing!' (Russell, 1986, p. 202). Empowered by repeated appeals to scripture, she inferred that the pope and his councils were no longer the arbiters of true religion. 'The Word of God alone is important,' she insisted, 'but monks and priests know nothing of this. They use lies, which the false and devilish papal church tells them' (Russell, 1986, p. 202). There was not much separating this basic conviction from later accusations that other aspects of the Catholic faith, from good works to the sacraments to the authority of the Church, were built on false premises. Many other lay pamphleteers, among them the soldier Haug Marschalck, the shoemaker Hans Sachs, the weaver Utz Rysschner and the artisan Steffan Büllheym, would draw conclusions of this kind.

Another notion of Reformation, and one which was crucial for the social dynamic of the movement, was the widespread sense of anticlericalism. From the very beginning of the Luther affair, antagonism against Rome and the Catholic clergy had been a powerful feature. Indeed, for many of the early supporters, anticlericalism was the sum and substance of the event. Certainly the background of medieval grievances against the clergy flowed naturally into the reform endeavours. The earliest spokesmen of reform were able to draw on this tradition of anticlericalism to give voice to their views. In this manner the sentiment provided a means of expression for the early movement, a vehicle for ideas, and it helped to channel the sense of grievance. Nor should we forget that anticlericalism was an emotion bound in experience and could thus be turned to common action. As Hans-Jürgen Goertz has noted, 'without the anticlerically motivated movements of the "Common Man," the Reformation would have remained an idea' (Goertz, 1995, p. 19).

In the beginning, the attack against the clergy cut through the different social and intellectual dimensions of the movement. All of the leading reformers, following the examples of Luther and Zwingli, joined the campaign against Rome and the Catholic clergy. It was a form of anticlericalism rooted in theological antipathies, though in the case of the radical reformers, men such as Thomas Müntzer, Hans Hut and Balthasar Hubmaier, it was little less than a declaration of war. When the literate laymen joined the fray, however, the social aspects came to the fore (Goertz, 1995, pp. 47 ff.). Ulrich von Hutten raged against the expropriations of Rome and the venality of the monastic orders, while Hartmut von Cronberg referred to the pope as the vicar of the Antichrist and the Devil's vice-governor for the ruin he had brought on Germany. And when the peasants rose up in revolt during the 1520s, the Church and its clergy likewise emerged as the main targets of the military assemblies. Peasant manifestos made repeated references to the perceived misdealings and misappropriations of the Church and demanded a reform of the clerical estate. Many of the rural peasants and the urban layfolk looked to the reformers and their religious proposals to remedy the unsuitable state of affairs. Their interest in the evangelical movement was aroused by this concern, and in the eyes of many it was the central issue of the movement – for both parties. 'If the teaching of Martin Luther had not threatened their [the clergy's] power, honour, their food stores, cellars and kitchens,' wrote an evangelical pamphleteer, 'they would not be so opposed to him' (Matheson, 1998, p. 95).

Closely associated with the prevalent mood of anticlericalism was a growing confidence in the ability of the average parishioner to understand the Word of God. Clearly, this confidence was derived, in part, from the principles of Reformation thought (the trust in scripture, the priesthood of all believers, the centrality of personal faith to salvation) and it was quickly tied to traditional social grievances. The parishioners welcomed the chance to reduce the power of the clergy and assume a greater role for themselves in religious affairs. There is thus much truth in the suggestion that the laity turned to the movement because it 'flattered' them; it placed their spiritual destinies in their own hands. 'From being hesitant trespassers on the margins of the spiritual domain, laymen were actually *invited* to judge issues at the very heart of their dealings with the Almighty, and by clerics at that!' (Cameron, 1991, p. 312). One of the main motifs of the early literature was the emergence of the learned layman, the common parishioner of simple faith who was able to recognize the truth of scripture. Even the peasants were afforded this insight, as the famous figure of Karsthans attested. Numerous pamphlets playing on this theme appeared during the first decade of the movement. Authors would contrast the honest faith of the average parishioner with the greed, deception and falsehood of the Roman clergy. And at the heart of the revolution was a growing familiarity with the Word of God. Witness the sense of discovery and confidence at the heart of this dialogue:

Shoemaker:	I have just written a book about your church services and teaching to explain them to the common man [*gemain man*].
Canon:	What does a shoemaker know about such things? He works with leather, not with Scripture ... I must tell you it is not proper for the laity to occupy themselves with Scripture.
Shoemaker:	Didn't Christ say in Matthew 7, guard yourselves from false prophets ... and Paul in Philippians 3 warned us to look out for the dogs. If it isn't appropriate for us to know the Scriptures, how will we recognize such things?
Canon:	That belongs to the bishops, as Paul says in Titus 1 ...
Shoemaker:	Yes, but they don't do that. They do just the opposite.
Canon:	What can you laymen learn? Many of you can't even read.
Shoemaker:	Christ said, 'You are all learned in God.'
Canon:	Yes, but there is an art to it. Why otherwise have universities?
Shoemaker:	What university did John graduate from? He was just a fisherman, like Mark.
Canon:	They had the holy spirit.

(Chrisman, 1996, p. 161)

Finally, a common concern during the initial stage of the movement was the need for a return to order. It is worth remembering that the movement took shape in a climate charged with the expectation of reform, and well before the Luther affair people were speaking of the fragility and uncertainty of the times (Strauss, 1995, pp. 1–30). Prophets and advocates of change spoke quite specifically about types of reformation (*reformatio*) or renewal (*renovatio*), but the terms were also used indiscriminately and applied to a variety of causes, from political systems and university regulations to the general order of being and the constitution of the Catholic Church. Most talk of *reformatio* took on meaning within the context of the Christian tradition. In the medieval period religious movements had emerged projecting a notion of *reformatio* which looked to original apostolic Christianity as its guide. The Franciscan spirituals in the thirteenth century belonged to this tradition, as indeed did the conciliarists of the late medieval period. Ideas of *reformatio* were also common to medieval political culture. Notions of political reform did the rounds as ominous prophecies, such as the return of the reforming Emperor or the plans associated with the *Reformatio Sigismundi* (1438). There were also quite deliberate and determined efforts to change the basic system of rule in the Empire. The reign of Maximilian I (1493–1519) bore the brunt of these, culminating in the reform programme submitted at the diet of Worms in 1495. In general, however, contemporaries did not think of reformation in exclusively political or religious terms, and while there were certain traditional notions in circulation, this did not limit public dialogue. *Reformatio* was a word charged with a variety of meanings, and its essential power lay in the range of its possible associations rather than any real normative weight.

Thus when the followers of the evangelical movement first came forward they often spoke in general terms about the need for reform and renewal. The appeal to scripture was invoked as a panacea for the ills of the German Nation, and those ills could include almost anything, from the condition of the Church to the state of morality to more specific allusions to governance, marriage, education and public welfare. The essential consideration was the need for order, a return to faith, morality and justice, and for many people the only solution lay in a reform of the community based on the Word of God. As we will see, the idea of the holy community could mean different things in different contexts, but the inclination to judge earthly affairs according to the measure of scripture was common.

When the imperial knights first came out in defence of Luther, a central feature of their interest was the need to restore order and unity to the German lands. For Ulrich von Hutten, the papacy was at the root of the Empire's afflictions. End the tyranny of Rome, he advised, and restore German liberties – at the very least, reform must begin with this. Franz von Sickingen also wrote in support of the movement, emphasizing the need to set things right in the German Church. Others followed suit. 'I, Eckhardt zum Drübel, am certainly not a Lutheran nor an agitator,' wrote another of Sickingen's circle, 'but I am a Christian and a layman and my conscience has been uneasy for many years . . . with regard to the . . . disorder in our Christian faith' (Chrisman, 1996, p. 102). The same concern was paramount in the towns and cities, where reformers such as Huldrych Zwingli and Martin Bucer preached in explicit terms about the need to create the godly community. In response, the faithful tied their reading of the Gospel to the world of social experience. In *The Three Christians* (1523) Pamphilus Gegenbach revealed this cast of mind by projecting the utopian image of a town built in the image of God's commandment of brotherly love. A few years later, radicals such as Hans Hergot and Michael Gaismair would take the same approach to extremes in their visions of the godly community on earth, but the concern with order did not have to lead down such radical paths. Many of the urban laity also turned to the evangelical movement because it spoke to their need for general reform, whether that meant a reform of Church, State, morals or belief. Some parishioners were quite specific about what they had in mind. When the Strasbourg artisan Steffan Büllheym spoke up in defence of the movement, he emphasized the need to reform the moral quality of the Roman clergy. And he pointed to the culprits – the Strasbourg priest and his fat wife, the canon at Old Saint Peter, the Dominican Thomas Schwein, the vicar of the Cathedral (Chrisman, 1996, p. 183). For Büllheym, it was clear that God's Word spoke directly to the disorder of the Strasbourg commune.

Lazarus Spengler, Nuremberg's long-term municipal secretary, approached the movement from this perspective. When the Luther affair first surfaced, Spengler had been in office for over a decade. He was thoroughly familiar with the rights, traditions and obligations of the city government, including the minutiae of its ecclesiastical affairs, and he was often privy to Nuremberg's most important political concerns. In 1519 Spengler published *Defence and Christian Reply of an Honourable Lover of Divine Truth*, the first public defence of Luther written by a layman. For Spengler, Luther's message was prized for its reliance on scripture, and thus its proximity to the Word of God, and its ability to expose the 'false doctrines and teachings' of the Catholic Church. In his second defence, published anonymously in 1522, Spengler drew on evangelical theology to bring to light the supposed errors of the Catholic Church. Belief in free will is false, he advised the reader, as is the notion of salvation in good works, the authority of tradition and the idea that scripture belongs to the clergy alone. In addition to his theological insights, Spengler stressed the importance of godly norms. 'Believe in Christ and do for your neighbour as you believe Christ has done for you. That is the singular way to become pious and blessed; there is no other' (Ozment, 1975, pp. 78–9). This final admonition exposed the social dimension of Spengler's religious thought, for his vision of reform was strongly influenced by the notion of community. This was common to many of the lay leaders of the urban Reformation, this fusion of law and Gospel, the belief that the urban community had a spiritual foundation and a spiritual goal. Spengler imagined a Reformation guided by the Word of God, but realized in the urban commune. In doing this, 'Spengler moved completely within the mental horizons of his civic world,' for he anchored social values to sacred norms and saw a fluid continuum between matters of the spirit and matters of the flesh, 'between private and public, between spiritual and secular, between Christian morality and upright civic virtue' (Hamm, 1996, p. 156). In this vision of reform the evangelical movement was imagined in part as a confirmation of traditional values of community. It would bring with it a return to order.

People like Ulrich von Hutten, Steffan Büllheym, Lazarus Spengler and Ursula Weyda are proof that the Reformation engaged the laity as much as it did the clergy. And they are also testimony to the variety of perspectives that informed early notions of reform. But this survey of poets and pamphleteers should not be taken as representative of the laity as a whole. Most people in the sixteenth century lacked both the opportunity and the ability to express themselves in print. For the vast majority of people, the only way to demonstrate religious conviction was through public action. This was especially true for the rural parishioners, the faithful in the villages and hamlets, where the evangelical message also found a ready audience.

The Rural Reformation and the Peasants' War

In 1524 a short manifesto was published in the name of the Franconian village of Wendelstein. The manifesto, which is now referred to as the *Wendelstein Church Ordinance*, was read aloud to the newly appointed pastor as he came to assume office. Claiming to speak for the Christian congregation, the ordinance related how 'according to the testimony of Holy Scripture' the commune had the right to seek a pastor for its church and the power to dismiss him if he were found unsuitable (Krodel, 1964, pp. 151–2). As they informed the pastor, 'we shall acknowledge you not as a lord over, but only as a servant . . . of the congregation; you are not to give us orders, but we will give you orders.' The first task of any pastor, the ordinance continued, was the preaching of the Word. 'And so we command you to present the gospel to us faithfully . . . in its purity . . . according to the truth,' free of all human additions. It ordered the pastor to lead a Christian life and administer baptism in the German language. For this, he will receive the traditional tithe, but not the unwarranted fees and dues exacted by the Catholic clergy. The manifesto ends by reminding him that he is both a servant of the commune and a subject of the neighbouring prince. He should pay heed to their wishes, it reads, or 'we shall not only brand you as an unfaithful servant but shall also drive you as a ravenous wolf into the net and shall under no circumstances tolerate you in our midst.'

The first thing that strikes the modern reader about the *Wendelstein Church Ordinance* is its claims to sovereignty. The clergyman had become a servant of the commune. In part, this was a new political language, shaped by the principles of evangelical theology. But the ordinance was also a natural expression of the political culture in this age. Throughout the late medieval period (1300–1500) the village commune had been evolving into a new type of political association (Blickle, 1997, pp. 11–50; Wunder, 1986, pp. 33–79). The process was most pronounced in south-west Germany and Switzerland, less so in the north, but certain features were fairly widespread. Exploitation of natural resources, intensified agricultural relationships, and the gradual breakdown of the manorial system forced local settlements to join together in social and political organizations. The result was the evolution of the village commune (*Gemeinde*), a unit of governance with its own norms and institutions, its own traditions of law and order, and its own public servants. By way of example, Wendelstein had a core of local officials empowered to rule over village affairs and its own judicial court for lesser crimes. Every male householder, in theory, had the right to attend the village assembly and cast his vote. It was a far cry from our modern notions of democracy, for not only were women excluded but the landless, the homeless, the jobless and the poor. But it was a widespread form of political culture in Germany, and it did represent an alternative to the culture of feudal lordship. When the Reformation first developed, communalism was a powerful reality of political life.

The other thing that strikes the reader is the ease with which the ordinance subjects the clergyman to the secular order. Indeed, the ordinance ends by reminding the pastor that he was no longer subject to the ecclesiastical courts in Eichstätt, but rather to the princely courts of Ansbach. This too, in large part, was the expression of a new sense of social and political consciousness given voice by the evangelical movement. But it also had a historical provenance, for just as the local communes were developing into fairly autonomous political associations, so too were the communes extending their control over the local church. Canon law provided the framework for this development. Once a candidate was ordained and appointed to office, he offered his clerical services in return for a living. In most instances this meant assuming the office of parish priest, with the notion of parish (*parochia*) encompassing a distinct legal domain of land and people. With the passage of time, however, the office itself began to assume a worldly character. Clerical income often fell to the supervision of secular officials, while local lords and parish associations acquired rights of patronage. At the same time, villagers appointed churchwardens to watch over the parish church and assume responsibility for its inner and outer fabric. Moreover, by way of endowments and foundations, the community could not only tailor the local church to their needs but determine the type of religious services required (Fuhrmann, 1995, pp. 436–51). Thus the late medieval parishioners were no strangers to the idea that the parish church should be subject to temporal regulations. On the contrary, on the eve of the Reformation, many German villagers thought of the church as a local, communal institution.

Thus, to understand the Reformation as the peasants understood the Reformation, as the historian Peter Blickle has observed, we have to imagine religious culture in terms of the commune. (Blickle, 1992, 1999, pp. 136–67). Using such an approach, three distinct characteristics of the rural Reformation stand out. First, like their urban counterparts, the rural parishioners demanded the preaching of the Gospel and the creation of an evangelical church. In addition to this spiritual concern, the rural communes demanded the right to appoint and dismiss the pastor, the right to judge his teaching and the right to manage church funds. All of these claims were drawn from scripture and all imagined the church as a communal institution. Second, the rural parishioners tended to read scripture tropologically, which meant they abstracted norms from the Gospel or the evangelical message and applied them to social and political relations. 'To hear the Gospel and live accordingly' was a frequent refrain in the peasant supplications, and it was evidence of their tendency to relate the abstract religious message to the central concerns of daily life. The most fateful association was the biblical invocation of brotherly love and the political idea of the common good (*Gemeinnutz*), a marriage of religious teachings and political values with obvious appeal for the rural commune. Third, the idea of a reform movement tied to the values and aspirations of the parish commune was not just an unforeseen corollary of the evangelical movement. In many ways, the idea of a communal Reformation was present in the very thought of the leading reformers. Luther empowered the commune in his early works, even if he drew back on the eve of revolution, while many of the south German and Swiss reformers, men such as Huldrych Zwingli and Martin Bucer, spoke in quite explicit terms about the need for God's Word to bring about the godly community on earth. All of these aspects of the evangelical movement in the rural parishes supported the idea of a reformation located and developed at the level of the commune.

Not all historians agree with the notion of a communal Reformation as Blickle has articulated it, and there has certainly been doubt cast about the scale of its application (Scott, 1991, pp. 183–92, 1992, pp. 175–92). Critics suggest there was no necessary relationship between the evangelical faith and the desire to control the local church, and the model of a parish working to realize communal goals does not really take the tensions or complexity of local rule into account. And yet there is no doubt that in some parts of the Empire there is strong evidence that the early Reformation found a ready audience in the rural parishes. In some instances, as in the parish of Wendelstein, for instance, the commune itself formulated its own understanding of reform. In the rural parishes near the city of Zurich, the villagers surfaced very early on as supporters of the movement. In Upper Swabia, the rural parishioners repeatedly demanded the right to appoint pastors, the right to control church finance and the right to have a clergyman who would preach the Word of God 'clearly and purely'. Similar demands were voiced in the parishes of Salzburg and the Tyrol. In Alsace, the peasants were the earliest supporters of the evangelical movement, demanding a reform of the Church based on the principles of scripture and rooted in the communes (Blickle, 1992, pp. 12–53; Conrad, 1984, pp. 91–114). As the new ideas spread through the parishes in the Tyrol in the early 1520s, it was the peasants and their unique understanding of religious reform who stood at the forefront of the movement. When Jacob Strauß began preaching the faith in Hall, the local chronicler observed how his sermons soon attracted a huge following of people from the town, but also 'those from the neighbouring villages . . . the peasant folk' (Bierbrauer, 1993, p. 50). In time the council of Hall allowed Strauß to preach in a larger church. When the authorities found a stash of Lutheran publications in the monastery at Stams, the Innsbruck officials were reluctant to act, for they feared the peasants might turn violent if the books were confiscated. Similar concerns were raised following investigations in the parishes of Breitenwang, Zillertal, Imst and Schwaz, where a group of Franciscan monks were preaching the new faith to the resident miners. In these parishes, as elsewhere, the combination of evangelical theology and peasant expectation accounted for much of the success of the early Reformation. It also proved to be a large part of the formula which transformed the reform movement into a social and political revolution.

For over a year, from mid-1524 to the early months of 1526, the common man took up arms against the local lords in an event historians have labelled the Peasants' War of 1525. The course of battle is well known. On 30 May 1524 subjects of the Black Forest abbey of St Blasien refused to pay traditional dues or to render feudal services. In June the peasants of Stühlingen followed suit, rejecting requests for customary exactions and demanding self-government. Peasants joined up in the Black Forest and Upper Swabia, taking revolution to the cities of Waldshut, Zurich and Freiburg im Breisgau. Armed bands marched through the lands of Swabia and gathered together near the shores of Lake Constance. By the spring of 1525 the area of revolt had spread to the environs of Ulm, Biberach, Lindau and the abbey of Kempten. A peasant assembly met in Memmingen, and the Christian Union of Upper Swabia, a sworn association of rebel peasants, was declared on 27 February 1525. To the north, in the lands of Franconia, peasant bands began forming in March and April (Tauber Valley, Odenwald-Neckar, Bildhausen). After taking the city of Rothenburg, the Tauber Valley band, with many Rothenburg artisans in tow, marched through Franconia, razing noble strongholds and ultimately setting siege to the bishop's palace in Würzburg. The Odenwald-Neckar band, with subjects of Mainz, Hohenlohe and Württemberg, invested the town of Heilbronn and surrounded the castle of Aschaffenburg. Further north, in the lands of Thuringia, where an urban revolt had occurred in Mühlhausen in 1524, a still more threatening movement followed in April 1525, as the peasants, encouraged by the preaching of Thomas Müntzer and marching under the banner of the Eternal League of God, took up arms in Fulda and the Werra valley. Similar events occurred in Alsace and the Palatinate. Indeed in Alsace, where the bishop of Strasbourg was the object of peasant grievance, violent anticlericalism shadowed the event. Abbey after abbey was taken by the peasants, while bands marched through the districts of Saverne, Strasbourg, the Sundgau and Montbéliard. In the Tyrol the miners of Schwaz showed the first signs of unrest in January 1525. By May the rebel movement,

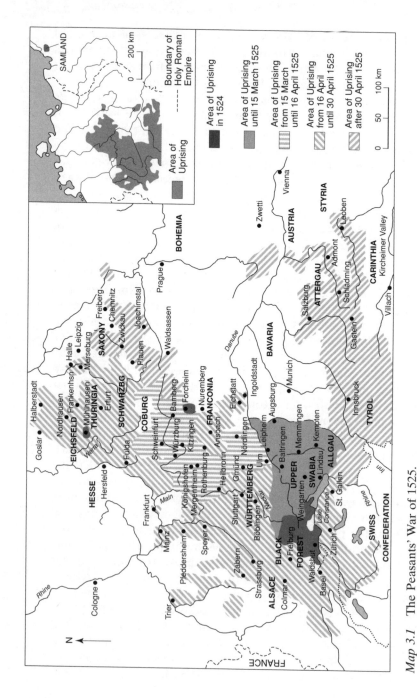

Map 3.1 The Peasants' War of 1525.

Source: Bob Scribner and Gerhard Benecke (eds), *The German Peasants' War of 1525: New Viewpoints* (London: George Allen & Unwin, 1979).

having shifted south, was consolidated enough to hold its own provisional assembly at Merano (30 May 1525), while to the east, in the Catholic heartland of imperial Germany, the peasants of Inner Austria went so far as to lay siege to the archbishopric of Salzburg. By 1525 most of the central and southern German lands, as well as Switzerland and Austria, were in the grip of revolution (Scott and Scribner, 1991, pp. 19–53).

Contemporaries were quick to blame the preaching of the reformers for the unrest, but at one level the revolution was just one stage (albeit the most threatening) in a series of popular revolts which had occurred in the southern Empire for over a century. Unrest, to some extent, was unavoidable in this age. In the absence of political dialogue, or indeed any sign that the authorities were willing to heed peasant demands, the subject population took up arms – against taxes, against feudal dues, against arbitrary rule. On occasion, as in Salzburg, a revolt might force through some concessions, but the majority of uprisings, even one as large as the Poor Conrad revolt in Württemberg (1514), ended in defeat. Yet all the major peasant revolts in the Empire, whatever the outcome, developed out of similar social and political conditions. Late medieval Germany witnessed the rise of the territorial powers, a process which necessarily occurred at the expense of local autonomy. For the peasants, this meant further burdens brought on by the legal and administrative apparatus, as well as an increase in the related financial demands. Faced by an agrarian crisis, and affected by the problems of overpopulation, the territorial rulers 'used every possible opportunity to bind "their" peasants more closely to themselves by intensifying the forms of personal dependence' (Blickle, 1981, p. 30). Hunting, fishing and the use of common lands were now restricted by the lord's forest administrators; common law was replaced by Roman law and communal traditions were ignored; feudal dues and rents increased, as did customary feudal requirements such as forced labour and death duties; and the lords, desperate for income, restricted peasants' access to the markets of their choice. Agricultural conditions worsened, while the territorial rulers claimed a monopoly of stock-rearing, viticulture and the cultivation of industrial crops. The result was a process of disenfranchisement as the peasant community was gradually divested of its local sovereignty, and the claims of the territorial state become more and more exclusive and absolute. Peasant revolution, conceived and articulated within the framework of the commune, was a response to this historical process.

Many of the rebel manifestos drawn up during the Peasants' War spoke directly to these medieval developments. The most widely circulated programme of the revolution, *The Twelve Articles of the Upper Swabian Peasants* (1525), articulates the secular concerns at the root of the insurrection. The manifesto begins by referring to the 'basic and just articles of the whole peasantry and the subjects of spiritual and secular lords, by whom they feel themselves burdened' (Baylor, 1991, pp. 231–8). Article three disputes the justice of serfdom and the notion that the peasant can be regarded as 'a lord's personal property'. Where was this written in scripture? 'Without a doubt,' the authors resolve, 'as true and just Christians, you will also gladly release us from serfdom, or show us from the gospel that we should be serfs.' Article four speaks of the great detriment caused by the unjust laws against 'the right to hunt game or fowl or to catch fish in flowing water'. Nor should the woodlands be restricted, as article five relates, but rather the community should have the right to use it freely. The remaining articles address similar themes, from the gradual exclusion of 'ancient laws' to the reduction of the common lands. *The Merano Articles* (30 May 1525), drawn up by the rebels in the Tyrol, also spoke of the many 'evil abuses [which] have arisen in the secular and spiritual estates for some time now'. Numbered among the list of complaints were the unwarranted mortgages and revenues demanded by the clergy, the growing complexity of the law, rising fees and dues, the threat posed by an unchecked nobility, labour services, and the damage done to the local communities when the waters and woodlands are enclosed. Even in the cities, as the *Articles of the Peasants of Memmingen* suggest, the subject population looked to the authorities for the redress of grievances inherited from the fifteenth century (Scott and Scribner, 1991, pp. 78–95).

Yet there was a completely different quality to the revolution of 1525, a quality derived through its association with the evangelical movement. Unlike the revolts of medieval Europe, the Peasants' War was supra-territorial, a movement with common grievances, common ideas and a common field of action. And fundamental to both its evolution and its constitution was the peasant reading of the religious message. Paramount was the demand for the Word of God, registered, for instance, with force in the *Twelve Articles*, where it was written that 'the peasants want to be taught and to live by such a gospel' and thus the pastor 'should preach the gospel to us purely and clearly'. In Alsace the peasants made similar demands for the preaching of the Word, the only 'light of truth', as did the rural parishioners in the Tyrol, who understood the rise of reform as the advent of God's Word, which 'due to the grace of the Lord is once again in evidence, clear, pure, and unblemished' (Bierbrauer, 1993, p. 93). Closely associated with the peasant trust in God's Word was the belief in the commune's right to appoint and dismiss the pastor, a demand which surfaced in a number of peasant manifestos, including the *Twelve Articles* and the articles of Memmingen, Tyrol and Salzburg. It was also a demand with affinities with the conviction that the introduction of the evangelical faith would lead to a reform of the local clergy and the elimination of traditional abuses such as absenteeism, incorporation, pluralism, simony and unwarranted tithes (Blickle, 1981, pp. 12–40). The *Merano Articles* (30 May 1525) made reference to these 'evil abuses' and called for a new territorial ordinance to remedy the state of the Church, while many other regional manifestos imagined a communal solution to the general crisis. With the rise of violence during the Peasants' War these demands, though inspired by the Word of God and largely concerned with the reform of religion, came to threaten the very fabric of governance.

There was no more powerful witness to the influence of evangelical ideas during the Peasants' War than the repeated appeals to the authority of scripture. The conviction first surfaced in the early 1520s, when the peasants called for the Word of God preached 'clearly and purely'. By early 1525, however, as unrest swept through most of southern Germany, the teachings of the Gospel were drawn upon to support detailed and often revolutionary visions of social and political change. In the most radical of these published tracts, *To the Assembly of the Common Peasantry* (May 1525), traditional authority was rejected because 'so far God has never enlightened them [the rulers] with his grace so that they recognise what authority really is' (Baylor, 1991,

p. 103). Only a true reading of scripture could grant this knowledge, a reading which elevated the commune above the existing relations of rule and abolished the traditional hierarchies. Moreover, should the authorities not recognize the truth as revealed by the Word, the author related the necessary conclusion: 'I will prove that a territory or community has the power to depose its pernicious lords, by introducing thirteen sayings drawn from divine law, which the gates of hell with all their knights cannot destroy' (Baylor, 1991, p. 119). Taken to such extremes, scripture provided the peasants with an appeal to 'godly law', a source of authority which superseded all traditional civil and ecclesiastical traditions. In place of tyranny and princely rule, the rule of godly law would be realized on earth and with it the principles of personal freedom, equality before the courts, brotherly love and natural rights. Serfdom, for instance, was rejected on the grounds of revealed religion. Christ's saving death, the command to love one another as brothers, and the natural laws associated with divine creation ruled against it (Blickle, 1998, pp. 35–69). Similar conclusions were drawn by referring to the nature of the worshipping community in the New Testament, with the result that many conventional seigniorial rights (hunting, fishing, fees and dues) were rejected as unchristian.

According to Luther, this was a false reading of God's Word, blinded and befouled by worldly concerns. For the peasants, however, there was no distinction between the promises of scripture and the world of experience. Evangelical preaching had taught the rural parishioners that scripture alone was the sole standard of sacred and secular truth. There was no higher authority than the Word of God, and that meant that both Church and State had to comply to the norms of Holy Writ. As a result, both the clergy and the Church were shorn of their special status, while the peasants, with centuries of local tradition in mind, imagined a Reformation realized at the level of the commune. Similarly, inspired by the rediscovery of scripture, the rural parishioners began to rethink the social and political relations of the realm and challenge the basic structures of rule. Actions, rather than words, bore witness to this cast of mind, but the few written works associated with the rural Reformation, from the *Wendelstein Church Ordinance* to the more radical *Twelve Articles*, articulated the essential themes. This was a worldly reading of the evangelical message, just as Luther had charged, but it was no less fundamental to the character of the Reformation as it took hold in the German lands.

The Theology of Revolution

In April, 1525 the Swabian League launched its military campaign against the rebels. It was a success. By late May, most of the main peasant bands had been driven back or overthrown and order was restored to the Empire. In the same month Luther published *Against the Robbing and Murdering Hordes of Peasants*, a work which denounced the rebels for implicating the gospel 'selfishly in . . . sedition' and admonished the princes to 'smite and punish these peasants.' Abandoned by the reformers and defeated by the authorities, the surviving rebels returned to their parishes to wait for the retribution of their lords. From this point forward the Reformation fell subject to the control of the ruling elite. But the ideas and the aspirations at the heart of the peasant movement had not been extinguished by military failure. An alternative tradition of evangelical thought, shaped in large part by the very men who had drafted the peasant manifestos and led the rebel bands, continued to take root in the rural parishes of the German lands. Historians have referred to this as the radical Reformation, a movement distinguished by its apostolic ideals, its literal readings of scripture, its rejection of secular and ecclesiastical tradition, its social and religious meliorism, and its prophecies, preaching and visions of the pending apocalypse (Stayer, 1995, pp. 249–78).

A narrative account of the radical Reformation begins in Wittenberg, where Andreas Karlstadt, inspired perhaps by Nicholas Storch and the Zwickau prophets, withdrew from traditional theological debate and began a search for alternative sources of inspiration and authority. Karlstadt's reliance on the Word of God intensified, to the point where he would recognize no authority other than scripture. 'If a peasant from his plough could show the Council by Scripture that his meaning was right,' he wrote, 'and that of the Council of the Church was wrong, then the Council ought to yield to the peasant and give him honour on account of the Biblical writing' (Rupp, 1969, p. 83). By 1520 Karlstadt had rejected the papal claims to primacy, especially its presumed sovereignty in matters of interpretation, and a marked anticlerical tone crept into his writing. Turning away from the Church, he sought reassurance in the language and ideas of the German mystical tradition. He drew from the works of Johannes Tauler and Johann Staupitz, and he spoke of how complete resignation (*Gelassenheit*) in the face of the divine will was the highest virtue of true belief. Church reform remained a priority, but it soon became clear that his vision of reform went beyond the limits established by Luther's theology. Karlstadt looked inward for religious truth, speaking of revelation and the mystical marriage between God and the believer; he criticized Luther's trust in a magisterial Reformation, projecting a Christian community bound in the norms of brotherly love and the principles of social equality; and he preached of the elect, the chosen community, and how the true Christian congregation 'be it great or small shall make up its own mind what is right and shall do it without tarrying for any' (Rupp, 1969, p. 138). With this final point Karlstadt blurred the distinction between reformation and revolution, stating clearly in his work *Whether One Should Proceed Slowly* (1524) that the reform of God's Church must not wait for the weaker conscience, as Luther had advised. The reform of worship, and in particular the removal of images, the suspension of infant baptism and the reform of the Mass, must be introduced without delay.

At the same time, in the Saxon towns of Zwickau, Allstedt and Mühlhausen, the clergyman Thomas Müntzer was preaching a faith steeped in intuition and allegory, informed by his own mystical reading of God's Word. Müntzer's career as an evangelical preacher originated in Zwickau. Soon after his arrival he began to stir up the congregation with anticlerical sermons and visions of the godly community on earth. Eventually his preaching led to unrest and Müntzer was forced to move on to Prague, where he published the *Prague Manifesto* (1521), the first explicit declaration of his reforming ideas. In this work Müntzer compared the 'scholars, priests, and monks' to the 'thieves and murderers from the Bible' for their crime of robbing the faith of its meaning. True religion was not found in the learned tracts or the dead letter of scripture; it was written on the hearts of men. He spoke of a mystical union with God, as Karlstadt did, though with a much stronger emphasis on the necessity of fear and 'the suffering of creatures' as preparation for true faith. In addition to his spiritualism, two other themes central to Müntzer's thought also appeared in this tract: the idea of the elect community and the conviction that the age of the Antichrist would soon begin. 'The time of the harvest is at hand!' he claimed. 'Thus God himself has appointed me for his harvest. I have made my sickle sharp, for my thoughts are zealous for the truth and my lips, skin, hands, hair, soul, body, and my life all damn the unbelievers' (Baylor, 1991, p. 10). Enraged by Luther's willingness to compromise with the authorities, he began to attack the reformer in print. Luther, for his part, thought Müntzer more dangerous than the Romanists. In Müntzer's talk about the spirit, his misgivings about scripture, his notions of the elect community and his visions of the coming harvest, Luther believed the Devil was at work.

Müntzer's preaching became even more aggressive and intolerant, his theology more mystical and internal, and his visions more revolutionary. He spoke of the elect friends of God 'united in the poverty of the spirit,' and he saw himself as a prophet, come to deliver the 'poor, wretched, pitiable Christian people' from the godless authorities. He began to speak openly of violence in defence of the elect (Scott, 1989, p. 60). There was no greater testimony to the radical tenor of his theology than his *Sermon to the Princes* (1524), a public address held in the presence of both Duke Johann and the crown prince Johann Friedrich of Saxony. Drawing on dreams from the second chapter of Daniel, Müntzer spoke of the deceit of the clergy, the decline of the Church, the downfall of earthly kingdoms and the coming reign of Christ. He admonished the princes to prepare for the impending struggle between the godless and the elect, and he reminded them that God had placed them in power to wield the sword against non-believers. 'For a godless man,' he raged, 'has no right to live if he gets in the way of the godly' (Rupp, 1969, p. 203). After one aborted attempt at reform, Müntzer settled in the Saxon town of Mühlhausen, and it was there, together with Heinrich Pfeiffer, that he finally realized his theology of revolution. He formed the Eternal League of God (April 1525), an openly military association of true believers convened in order to smite the godless. On 11 May 1525 Müntzer set out under the banner of the Eternal League and joined up with the peasants in Frankenhausen. The intention was clear: once victorious, the League would bring down the mighty, give power to the poor in spirit, and overthrow the false clergy and their godless throng (Scott, 1989, pp. 127–80). In the

end, however, the combined forces of Saxony, Hesse and Braunschweig routed the rebel army. Müntzer was captured, tortured
and executed, his body left on display as a warning. For Luther,
the defeat served as a parable of wayward faith and earthly
conceit. For the Saxon authorities, in contrast, it was a timely
reminder that religious ideas, if stretched too far, could lead to
other worlds of thought.

A similar strain of radical evangelical belief evolved in the
lands of south Germany and Switzerland, where Zwingli, no less
than Luther, faced growing opposition from within his own
ranks. The first to defect publicly (and in essence the founder of
Swiss Anabaptism) was Conrad Grebel. Grebel had been a close
associate of both Zwingli and Leo Jud, but he soon came to dis-
agree with the Zurich reformers over questions of duty and
authority. The issue was similar to the point of dispute between
Luther and Karlstadt: Grebel rejected Zwingli's readiness to
compromise the Gospel in order to secure the cooperation of
the magistracy. 'Zwingli,' he wrote, 'the herald of the Word, has
cast down the Word, has trodden it underfoot, and has brought
it into captivity' (Williams, 1962, p. 96). In his eyes, the reform
of the faith must be immediate, undiminished and without concession, and that meant, in the first instance, abolishing the
Catholic Mass and cleansing the churches of all images. The
matter surfaced publicly at the Second Disputation in Zurich
(October 1523), where Grebel's objections were also voiced by
Simon Stumpf, Balthasar Hubmaier and Ludwig Haetzer. In
short order a community gathered as other reformers, including
prominent Anabaptists such as Felix Mantz, Georg Blaurock,
Johannes Brötli and Wilhelm Reublin, renounced the Reformation in Zurich and took refuge in the voluntary church, a
separate community of like-minded believers which began to
distance itself from the Zwinglian settlement. A brotherhood of
radical reformers thus evolved in the Swiss lands at the same
time as the Reformation took shape in the city of Zurich.

Grebel first articulated the beliefs at the heart of this community in his *Letter to Thomas Müntzer* (5 September 1524), a
document which made it clear that the Swiss community held
many of the views shared by the Saxon enthusiasts. But it was
really the drafting of the *Schleitheim Articles* in February 1527
that synthesized the basic tenets of the religion. The *Articles*,
written in the main by the Anabaptist Michael Sattler, set out

the principles of an exclusive faith. Baptism was reserved for those who understood repentance; it was a spiritual passage, a decision 'to walk in the resurrection of Christ'. Infant baptism, it followed, was an abomination. Discipline and communion were restricted to the baptized elect, those who had been called to God in one faith, one baptism, one spirit. The Church and its faithful must separate from the world and its evils. There could be no association, no participation. 'For there has never been anything in the world and among all creatures except good and evil,' read article four, 'believing and unbelieving, darkness and light, the world and those who are out of the world, God's temple and idols, Christ and Belial, and neither may have anything to do with the other' (Baylor 1991, p. 175). Unlike Müntzer, the Swiss radicals did not speak in terms of force or resistance. But there was the same sense of mission, the same depth of spiritual conviction and the same association of God's Word with the realities of Christian life. There was also the same note of disquiet and impatience, the conviction that the initial Reformation had not gone far enough.

The radical reformers did not agree among themselves. There was no core theology or canon of the faith, and no single figure united the later Anabaptist communities. Nevertheless, there were four basic features of the movement held in common (Goertz, 1996, pp. 36–84). First, in both Saxony and Switzerland, the radical reformers employed an extremely literal approach to scripture. Indeed, Grebel and his Swiss followers first moved away from Zwingli because they thought he had betrayed the principle of *sola scriptura*. They formed interpretative communities, abandoned traditional approaches to Holy Writ and adopted a reading of scripture so literal the magisterial reformers accused them of being legalistic. The upper German radicals, in contrast to the Swiss, were less reliant on the letter than the spirit, but even in the case of the spiritualists the visions conformed (if only figuratively) to the Word of God. The most famous literal reading of scripture (Mathew 7:14) was the rejection of infant baptism (a corollary to the conviction that faith must precede admittance to the worshipping community). Not all of the radical reformers made this distinction in print, but in a very short time the rite of adult baptism (or rebaptism, which is the meaning of the term Anabaptism) became the distinguishing mark of the radical tradition. The same hermeneutical approach also led to attacks against the Mass, the sacraments and sacramentals, images of worship and the status of the ministry. The radicals held that the Church had fallen prey to a reliance on 'outward works' far removed from the teachings of Christ 'and the pure and chaste doctrine of the holy apostles'.

Second, many of the radical reformers sanctioned an aggressive anticlericalism. Again, this was a common enough feature of the early evangelical movement, but both Luther and Zwingli drew back from anticlericalism once it passed into violence. The radicals, in contrast, encouraged their followers to wage a war against the clergy. It began as an attack against the Catholic priesthood, with men such as Balthasar Hubmaier railing against the 'courtesans, fools, whores, adulterers, procurers, gamblers, drunkards, and buffoons' of the German Church. Other voices were even more extreme. Simon Stumpf, for instance, went so far as to vow that a Reformation would not take hold until 'all the parsons were beaten to death' (Goertz, 1996, pp. 39–40). In time the radicals began to direct their published attacks against the mainstream reformers as well. Both Luther and Zwingli were subject to harsh criticism on the eve of the Peasants' War. Moreover, by this stage the anticlericalism voiced by the radicals had become profoundly sympathetic to the common man. Catholic priests were condemned as wayward shepherds and vassals of the Antichrist, while the clerical office, divested and disenchanted by the priesthood of all believers, lost its former status. As a consequence the laity replaced the clergy as the true followers of Christ, and the common man became the interpreter of God's Word. Social revolution inhered in anticlericalism of this kind.

The radical Reformation remained on the margins, and the third feature of the movement was its exclusiveness. In part this was a product of circumstance. Wittenberg rejected the Saxon enthusiasts, while the Swiss Anabaptists soon realized they had no place in the Zwinglian settlement. But the principle of separation was fundamental to the faith. In the *Schleitheim Articles* (1527), Sattler projected a community forced into separation by the Word of God. There could be no dialogue with the existing Churches, only the hope that the true believers 'armed with patience and self-knowledge' might find their way into the fold. In Saxony, Thomas Müntzer also thought in terms of the exclusive community, though he did not counsel patience or voluntary exile. Müntzer spoke of the elect in Christ, and he envisioned a final battle between his army of the Eternal League and the godless on earth. This was an extreme vision of separation, but all radical communities necessarily broke with the broader *corpus Christianum*.

The fourth and final religious feature follows from this: the radical Reformation was coloured by the language of mysticism, spiritualism and apocalypticism. Examples of the mystical and spiritual aspects of the movement have already been provided in the discussion of Karlstadt and Müntzer. In both cases, the radicals rejected traditional interpretations, subjected the Gospel to an intensely personal reading and used vague, poetic language to express their revelations. This approach reached its apogee in the thought of the Spiritualists, thinkers such as Caspar Schwenkfeld and Sebastian Franck, who believed that all truths of the faith must be distinguished by the spirit. In the eyes of the more conservative clergy, Catholic and Protestant alike, it seemed a totally subjective, whimsical and dangerous approach, and it left little room for dialogue. It also led to a marked tone of apocalypticism – for visions and vague language, in order to have a sense of urgency, must have a sense of ending. Hans Hut, for instance, began his work *On the Mystery of Baptism* with the claim that 'the last and most dangerous age of this world is now upon us' and later took this message to the rural parishioners of upper and central Germany, Austria and Moravia (Baylor, 1991, p. 152). In this apocalyptical theology, the persecuted community found both the language and the ultimate message for its ideals.

Another general characteristic of the radical Reformation was the close association between religious ideas and social context. In essence, the movement first emerged as a social phenomenon in the rural parishes of Switzerland and southern Germany, and recently historians have made much of the 'significant connection' between the Peasants' War and the growth of Anabaptism (Stayer, 1994, p. 86). The same themes of social justice and religious purity surfaced, the same attack against tithes, the same demands for communal control of the church, often penned and preached by the same men. All of the radical reformers set out to renew Christian society, and all believed that there was (and must be) a direct and dependent relationship between the norms of the Gospel and social reality. As a result there was a marked stress on moral improvement, an ongoing conviction that the reform of belief must entail a reform of life. Hans Denck, for instance, professed that there was no divide between justification and holiness, Felix Mantz counselled that 'everyone would receive remission of his sins, if he believed in him [Christ], changed his life, and did suitably righteous works,' while Hans Hergot, in his work *On the New Transformation of the Christian Life*, envisioned a Christian society fashioned by the dictates of scripture (Goertz, 1996, p. 62; Baylor, 1991, pp. 210–25).

Attitudes towards governance varied, but most radicals kept the state at a distance. Aside from protecting the good, the government had no substantial role to play. Equally, the true believer had no role to play in secular affairs. Anabaptists refused to swear oaths, pay tithes, become magistrates, bear arms, render judgement in secular courts, or participate in assemblies. As Hans-Jürgen Goertz has noted, 'the basic principles of Anabaptism attacked the foundations of the spiritual and temporal social form of the *corpus Christianum*' (Goertz, 1996, p. 129). It was extreme at two levels. On the one hand, in matters of religion, it placed the individual believer above the sovereign powers, pitting personal conviction against the traditional values and gestures of association in early modern society. On the other hand, it projected the Church as a community of equals. There were no hierarchical distinctions – no princes, prelates, nobles or priests. (As the authorities noted with considerable unease, Anabaptist congregations were made up of craftsmen and peasants.) All power was rooted in the community (more explicitly, in the common man) and all sovereignty was subject to the Gospel. Taken to extremes, as in the works of Thomas Müntzer, Balthasar Hubmaier and Hans Denck, this belief could be translated into revolutionary models of rule that included popular sovereignty, elective government or the suspension of social privilege. Indeed, there is evidence that in the earliest Anabaptist settlements the faithful went so far as to eliminate distinctions of wealth and practised the community of goods. (Packull, 1995, pp. 37–75; Stayer, 1994, pp. 95–159). This was yet another attempt to translate biblical norms into social reality, and it was yet another revolutionary challenge to the traditions of order and rule.

From the very outset of the movement, and in equal degrees in both southern Germany and Switzerland, the Anabaptists were suppressed and persecuted. As early as the mid-1520s Luther turned against Karlstadt and Müntzer, later encouraging the authorities to root out the rest of the 'Heavenly Prophets' and the enthusiasts (*Schwärmer*) gathering in their name. Similarly, soon after the first adult baptism in Zurich (1525), Zwingli condemned the teachings of Grebel and the Swiss Brethren. The following year rebaptism became a capital crime in Zurich and its dependent lands. Three years after this, at the imperial diet gathered in Speyer (1529), the Estates agreed unanimously to make Anabaptism a crime punishable by death. The Swiss radicals were compelled to leave Zurich in order to practise the faith. Conrad Grebel, Wilhelm Reublin and Johannes Brötli moved through northern Switzerland, Alsace, Swabia and the southern Tyrol, preaching the faith and performing adult baptisms. Once condemned by the Wittenberg reformers, the followers of Müntzer left the lands of Saxony and looked for shelter in the south. Hans Hut, for instance, became a wandering preacher, taking his beliefs to the parishioners of Franconia, Swabia, Upper Austria and Moravia. Indeed, the eastern fringe of the Empire became an important point of refuge for the early communities. The Philippites, followers of the Anabaptist Philip Plener, sought security in Moravia; Gabriel Aschermann's community of believers, termed the Gabrielites after their inspirational leader, settled in neighbouring Silesia; while the Hutterites (named, naturally, after Jacob Hutter) moved between the lands of south Tyrol and Moravia. (Packull, 1995). Far from the centres of mainstream reform, these apostles of the radical reformers gathered to develop their godly communities. Yet even in these lands, in the few places where the local authorities granted some toleration, the Anabaptists were ultimately forced to seek new lands.

Long after the threat presented by the radical Reformation had faded away, a powerful memory lived on in the minds of the German people. Above all, the movement was remembered for the Anabaptist episode in the Westphalian city of Münster (1534/5). For Münster had been identified by the radicals as the New Jerusalem, the city where the godly community would gather and await the second coming of Christ. The idea was first sounded by the lay preacher Melchior Hoffmann, a furrier from Schwäbisch Hall, who taught that the godly must assemble in preparation for the final apocalyptical struggle between the true believers and the godless. His teachings soon gathered a following in the northern lands, Westphalia and the Netherlands in particular, but it was Münster (not Strasbourg, as Hoffman predicted) where the godly began to assemble. By the year 1534 the Anabaptists had secured the city and soon began to fashion Münster in the image of their beliefs. No other event in the century of Reformation was such a stark reminder that the world was now open to interpretation. That is why the episode in Münster lived on so long in the collective memory: it was manifest proof that religious ideas could be translated into social reality, that these ideas could create alternative social worlds and that scripture could serve the most radical agendas. In the end, the community in Münster was defeated under siege, its leaders punished and executed. The episode, as Richard van Dülmen has noted, 'let loose a wave of persecution which marked the end of the radical movement . . . and even the end of Anabaptism in southern Germany' (Dülmen, 1987, p. 325). But the Kingdom of Jerusalem in Münster was not quickly forgotten by the ruling elite, nor was it forgotten by the subject population, and many of the later religious settlements in the towns and the territories were drafted with one eye on the dangers of the radical alternatives.

4

Political Culture and the German Reformation

When the Reformation first surfaced, very few of the early leaders were explicitly concerned with the practical dimensions of religious reform. Of course, there were principles at the heart of their theology with clear implications for the structure of the Church; but ecclesiology, the formal constitution of the Church, was a secondary concern when measured against themes such as grace or justification. Luther declared that he was certain of God's Word and certain he had been called forth to preach it, but he did not consider himself equal to the task of building an earthly Church. Yet the Reformation movement would not survive without the security of an institutional framework. Nor would evangelical theology take root among the Christian congregations unless its abstract ideas were translated into religious experience. In the absence of suitable ecclesiastical support (and little wonder, given that evangelical theology was in essence a rejection of the existing Catholic Church), the reformers called on the secular officials. In the German lands, as the clergy quickly realized, only the urban communes and the princely territories could offer the political support and the institutional framework for the evolution of the new Church. Concession and compromise was necessary, but in the end it was a relationship of mutual benefit and mutual dependence. The secular authorities looked to the reformers to secure their faith and justify their rule over the Church, while the evangelical theologians turned to their godly rulers in order to survive in the face of a hostile Catholic reaction. The Reformation, as a consequence, was quickly absorbed into the nexus of political relations, first at the level of the urban communes and the secular territories, and then ultimately at the level of imperial politics and the theatre of European intrigue. Scholars have been aware of this relationship since the age of Reformation itself, when histories of Protestantism first appeared. As Johannes Sleidan, historiographer to the Schmalkaldic League and author of the first substantial history of the event, remarked in his *Apologia*: 'I could not omit what concerned civil government, because ... they are interwoven with the other, especially in our own times, so that it is impossible to separate them' (Dickens, 1977, p. 27).

The Urban Reformation

Long before the Reformation, the ruling elite in the towns and cities had been working to integrate the local Church into the framework of civic relations. Throughout the late medieval period, urban governments had chipped away at the powers of the diocesan system, to the extent that we might speak of a self-sufficient urban Church in the medieval age. With time communes acquired rights of patronage over the parish churches, lay officials were placed in charge of local ecclesiastical affairs, city councils assumed control of the foundations and dependent clergy (Mass priests, vicars, chaplains), preaching posts were created independent of the bishops, and the councils, often in the name of the commune, openly criticized unsuitable clergy, going so far as to request their dismissal and appoint others in their stead (Blickle 1992, pp. 153–84; Isenmann, 1988, pp. 210–26). Few Church prerogatives escaped the advance of the urban commune; indeed, even the higher matters of morality and sexual deviance, traditionally the preserve of the spiritual authorities, fell prey to lay regulation. With increasing frequency in the late medieval period, the civic authorities assumed the right to arbitrate the moral relations of the Christian community. As the Basle city council declared in the fifteenth century, 'the government of every city is established primarily to augment and support the honor of God and to prohibit all injustice and especially the grossest sins and crimes according to the ordinance of holy Christianity' (Moeller, 1972, p. 46). Much more than pure political calculation lay behind this process. In the medieval urban commune there had long been a strong association between religious belief and the social constitution. True religion was not just a matter of personal conviction, but something manifest in the community. The proofs of faith would be evidenced and justified by the godly commune. When the city fathers acted as arbiters of Christian morality or intervened in local religious affairs, the concern with collective salvation was no less real than the desire to rule over a peaceful community. This idea of a sacral community was an important precondition for the success of the urban Reformation.

From the very outset, a relationship existed between the evangelical movement and urban culture (Hamm, 1995, pp. 198–206). In part, this was a natural alliance. The presses were in the towns and cities, as were the reformers and their reader-ship. But it was also the result of a deliberate attempt to estab-lish a dialogue between an urban audience and the new vision of reform. Luther himself addressed over twenty towns and cities in open letters and pamphlets. In his work *To The Coun-cilmen of All Cities of Germany* (1524) he imagined a pro-gramme of educational reform unique to the urban setting. Most of the other reformers shared a similar cast of mind. Huldrych Zwingli wrote as a pastor to a civic congregation, as did Johannes Brenz in Schwäbisch Hall, Andreas Osiander in Nuremberg and Martin Bucer in Strasbourg. Some evangelical tracts were explicitly directed at a particular commune (Stack-mann and Moeller, 1996, pp. 202–48). Luther wrote an early work for the town of Leisnig; Jacob Strauss drafted a defence of the faith for the people of Eisenach, as did Johannes Briess-man for Cottbus and Johann Fritzhanns for Magdeburg; Johann Rothmeler sent an open letter of consolation to the people of Mühlhausen; while Andreas Althamer published *A Sermon on the Holy State of Matrimony* (1525) with the people of Schwäbisch Gmünd in mind. Indeed, at one stage a type of pam-phlet emerged which was little more than a dialogue between an evangelical preacher and his urban congregation. Johann Eberlin von Günzburg wrote a tract of this kind, consoling his parishioners that he had returned to preach, even if it was 'not in body but in spirit' (Moeller, 1999, p. 49).

The text was thus a powerful vehicle for the spread of the evangelical message. Yet it is worth remembering that very few people could read, and historians are right to question the effect of the word on an age with such a low literacy rate. One estimate suggests that less than 5 per cent of the population could actually read (Scribner, 1986, p. 19). Print may have set the terms for theological discussion and given meaning and direction to Reformation discourse, but it was oral culture, as much as anything else, that took the message to the people. Books and pamphlets were read aloud in homes, schoolhouses, inns, workplaces, open fields, cemeteries and market squares, thereby allowing an illiterate audience to engage in a dialogue with the new religious ideas. Most important of all, however, and by far the most effective way of spreading the message to the urban audience, was the sermon. In the early years, evangelical sympathizers would preach the faith wherever the people could gather and hear them. Famous examples would include Matthäus Zell in Strasbourg, who was forced to use a portable pulpit in order to address the crowds, Sebastian Fröschel in Leipzig, whose pulpit was placed in the churchyard, and Johannes Zymler, who preached from the windows of his schoolhouse. Most major centres of reform had a powerful preacher. Wittenberg had Luther, Zurich had Zwingli, Strasbourg had Bucer, Nuremberg had Andreas Osiander, Memmingen had Christoph Schappeler – a comprehensive list would include both the large imperial cities and the smaller territorial towns. Some cities, once set on reform, tried to coax a leading preacher to reside within their walls, as evidenced by the efforts of Braunschweig, Lübeck and Hamburg to win the services of Johannes Bugenhagen. (Cameron, 1991, pp. 226–34; Scribner, 1986, pp. 17–24). On occasion the Reformation itself first came to the attention of the urban congregation as a battle between antagonistic preachers. The people of Erfurt witnessed a number of debates in the church, as did the congregation of Augsburg, who watched on as Urbanus Rhegius and Michael Keller quarrelled over the faith. The townspeople of Ansbach, where the Catholic archdeacon Dr Johann Weinhardt and the Lutheran sympathizer Johann Rurer traded religious opinions from the pulpit, soon found themselves caught up in the clerical dispute. As Rurer himself protested, Weinhardt's censures did not just question his faith, 'but rather the Christian honour of my audience, noble and non-noble, learned and unlearned, those of high and low estate. For if I am an unchristian preacher, so too must my listeners be unchristian as well' (Dixon, 1996a, p. 14).

Civic culture was unique, as Rurer implied, because there was a congestion of so many different social estates in one place. Moreover, cities and towns were also home to sophisticated forms of social organization, ranging from Church and university institutions to learned sodalities, monastic foundations, artisan guilds, traditional associations of honour and prestige, communal assemblies and privileged councils of rule. These collective associations set a stamp of social order on the city and thus, to some degree, restricted the range of public action; but in turn they also gave rise to new forms of solidarity, making it possible for different forms of collective action to develop. The Humanist sodalities, for instance, were quick to embrace Luther's early works and offer support, even before they realized the full implications of his ideas. Other subgroups or associations of the learned elite could effect similar forms of collective action. Throughout the German lands, it was often the urban clergy who first responded *en masse* to the Luther affair. Forms of clerical action ranged from the organized disruption of Catholic services, the introduction of changes in church services and liturgy, public debates against conservative or oppositional clergy, open letters to princes or city councils, to more dramatic (and often illegal) acts of defiance, the most famous being Luther's burning of the papal Bull in front of the gates of Wittenberg.

On occasion urban citizens participated in clerical campaigns, but most of the lay followers did not rely on the clergy for direction. The townspeople saw no necessary contradiction in their secular status and close association with the movement. The Reformation's earliest supporters represent almost every imaginable social category. Augustine Bader of Augsburg, for example, was a weaver, as was Utz Rysschner; Hans Sachs of Nuremberg was a shoemaker; Pamphilus Gegenbach, author of the evangelical tract *The Three Christians* (1523), was a printer in Basle; Hans Fürsli was a Swiss bell-founder; Steffan Büllheym was an artisan in Strasbourg. In Dinkelsbühl, the innkeeper Hans Harscher kept up a lively correspondence with the Crailsheim reformer Adam Weiss and did much to encourage reform. The list could be extended, from schoolteachers to furriers, tanners to wine merchants. But perhaps more significant than these examples of individual commitment was the *collective* action of the urban laity. Sympathy was often demonstrated by a show of common public action. This collective dimension has moved scholars to speak of the Reformation as a 'social movement', by which they mean that the essential force was not the logic of a single inspirational vision or the charisma of a gifted leader, but rather the strength of group dynamics (Scribner, 1987, pp. 154–74).

Collective action of this kind could assume various forms. In Strasbourg, the members of the gardeners' guild provided the most active support for the early reform movement. In the town of Schwäbisch Gmünd, the smiths, in a similar manner, were essential to the spread of the faith. In Zwickau, the collective action of the local guilds (the weavers in particular) forced the council to call a complete assembly of the commune in an effort to find a solution to the religious disturbances in the town. And in Memmingen, when one of the local bakers was imprisoned for refusing to pay tithes, several hundred citizens gathered before the town hall and demanded his release. Forced to give way to collective demands, the Memmingen council later staged a public disputation attended by the clergy, four doctors, the town councillors, and 'one man out of every guild, representing them all, and chosen for that purpose by a free vote in every guild'. Soon after the disputation, the evangelical service replaced the Catholic rites in the church (Blickle, 1999b, pp. 16–79; Cameron, 1991, pp. 239–46). Even after the first flush of reform activity, these urban collectives and secular associations played a decisive role at the early stage of the Reformation. In Ulm the question of religious reform was put before the guilds, fraternities and master craftsmen, and a vote was taken. Esslingen adopted a similar strategy, as did Constance, Goslar, Heilbronn, Weißenburg and Kempten, where a survey helped to decide the fate of the town's religious images. No doubt historians are right to question the integrity of ballots and referendums of this kind. Councils often rigged them, limited the range of questions, or excluded the majority voice (Scribner, 1986, pp. 29–30). But they are evidence of the communal dimension nonetheless.

The early Reformation in Wittenberg is a good illustration of how civic history, evangelical ideas, powerful personalities and collective activity determined the character of urban reform. Throughout the medieval period Wittenberg had assumed a special status in the eyes of the ruling house of Saxony and had thus secured liberties and privileges. On the eve of the Reformation, the council, made up of local patricians, electoral officials and representatives of the prominent guilds, held sway over both the townspeople and the local clergy. Since 1502 Wittenberg had also been the site of the first university in Germany founded without papal approval. There was a spirit of independence shared by its faculty members, or at least a sense of local identity given expression by such resident Humanist luminaries as Nikolaus Marschalk, Georg Spalatin, Christoph Scheurl and Andreas Meinhardi, whose imaginary student dialogue (published in 1505) identified Wittenberg as one of the centres of the new learning in Germany (Grossmann, 1975, pp. 56–70). Of course, the town was also home to a number of prominent religious thinkers, many of whom were quick to support the reform movement. Luther himself was both a professor of theology and the municipal preacher (the latter office given to him by the town council). Philipp Melanchthon, one of Germany's leading linguists, was appointed to the chair of Greek in 1518, and went on to provide both Luther and the Reformation with lifelong intellectual and spiritual support. Similar encouragement would be offered by Nikolaus von Amsdorf, Johannes Bugenhagen, Justus Jonas and the hundreds of other clergymen who later gathered at Luther's table. But two other resident figures are worth particular mention: the Augustinian friar Gabriel Zwilling and the theologian Andreas Karlstadt. Both men used all the means available to disseminate the new religious ideas (books, sermons, debates, public actions) and both eventually became the leaders of what historians term the Wittenberg Movement (1521–2), the first urban Reformation in Germany.

In 1521, with Luther sequestered in the Wartburg, Karlstadt and Zwilling assumed the leadership of the evangelical movement in Wittenberg. By early October, Zwilling was preaching against monasticism; by December he was directing his sermons against the Catholic Mass. Johann Dölsch, prior of the Augustinian monastery, claimed that Zwilling's words were giving rise to unrest and dissension, and he feared it would end in a revolt against the clergy. For his part, Karlstadt emerged as a public figure in a disputation against the Mass on 17 October 1521, when he called for a general reform based on the teachings of Luther. His demands did not end there, however, and on Christmas Day of the same year he offered the townspeople an early form of evangelical Communion. In the eyes of the local authorities, these two men were clearly responsible for the unrest that now gripped the town. The Augustinian clergy cited Zwilling before the electoral court on a number of occasions for 'heaping considerable abuse on the spiritual order' and giving sermons which led to 'horror, outrage, and unrest of the common man' (Bubenheimer, 1985, pp. 163; Scribner, 1987, pp. 145–8). Preaching was having its effect on the local parishioners, and they began to translate words into action. In October 1521 university students gave vent to public displays of anticlericalism. Crowds pelted the hermits of St Anthony with dung and stones, heckled sermons and disrupted services. On 3 December 1521 students and burghers interrupted the Catholic Mass, forcing back the clergy and ripping the missals from their hands. And finally, on 6 December, armed students and nobles marched through the streets with pipes and drums, while a citizen committee pushed into the town hall and presented the council with a list of religious demands. Ultimately, the councillors were forced to cede agreement to their proposals, and on 24 January 1522 a new church ordinance was introduced in the town. Inspired by Karlstadt, the ordinance called for a new order of Communion, the removal of images and the creation of a common chest. In the end, Luther's return and the intervention of the prince would put an end to Karlstadt's efforts, but not before the revolutionary potential of the movement had been demonstrated.

Given the complexity of civic culture in the Empire, it is not possible to reduce the historical variety of the urban Reformation to a single exemplary model or paradigm of reform. Wittenberg provides a vivid illustration of some of the figures and forces at work, but this local history is far from a general explanation of events. In towns where there was a different matrix of rule or a different social character, the Reformation ran a different course (Greyerz, 1985, pp. 1–63). In the Hanseatic towns in the north, for instance, including centres of merchant wealth such as Rostock, Stralsund, Greifswald, Lübeck, Hannover and Lemgo, the evangelical movement heightened the tensions between the closed patriciate, whose members remained true to the Catholic religion, and the politically isolated bourgeoisie, who emerged as the supporters of the new faith. The Reformation could thus threaten the very nature of rule. In a similar

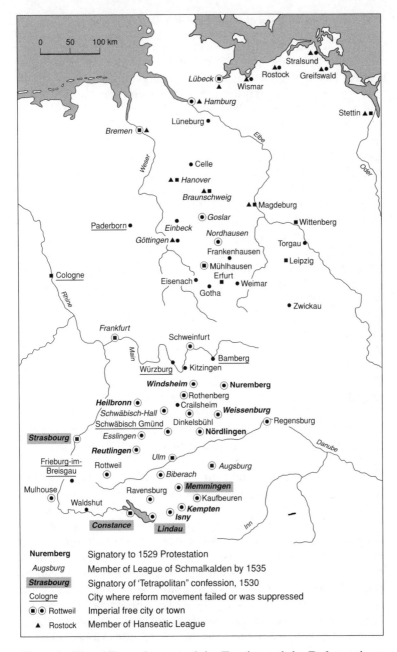

Map 4.1   The cities and towns of the Empire and the Reformation.

Source: Euan Cameron, *The European Reformation* (Oxford: Clarendon Press, 1991), p. 211.

manner, towns and cities with a strong tradition of burgher participation often ran the risk of public disorder. In Ulm, Strasbourg, Esslingen, Colmar and Augsburg, to cite a few of the more prominent examples, the urban Reformation evolved in the exchange between the guilds and the ruling elite. On occasion this could decline into violent confrontation, as happened in the city of Memmingen, where guild solidarity was transformed into public action and forced the council to implement religious change. By way of contrast, in the smaller territorial towns the crucial dialogue was often not between the council and the commons but rather between the magistracy and the urban overlord. Kitzingen, a territorial town in Franconia, realized this to its cost after the Peasants' War, when the lord rode into the town, assembled the council and commune, arrested the alleged ringleaders of the unrest, put out the eyes of sixty-two of them and imposed a preaching mandate (Demandt and Rublack, 1978, pp. 9–34). Even in powerful imperial cities the ruling elite had to balance domestic initiatives against the broader relations of power. Ultimately, the introduction of the Reformation was a political issue, for 'any "established" reformed settlement,' as Euan Cameron has observed, 'required the participation, even if only a reluctant, passive, or late participation, of the official governing body of the community' (Cameron, 1991, p. 239). In order to effect a lasting settlement, the governing body had to negotiate between many different and contending configurations of power, both within the community and beyond the city walls.

As an example we might turn to the imperial city of Nuremberg, where the evangelical movement forced the ruling elite to moderate between the demands of the commune and the Catholic Empire. Nuremberg's only effective (and constitutional) overlord was the emperor. Consequently, as soon as the Luther affair became an issue, it was no less than Charles V himself who advised the city to suppress the movement. But his counsel came too late. The Reformation had pressed in on the ruling elite from all sides. The early support offered by the Humanist sodality, whose members included Willibald Pirckheimer, Christoph Scheurl, Caspar Nützel and Albrecht Dürer, was given public voice when prominent local artists and authors such as Hans Sachs, Hans Greiffenberger, Sebald and Bartel

Beham, and Georg Pencz championed the evangelical faith
(Schindling, 1989, pp. 36–9). The message spread, resulting in
popular and widespread agitation in favour of religious reform.
Throughout the early 1520s, in an effort to maintain public
order, the city council was forced to intervene. Preachers were
told to leave off incendiary sermons, restrictions were placed on
the printing of books, and the posting of anticlerical placards
and pamphlets in the public squares was forbidden. And yet
these measures could not put an end to public sympathy or the
strength of support, especially as both Andreas Osiander and
Dominicus Schleupner preached in favour of the new faith in
the two parish churches. Visiting the city in 1524, the papal
legate witnessed the depth of public conviction:

> In this city the sincere faith in Christ is utterly abolished. No
> respect is paid either to the Virgin Mary or to the saints. They
> ridicule the papal rites and call the relics of the saints bones of
> men who have been hanged. In Lent they eat meat openly. Con-
> fession is neglected, as they say it should be made only to God.
> They generally communicate under both forms. They make a
> laughing stock of Pope and Cardinals by circulating drawings and
> caricatures. In short, they consider Martin [Luther] their enlight-
> ener, and think that until now they have been in darkness.
> (Strauss, 1966, p. 174)

Once the Emperor learned of the state of affairs in Nuremberg, he ordered the council, under a veiled threat of force (and
a more direct caution that he might rescind Nuremberg's imperial privileges) to put an end to the movement. The council was
thereby faced with a political dilemma. Approval of the movement was, in essence, a form of rebellion; but refusal to compromise with the commune could be, in effect, political suicide,
for the peasants were gathering in strength and there was no
certainty that the residents of the city would remain calm. For
even in Nuremberg, where a closed patrician class dominated
urban politics, the ruling elite was in place, to cite the words of
the city lawyer Christoph Scheurl, to watch over the 'government of our city and the common weal'. The commune could
not be ignored. In the face of this dilemma, the council adopted
the most appropriate political solution. It gave a show of

obeying the imperial requests, and this included censorship and the control of public preaching, while at the same time, as the magistracy waited on the proposed general Church council, it allowed for religious observance according to 'the holy gospel, as it is written in scripture'. This formula was in effect a concession to the movement, and the Reformation soon followed in train. By March of 1525, in a series of prudent, deliberate steps, the Catholic faith had effectively been replaced by an evangelical alternative. When reprimanded by the imperial authorities for allowing this to happen, the council made reference to the fact that 'the Nuremberg commune has become hungry for the Word of God.' The council did not think it was possible to put an end to the movement or the innovations that had been introduced (Schmidt, 1986, p. 163). The threat presented by the commune, at least in the eyes of the ruling elite, posed a greater political risk than the disapproving, but distant, imperial government. The Reformation in Nuremberg took shape within the parameters of this political dynamic.

A different set of considerations shaped the Reformation in the neighbouring town of Schwabach. Unlike Nuremberg, whose direct overlord was the emperor, Schwabach was subject to the Margrave of Brandenburg-Ansbach. The town was governed by a council which acted in the name of the commune; but the council itself was closely controlled by the margrave, and indeed many of the higher offices in Schwabach were held by representatives of the prince. The town council enjoyed some influence over the local church, but real power was shared between the margrave and the Bishop of Eichstätt. Thus when the movement took hold it gave rise to a different type of urban Reformation (Dixon, 1996b, pp. 123–40). Like Nuremberg, there was a broad spectrum of support for the new teachings. The movement first became a threat to civic order on 27 September 1523, when a renegade monk, dressed as a clothworker, usurped the pulpit in the church and shouted down the parish priest. His actions gave rise to public demonstrations in support of the faith, soon prompting the Schwabach officials to fear for the safety of the Catholic clergy in the town. The movement also won the support of two local secular officials who worked to introduce reform. In contrast to the course of events in Nuremberg, however, the Schwabach officials did not rule over a sovereign political community. Nor was the town overlord the distant emperor of the German Nation. Ultimately, all decisions had to be sanctioned by Margrave Casimir of Brandenburg-Ansbach-Kulmbach, a lord who could march on the town within the space of a day. Every attempt to reform or restructure the Church, from the appointment of preachers, the dismissal of the Catholic clergy, the introduction of an evangelical service, to the establishment of a common chest, was ultimately at the margrave's discretion. And as Casimir did not adopt the faith, the town of Schwabach could not introduce a lasting Reformation until after his death (27 September 1527), when his brother Georg the Pious assumed rule and converted the margravate to Lutheranism. Only then, with the conversion of the entire territory, could the Schwabach authorities undertake an urban Reformation.

Quite often the fate of the Reformation in the urban communes was dictated by the broader context of political relations. For those communes in the south of the Empire that remained Catholic, for instance, both internal and external affairs favoured a conservative approach. Rottweil was an example of an imperial city which decided in favour of Catholicism even though the evangelical movement had taken root in the town (Enderle, 1993b, pp. 215–30). Political considerations advised against a change of religion. Rottweil was the seat of the *Hofgericht*, the main court of justice in the Empire and the source of considerable wealth and prestige for the city. Many of its members were also members of the city magistracy. In addition, Rottweil had one of the largest territories of any commune in the Empire, and it was dependent upon the good faith of its neighbours to maintain its subject lands. Given that its neighbours included Ferdinand of Austria and the Bishop of Constance, a change of religion would have put this territory in jeopardy, just as an urban Reformation would have undoubtedly fulfilled the emperor's promise to remove the *Hofgericht* if the city went Protestant. Thus in the end, following a vote of the council and the guilds, Rottweil remained Catholic and the reform party was exiled. The Catholic cities of Überlingen and Schwäbisch Gmünd had similar experiences, as did the smaller communities of Offenburg, Gengenbach and Zell am Harmersbach. But the context of political relations might just as easily favour a turn towards the Reformation (Enderle, 1993a, pp. 195–212). In Ulm, also an imperial city in the south of the

Empire, the council adopted a similar conservative approach to the evangelical movement, going so far as to exile prominent reformers such as Eberlin von Günzburg and Heinrich von Kettenbach. Ultimately, however, the Reformation was adopted in the later years of the decade and instituted with the publication of a Church order in 1531. As in Rottweil, though with a different outcome, the context of political relations influenced the fate of the Reformation in the commune. As the movement took hold, the council turned to its neighbours, first to the Swiss, then to the emperor, finally deciding to look for security among the Protestant Estates. Ulm joined the Schmalkaldic League, assuming that an alliance with the Protestant princes of the north and the Lutheran cities in the south (which included Augsburg, Nuremberg, Schwäbisch Hall, Esslingen, Nördlingen and Biberach) would be enough to keep the Catholic forces at bay.

However broad the stratum of popular support, and whatever the relationship between the commune and the external powers, the introduction of the Reformation was ultimately a political decision, effected by the ruling elite and guided by the context of political possibility. Thus every Reformation, in the final analysis, was a magisterial Reformation, for every religious settlement was brought about by the intervention of the secular authorities in the name of public order. The consequence, at the most basic level, was twofold. On the one hand, civic governance, drawing on the notion of the common good, integrated religious developments into patterns of governance. The Reformation effected a communalization (or domestication) of the urban church. The clergy fell subject to secular rule, the council increased its control over clerical appointments, the ecclesiastical structure merged with the organs of civic governance, the legal immunity of the church was abolished, and religion and piety were more closely allied with urban values (Blickle, 1992, pp. 81–105; Moeller, 1972, pp. 54–89). This process was more marked in the imperial cities than the territorial towns, but the domestication of the urban church was a general trend throughout the German lands. On the other hand, the evangelical message itself provided the authorities with powerful ideological legitimization, for not only did it offer a blueprint for a new Church, but it also sanctified the entire undertaking. Once again urban tradition lay at the root, for there had long been a tendency to think of the commune as a type of sacral corporation, a *corpus Christianum*, with each member of the union contributing to the salvation of the whole. Reformation theology revived this vision. But more than this, for the first time in German history theology emerged as the dominant discourse in public affairs. Religious language became the most powerful medium of expression and negotiation, in both communal and individual terms. As the Strasbourg reformer Caspar Hedio observed, scripture offered 'a vital, certain unerring guide against false doctrine, divisions and sects, and how one can survive dangerous times' (Brady, 1988, p. 20; Hamm, 1996, pp. 125–7). No one appreciated this more than the ruling elite of the German towns, whose biblicism was the working logic behind the conception, and then the preservation, of the urban Reformation.

Despite the affinities, however, this close association between evangelical thought and urban culture did not always promote consensus. In many instances, as we have seen, the Reformation brought dissension and disorder to the urban communes, even if the disorder did not last. The spread of the faith was often shadowed by social unrest, violent bursts of iconoclasm or anticlericalism, and even acts of political rebellion, especially in cities where there was already a history of social disquiet. Recognizing the disruptive potential of the movement, most city authorities took steps to control both private preaching and public displays of evangelical sympathy. The city council of Nuremberg published preaching mandates, forbade the posting of anti-Catholic propaganda, placed restrictions on the local printing industry, maintained control of the clergy and issued mandates designed to contain uprisings and exile suspect preachers (Vogler, 1988, pp. 33–49). In northern Germany, however, in towns such as Stralsund, Erfurt, Rostock, Lüneburg and Göttingen, the movement could not always be contained to the same degree. There had long been a political rift between the ruling patrician elite and the disenfranchised burgher population, and the disagreements over the Reformation brought about momentary political revolution. The most famous example is perhaps the town of Lübeck, where a reform-friendly burgher committee assumed rule over the commune, forced through the Reformation and drove the conservative patrician council into exile. Such revolts did not create lasting change; traditional forms of governance were soon restored. But the disorder, however fleeting, had been real. Similar displays of pro-Lutheran burgher movements sprang up throughout northern Germany, and many of the neighbouring towns suffered political disorder and social disunity as a result (Cameron, 1991, pp. 234–63; Dickens, 1974, pp. 156–76). This also holds true for some of the sophisticated urban communes to the south, cities such as Ulm, Memmingen, Esslingen and Strasbourg, where popular pressure for reform gave rise to serious tensions between the ruling elite and the subject population. Only a delicate policy of negotiation and concession, often ending in the formal introduction of the Reformation, staved off serious political confrontation.

Thus to a large degree, every urban Reformation was a dialogue between the rulers and the ruled over the meaning of community. And in a similar sense, every final religious settlement was both a confirmation and a legitimization of a system of governance or a culture of rule. At the centre of the dialogue were the norms and values of rule and how they should be understood (Rublack, 1984, pp. 24–60). Paramount was the idea of the common good (*Gemeinnutz*), a term with real meaning for most members of the urban commune and real points of reference to daily life. Yet the concept was very flexible, and its meaning often fell into dispute. All were in agreement that the common good had to measure itself against the Word of God, but widely different conclusions and fundamentally antagonistic political visions could be derived from the term – the communal Reformation and the Peasants' War of 1525 were evidence enough of that. In the end, however, it was not the promise of radical change but the force of order and tradition that won the day. The Reformation did not give rise to the social and religious vision of the common man, but rather confirmed the idea of order and governance held by the ruling elite. City councils drew on evangelical theology to sanction long-held urban values of peace, law, justice, unity and the common good, and they did so with reference to the words of scripture and the divine mandate of peace and brotherly love. 'In an age of uncertainty,' as Thomas Brady has remarked, 'the urban Reformation promised to convert civic religion from an unsettling, disruptive force into a supportive, legitimizing force for oligarchical rule

and basic civic values' (Brady, 1988, p. 28). Evidence of this is
borne out by the success of Lutheranism in the towns of northern and western Germany, where it took root at the expense of
the alternative evangelical traditions (Zwinglians, Sacramentar-
ians, Spiritualists). Only Lutheranism, with its close association
of the temporal and the spiritual, and its stress on the norms and
values of 'concord, peace, and love' (to cite the reading of the
Hanseatic diet) could work as a guarantor of civic and religious
unity. Even the Lutheran interpretation of the eucharist seemed
closer in kind to the habits of urban thought (Schilling, 1992b,
pp. 99–120).

The Reformation did not work wonders. There was no
alchemy of concord, peace and love in the sixteenth century, no
godly city born of the Word. Evangelical theology proved a powerful ally to many of the norms of urban culture as well as a
powerful support for the praxis of rule, but tensions and dis-
parities remained. Indeed, in many towns and cities the implementation of the Reformation lasted the better part of the
century. In Strasbourg, for instance, scripture and its interpreters
remained a dynamic force for many years after the city fathers
adopted the Augsburg Confession in 1536 (Abray, 1985, pp.
66–179). Less than two years later Strasbourg's principal clergyman, Martin Bucer, published *On True Care of Souls* (1538)
in an effort to clarify the rights of the Church and its ministers.
Bucer wanted to see the original vision of reform through to its
conclusion. That same year Strasbourg issued a mandate against
the Anabaptists and Schwenkfeldians seeking shelter in the
town. Their utopian ideas of reform, the magistracy believed,
were giving rise to unrest. Less threatening, but no less con-
frontational, were Strasbourg's resident Catholics, a community
which waxed and waned in step with imperial events and yet
remained a powerful visible minority in the city. Meanwhile, the
Calvinist refugees, most of whom were in exile from lands on
good terms with Strasbourg, could even boast of a French
service in the town. A plurality of religious cultures in Lutheran
Strasbourg remained the norm throughout the century, each
with a unique understanding of faith and community. As the
Jesuit Jacob Rabus wrily noted, 'In poor Strasbourg you now
have five or six sects among the common people. One fellow is
an out-and-out Lutheran, the second a half-Lutheran, the third
a Zwinglian, the fourth a Calvinist, the fifth a Schwenckfelder,

the sixth an Anabaptist, and the seventh lot is purely epicurean'
(Brady, 1988, pp. 28–9). The Jesuit's observations would have
been true for most cities, for the urban Reformation did not
come to an end with the official adoption of the faith or the publication of a Church order. The process of Reformation spanned
the century, as towns and cities worked to integrate the intan-
gibles of faith with the realities of rule.

The Princely Reformation

In his *Address to the Christian Nobility of the German Nation*
(1520), a vernacular treatise written in order to inspire a reform
of the Church, Martin Luther turned to the nobility of the
German lands in the hope that 'God may help his church
through the laity, since the clergy, to whom this task more properly belongs, have grown quite indifferent.' The tract detailed a
comprehensive plan of religious reform, all of which was to be
implemented and directed by the princes, nobles and ruling
classes of the German nation. Luther drew on his theological
principle of the priesthood of all believers to justify the intervention of the secular arm. For if all members of the Christian
Estate were consecrated priests through baptism, as Luther
charged, and if there was no fundamental distinction between
the spiritual and the secular Estates, then it was reasonable to
conclude that 'all are truly priests, bishops, and popes.' In such
a view, it was also reasonable to conclude that the reform of the
Church need not wait on the approval of Rome. On the contrary, Luther declared, 'it was God's will that this empire should
be ruled by the Christian princes of Germany,' and he called
on the ruling princes and nobles to effect a reformation of
the Church. 'God give us all a Christian mind, and grant to the
Christian nobility of the German nation in particular true spiritual courage to do the best they can for the poor church. Amen.'

Given the nature of politics and rule in sixteenth-century
Germany, it was natural for Luther to turn to the secular princes
and nobles of the realm. The Holy Roman Empire was in
essence a federation of princely states. The emperor, an elected
monarch, was the titular head of the federation, but the vague,
if venerable, notion of empire had little impact on political practice. The Empire remained a landscape of particular powers

rather than a consolidated monarchy. Real powers of rule lay with the territorial sovereigns, and that is why the Protestant Church in Germany was, in the first instance, a territorial Church. Indeed, in large part, the introduction of the Reformation in the princely state must be understood as a natural extension of medieval developments rather than a radical break with the past. Throughout the medieval period the German princes had been drawing together their lands and intensifying their powers of rule (*Herrschaft*) over the subject population. Government was becoming more 'absolute' as princes ruled with growing inflexibility, while the means of opposition, such as the resistance of the Estates or appeal to the imperial courts, were proving increasingly ineffective. At the same time, more modern features of governance developed. Councils of rule became standardized and less subject to princely whims; courts of justice emerged, observing quarterly sessions, staffed with jurists trained in Roman law; state treasuries evolved as the exchequer assumed responsibility for the wealth of the realm; while a new generation of public officials, most of whom were trained in universities, took office as councillors, treasurers, and chancellors (Press, 1990, pp. 510–3). Similar developments were taking place all over Europe, but usually on a national scale. In the German lands, in contrast, the princely territory was the setting for the rise of the modern state.

Along with the intensification of their sovereignty in the traditional spheres, the secular princes of Germany had also strengthened their control over the Church in their lands. It was a purely pragmatic or functional increase of power, rather than a foretaste of the ideological challenge that would come with the Reformation. Nevertheless, the increase of princely power necessarily meant that lesser sovereigns would fall prey to the emerging state – and this included many of the Catholic bishops. In the first instance, the princes weakened the Church through treaties and statecraft. In Saxony, for instance, a series of alliances signed with the bishops of Merseburg, Meißen and Naumburg in the thirteenth and fourteenth centuries developed into a military protectorship, with the bishops soon eclipsed as the weaker partners. Similarly, the rulers of the Electoral Palatinate forced the cathedral chapter of Worms to swear to an oath that it would never elect a primate who might bring harm to the land (Schulze, 1991, pp. 17–43). It was the politics of force, and it was no different in kind from the strategies of rule informing secular affairs. In a similar fashion, the princes extended their control over ecclesiastical foundations by exploiting the traditional rights of safeguard and patronage. This was an effective method, for the right of safeguard or advocacy granted the secular lord the latitude to act as guardian over a foundation or a church; and while it did not carry with it an increase in jurisdictional or sovereign power, the princes were able to turn the relationship to their advantage. In the duchy of Zweibrücken, for example, the dukes deliberately extended their powers of safeguard over the caritative foundations in order to control Church funding. At the same time, treaties of advocacy, such as the understanding between the ruling house and the foundation of St Fabian (confirmed in 1418), meant that the dukes could intervene whenever it seemed that the liberties of the foundation were under threat (Konersmann, 1996, pp. 73–90).

In some secular territories there is reason to speak of a princely reformation before the sixteenth century. In Württemberg, a land which later became a Lutheran stronghold, the dukes used their powers of advocacy to oversee religious reform some generations before Luther was born. The most zealous of the Württemberg sovereigns was Eberhard the Bearded, a man whose reforming vision inspired a papal-approved visitation of the monasteries, the foundation of the university of Tübingen (1477) and the settlement of the Brethren of the Common Life in his lands (Dykema, 1996, pp. 39–56). In Luther's own land of Saxony, religious conviction played a central role in Duke Wilhelm III's decision to intervene in ecclesiastical affairs. The *Reformatio Wilhelmi*, a reforming programme first implemented by the duke in 1446, was a fusion of secular and spiritual injunctions, and it spoke quite clearly of his intention to watch over the Church. Wilhelm's beliefs were further strengthened on 6 September 1452 when the famous Franciscan preacher, Giovanni de Capistrano, gave a sermon in Jena and called on the rulers to introduce reforms. Five weeks later Wilhelm published an ordinance reminding his subjects of his divine commission and how he had been 'powerfully moved through this preaching'. As a consequence, the duke resolved 'to act among our subjects with all necessary diligence, so much as it lies within us, to see that with the help of God, these weaknesses are corrected and transformed' (Bast, 1997, p. 179). Inspired by Capistrano's preaching, and fired by his own conviction that God's wrath would lie over the land if an improvement of faith and morality did not follow, Duke Wilhelm published an ordinance which bound Church and State to his vision of reform.

Thus well before the advent of the Reformation, and well before the Protestant reformers turned the secular rulers into caretakers of the faith, the German princes had been behaving, as the Duke of Jülich phrased it, like popes in their lands. The long-term process of state formation had weakened the autonomy of the Catholic Church. Bishops and chapters were often little more than subjects; Catholic foundations, for different reasons at different times, fell under the rule of the state; and the clergy, both secular and regular, were forced to implement and obey the religious ideals of the sovereign. Moreover, as many of the higher offices of the Church were frequently in the hands of the German princes or the lesser nobility, there was limited internal opposition to the interventions of the sovereign. In terms of practical politics, the medieval Catholic prince had much in common with his Protestant posterity. Both had the same aspirations of domestic rule, and both had leverage over the Church in their lands. Viewed from the perspective of local strategies of rule and governance, the Reformation was not a radical break with the past. As Manfred Schulze has noted: 'In the realm of church politics, the modern age already begins in the fifteenth century' (Schulze, 1991, p. 16). The difference between the type of rule enjoyed by a medieval ruler and the later Protestant prince did not reside in the intentions or the application of power. The difference, as we will see, was rooted in the ideology of governance. The Reformation introduced a new understanding of princely sovereignty, and this shift of ideas in turn gave rise to a reach and intensity of rule without precedent in German history.

With this historical background, it is easy to understand why Luther called on his prince, Friedrich the Wise, to supervise a reform of the Church. Certain features of German political culture made this inevitable. Moreover, with the evangelical principle of the priesthood of all believers, no fundamental theological obstacle stood in the way. Both tradition and scripture could be cited in support of the princely Reformation. To add to this, by the early 1520s Luther had developed a philosophy of rule (his notion of the Two Kingdoms) which argued that secular rule had been ordained by God to keep order and peace on earth. The prince had a duty to secure Christian worship in his land, and he was bound as a Christian brother to come to the aid of the Church in distress. Luther called on the Elector of Saxony to assume the role of an emergency bishop (*Notbischof*) and reform the Church, though with the proviso that the elector had no right to intervene in the spiritual realm. 'For although, Most Honourable Elector,' wrote Luther, 'you have not been commanded to practise spiritual rule, as the secular authority you nevertheless have a duty to make sure that dissension, riot, and rebellion does not break out among your subjects' (Schwarz Lausten, 1983, p. 61). It would be his followers, rather than Luther himself, who entrusted the Protestant sovereigns with full powers of rule over the Church. For the reformers Philipp Melanchthon and Johannes Brenz, the prince had the God-given duty to reform and protect the Church. Melanchthon spoke of the prince's status as the 'chief member of the church' (*praecipuum membrum ecclesiae*), an office which obliged him, out of Christian love, to intervene in Church affairs, while Brenz, turning to the Old Testament, spoke of the need for the German princes to preserve the Christian community on earth. This made them, in effect, the custodians of God's laws. By the end of the century, there was little practical distinction in Protestant lands between the rule of the Church and the rule of the State.

In the beginning, the princes were reluctant to assume the mantle of Church reformers. Prudent politics advised against it. Luther had been excommunicated in 1521 and placed under an imperial ban in the same year; the series of imperial diets held in Nuremberg (1522–4) granted the preaching of 'the holy Gospel according to Scripture', but made no real concessions to the idea of reform; and by the closing months of 1524 peasant unrest was proving how dangerous the evangelical movement could be in the hands of the common man. Public support for Martin Luther or the Wittenberg theology was, essentially, a form of rebellion, and there was no reason to doubt the strength or the determination of Charles V. For these reasons, princely support for the Reformation was relatively slow to develop.

In essence, there were three possible reactions to the evangelical movement in the early 1520s – a strongly conservative (anti-Lutheran) reaction, a neutral stance or a pro-evangelical approach (Wolgast, 1998, pp. 407–34). At the outset, the anti-Lutheran princes proved the most determined and active. Elector Joachim I of Brandenburg forbade the sale or circulation of Luther's works (including his Bible translation) and reissued the Edict of Worms, while Duke Heinrich of Wolfenbüttel published a mandate against Lutheran teachings (12 January 1522) and introduced a series of repressive anti-evangelical laws. Duke Georg of Albertine Saxony, later to become Luther's arch-nemesis, issued mandates against the movement in 1522, outlawed evangelical publications (including Luther's New Testament) and published laws against former monks, suspect preachers and subjects who communicated in both kinds. Georg also introduced a series of independent reform measures in an effort to strengthen the Catholic Church in his lands. This was also a policy adopted by Wilhelm IV of Bavaria, who matched repressive measures, such as the enforcement of the Edict of Worms, with constructive attempts to reform the Bavarian Church. On 2 October 1524 the duke published a religious mandate calling for a general examination of the clergy. He also forbade Bavarians to study in Wittenberg. In many ways the measures taken in Albertine Saxony and Bavaria were the first steps of the Catholic reaction in German lands. In the first instance it was these secular lords, rather than the powerful prince-bishops, who assumed leadership of the Catholic response. Indeed, some of the prince-bishops were slow to act against the evangelical movement. As an example we might look at the bishopric of Würzburg, later a bastion of Tridentine reform, where the early movement fell on fertile ground. Before the Peasants' War the bishop had tolerated evangelical sermons, and a number of reform-friendly clergy resided in the town (Rublack, 1978, pp. 1–74). Over time the movement would be neutralized (though a Lutheran community persisted) and repression would intensify later in the century when Catholic reform was in full flight. But in the beginning the bishop had been relatively slow to respond – in contrast to the most zealous of the secular princes.

Far more common than the commitment of Duke Georg of Saxony or the dukes of Bavaria was the policy of neutrality favoured by the majority of the German princes. For rulers such as Casimir of Brandenburg-Kulmbach, Heinrich V of Mecklenburg or Philipp of Baden, to name but a few (and we might even count Elector Friedrich the Wise of Saxony among their number), the issues raised by Luther at Worms had not yet been settled. The series of diets held in the German lands had not been able to effect a political solution, while the proposed national Church council, which lacked the support of both the emperor and the pope, seemed a distant possibility. Under these conditions, and in the face of widespread public demand, many German princes adopted an attitude of relative tolerance, at least until such time as the pope or the emperor could reach a final solution. (The pamphleteer Heinrich von Kettenbach referred to such men as 'keeping an eye on the wheel of fortune'.) Philipp of Baden, Casimir of Brandenburg-Ansbach-Kulmbach, Johann III of Jülich-Cleve-Berg, the dukes of Pomerania and Mecklenberg – all of these rulers tolerated the preaching of the Word 'clearly and purely' and the appointment of evangelical preachers, without, however, introducing the Reformation in their lands. In the Palatinate during the reign of Elector Ludwig V, the Saxon diplomat Hans von der Planitz observed how 'the gospel is being preached clearly and purely in Heidelberg, and nevertheless they do not want to become Lutheran' (Wolgast, 1998, p. 426). Yet there is no doubt that the evangelical movement was able to gather strength in lands such as these, where the rulers were willing to tolerate a degree of religious innovation. Waiting for a final decision from the imperial authorities, and pressed from below by the strength of popular interest, the neutral princes gave in to certain basic demands of the movement, even though they did not offer public support.

Far fewer in number were the princes who offered active and public support to Luther and his notions of Church reform. Johann of Saxony (who succeeded Friedrich in 1525), Philipp of Hesse, Ernst of Braunschweig-Lüneburg, and the princes of Mansfeld and Anhalt were among the few 'pro-Lutheran' princes in Germany before the year 1526. At this stage, supporting the movement was a dangerous political prospect. The evangelical sympathizers were isolated and defenceless, for there was not yet a league of Protestant powers to offer mutual military support. There was no clear structure to Protestantism, no clear political or legal framework, and no context for a common defence. Nor was there yet the theological consensus that would later evolve with confessional statements such as the Confession of Augsburg (1530) or the Schmalkaldic Articles (1537). In the early 1520s, it was still essentially the reformers and their reading of scripture against centuries of Catholic tradition. There was not yet the sense of certainty that faith and tradition acquire with time, let alone the practical security of a common public religion. No doubt Duke Georg of Saxony touched a nerve when he demanded to know how Martin Luther, a mere Augustinian monk 'out of such a hole', could dare challenge centuries of Catholic history.

The princely Reformation did not really begin apace until 1526, one year after the defeat of the peasants, when the diet of Speyer's recess (27 August 1526) ordered the Estates to conduct their affairs (in relation to the Edict of Worms) 'as [they] hope and trust to answer to God and his Imperial Majesty'. It was viewed by the majority as a compromise solution, and the Estates were advised that a future council would resolve the issue. But the evangelical powers interpreted the document in a positive sense and began to introduce reforms. One of the first to act was Philipp of Hesse, who gathered his secular and spiritual officials together at a meeting at Homberg (October 1526) as a first step in the reform of the Hessian Church. Inspired by the powerful presence of the reformer Franz Lambert of Avignon, the Homberg synod resulted in the drafting of a Church ordinance (*Reformatio ecclesiarum Hassiae*), but as it was rejected by Wittenberg it never had a chance to develop. Instead, the first process of territorial reform took place in the lands of Prussia, where Albrecht of Brandenburg, grand master of the Teutonic Order, decided to transform the order into a secular duchy. Albrecht had entertained this idea as early as 1523, the same year he had heard Osiander preach in Nuremberg and met Luther in Wittenberg. Albrecht issued a new Church order in 1525 and authorized a visitation committee the following year. But the evolution of the territorial Church in Prussia took place in unique circumstances. Albrecht was a spiritual lord transforming a religious order and placing it under Polish suzerainty. The Church order was provisional, a theological compromise, while the visitation was carried out in agreement with the bishops, more akin to the episcopal visitations of old. Prussia did not provide the German princes with a model of Lutheran reform.

For guidance, the evangelical princes looked to the Reformation in Electoral Saxony, for that is where Luther and Melanchthon were able to develop their visions of reform. The patronage of Friedrich the Wise (1486–1525) had already resulted in the preaching of the Word 'clear and pure' and a new order of service in the Castle Church of Wittenberg. But it was the reforming initiatives of Johann the Steadfast (1525–32) that did most to build a Reformation Church in the principality. During his years of rule a Lutheran service replaced the Catholic Mass (a change of worship given its theological stamp with Luther's *German Mass* of 1526); Catholic clergymen were dismissed and replaced by evangelicals; Church wealth, including the foundation wealth, was given over to the state; and a sophisticated system of territorial Church government gradually replaced diocesan rule. But perhaps the most important feature of the Reformation in Saxony was the visitation process of 1528, the parish-by-parish assessment of religion in the region. The visitation provided the foundation for both a unified statement of the faith and secular control of the Church. In the preface to the *Instructions for the Visitors of Saxony* (1528), Luther made the first reference to the relationship between Church and State that later characterized the Reformation Church:

> Preferring to follow what is certain and to be guided by love's office (which is a common obligation of Christians), we have respectfully appealed to the illustrious and noble prince and lord [Johann of Saxony] . . . constituted of God as our certain temporal sovereign, that out of Christian love (since he is not obliged to do so as a temporal sovereign) and by God's will for the benefit of the gospel and the welfare of the wretched Christians in his territory, His Electoral grace might call and ordain to this office [of visitor] several competent persons.

Thus from the very outset of the process, the Reformation in Saxony was an act of state. And in this, as in other things, the Saxon Church provided guidance for the rest of Germany.

Local circumstances would dictate how the Reformation developed in each territory, but certain features of the process were evident throughout. First, it is worth noting that no

German prince ever claimed the exclusive right to interpret scripture or pronounce on true belief. This was left to the theologians, even if the prince put the final stamp of approval on doctrine before it was published. Second, no prince among the first generation of rulers forced the new religion on an unwilling land. Aside from these reservations, however, the princes were quick to assume complete control of the reform process, and they took considerable liberties to secure the faith. In general, the following steps had to be taken in order to effect a lasting Reformation: there had to be a standard or orthodox notion of religious belief; there had to be a uniform Church service in the land; the parishes had to be staffed with the appropriate clergy, of the right religion and the requisite quality; there had to be an educational programme effective enough to maintain right belief; and there had to be a system of Church rule in place capable of replacing the Catholic inheritance (Rabe, 1991, pp. 317–35). This was the strategy adopted by the supporters of the early Reformation in territories such as Saxony and Hesse. And it was also the approach employed by the important mid-century Reformation movements in Württemberg (1534), Albertine Saxony (1539) and Brandenburg (1540).

Of all the measures at their disposal, the visitation proved the most effective way for the princes to implement the Reformation, for it provided them with a concise overview of parish religion (which could then be used to justify reform) *and* it subjected the clergy to the will of the state. It is thus not much of a surprise that a series of visitations followed the Saxon initiative, first in Hesse, Brandenburg-Ansbach-Kulmbach and Braunschweig-Lüneburg. By mid-century the visitation was an annual event in most Protestant principalities. Of equal importance were the Church orders (*Kirchenordnungen*), published statements of the faith that defined ecclesiastical norms and standards of belief. Once again the cue came from the Reformation in Saxony, where the first Church order (1528) soon evolved into a model for a number of others, including the Church orders of Brandenburg-Nuremberg (1533), Württemberg (1536), Albertine Saxony (1539) and electoral Brandenburg (1540). Once the faith was defined, the final steps of the Reformation process were in essence a matter of political expediency (Dixon, 2000, pp 158–62). Recalcitrant Catholic clergymen were dismissed and replaced by Protestant pastors. The wealth from the Catholic foundations was confiscated by the prince and then used, *inter alia*, to pay for the clergy or to support the new educational facilities. In all of this, the prince maintained control of the entire process, from the appointment of clergymen to the payment of tithes to the construction of the schools. By mid-century, maintaining the territorial Church proved too complex and extensive a task for the traditional organs of rule, and the final stage of the process, the completion of the Protestant Church as an institution of governance, brought the princely Reformation to a close.

The introduction of Lutheranism into the margravate of Brandenburg-Ansbach-Kulmbach was a fairly typical example of the princely Reformation (Dixon, 1996a, pp. 47–65). In the early 1520s, as the evangelical movement spread through the towns and the rural parishes, Margrave Casimir advised his clergy to preach the Word 'clearly and purely' and avoid all religious disputation. As the movement grew in strength, fearing that the evangelical sympathizers might storm the Catholic strongholds, the margrave began to invest the foundations and secularize the monasteries. But the Reformation did not really begin until Margrave Georg, Casimir's successor, confirmed the Lutheran profile of the territory in a meeting of the Estates in Ansbach (3 March 1528). Following this, regional officials monitored the sermons of the pastors, ensuring that the Word of God was preached, while the *Mandate for the Implementation of the Reformation* (1528) made it a crime for the clergy in the margrave's patronage to practise the old faith. That same year a visitation took the Reformation to the parish pastors and published a Church order which defined the essence of the new faith. All of these steps were taken at the expense of the Catholic Church, and indeed often in the face of its protests. In 1531, for instance, the Bishop of Bamberg observed that

[The margrave] continues to impair diocesan jurisdiction, invest churches, foundations, and monasteries and insists on enforcing the Lutheran teaching [in such places]; moreover he forces the clergy to accept the new teaching, and those who will not suffer it he chases [from their posts]; the interdictions issued by the Swabian League he simply abuses and mocks. (Dixon, 1996a, p. 29)

In the same fashion as their Saxon counterparts the margraves of Ansbach replaced the system of diocesan governance. Superintendents, and ultimately General Superintendents, watched over the Church, enforcing right doctrine, keeping up the maintenance of churches and disciplining the clergy. Yearly synods reported on the state of the Church, while the visitation progress, beginning in 1528, repeated in 1536, and ultimately turned into an annual event with the chapter ordinance of 1565, enforced the faith in the parishes. At the centre of it all was the consistory, an independent council established to govern the Church. It began as a marriage court in 1556, but by the end of the century the consistory ordinance (1594) spoke of an institution with control over the full run of ecclesiastical affairs. Indeed, the emergence of the Ansbach consistory, staffed by both secular and spiritual officials, and ultimately answerable to the margrave alone, represents the final stage in the construction of the territorial Church.

The introduction of the Reformation in the territories lasted the better part of the sixteenth century. The Church did not really assume its final form until Protestantism (which meant, in the first instance, Lutheranism) had legal security in the Empire. This explains why the sophisticated consistories and the annual visitations were products of the second half of the century, after the Peace of Augsburg (1555). Moreover, there was also a host of external factors – the course of theological developments, for instance, or the state of political relations – which necessarily limited the progress of territorial reform. But just as significant was the standing of domestic politics, for now that the Church was tied so closely to affairs of state it proved impossible to set religion off from the forces of political intrigue. As an example of this we might look to Heinrich Julius, Duke of Braunschweig-Wolfenbüttel (1589–1613), who discovered this to his cost when tensions between two antagonistic interpretations of Lutheranism threatened the stability of his rule. Increasingly, a Christian, irenic tone of Humanism was colouring the Lutheranism of Heinrich Julius and his chancellor, Johannes Jagemann. Against this reading of the faith, however, stood the defenders of Orthodox Lutheranism, a religious tradition strongly associated with the recent history of the duchy and its member Estates. The nobility, the burghers and many of

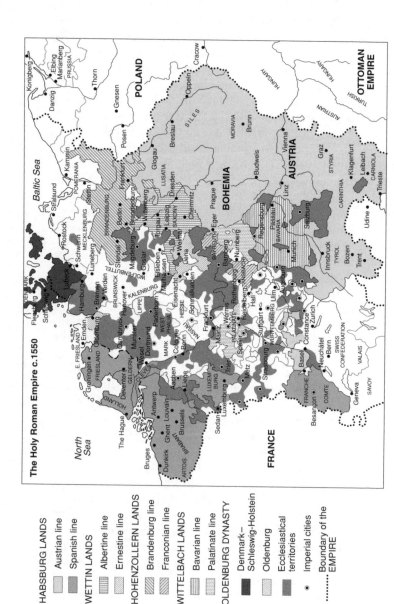

Map 4.2 The Holy Roman Empire c.1550.

Source: Volker Press, 'The Habsburg Lands: The Holy Roman Empire, 1400–1555', in Thomas J. Brady, Jr, Heiko A. Oberman and James D. Tracy (eds) *Handbook of European History* (Leiden: E. J. Brill, 1994), vol. 1, p. 438.

HABSBURG LANDS
  Austrian line
  Spanish line

WETTIN LANDS
  Albertine line
  Ernestine line

HOHENZOLLERN LANDS
  Brandenburg line
  Franconian line

WITTELBACH LANDS
  Bavarian line
  Palatinate line

OLDENBURG DYNASTY
  Denmark–
  Schleswig-Holstein
  Oldenburg
  Ecclesiastical
  territories
  • Imperial cities
  .... Boundary of the
  EMPIRE

the lesser clergy threw their weight behind Orthodox Lutheranism, for it seemed the only defence against the irenic feeling of Chancellor Jagemann and the growth of princely power. As a consequence, the duke and his Estates were at odds, both defending a vision of the Church in order to realize contrary political goals. Religion had been completely absorbed in power politics, and the Reformation in Braunschweig-Wolfenbüttel hung in the balance (Schorn-Schütte, 1992, pp. 163–94).

Due to the conjunction of religious confession and political aspiration, the process of Reformation lasted the century. Indeed, in the closing decades of the century there was a phase of princely conversions to the Reformed or Calvinist faith, which has encouraged historians to speak of a Second Reformation (Schilling, 1992, pp. 247–301). The heartland of this movement was the middle of western Germany (the Palatinate, Hesse, the Westphalian counties, Saxony, Brandenburg) and the teaching was derived from Huldrych Zwingli, Jean Calvin and Philipp Melanchthon, rather than the Lutheranism of the Augsburg Confession. Circumstances had changed. Theological controversy had divided Protestantism, confessional politics had turned religion into a matter of strategic importance, and the Catholic Church was on the march, sending missionaries into the German territories and winning back souls. Thus the Second Reformation was less compromising in its approach to reform; it granted the princes even greater powers of rule over the Church, and it tended to insist on manifest changes in outward belief and behaviour, the so-called 'reform of life'. In a sense it was an attempt to complete the first Reformation, a puritan approach bent on total reform, and as such it should be understood as part of the general evolution of Protestantism in the sixteenth century. 'Use of the term,' as Heinz Schilling explains, 'emphasizes the unity of the processes at work in church history from the beginning of the Reformation through confessionalization, on the one hand, and the differing concepts of "Reformation" that were expounded during the first and second halves of the sixteenth century on the other' (Schilling, 1992a, p. 259). The same methods of reform were employed: the formulation of unified confessional statements; the introduction of visitations; the publication of catechisms; the appointment of Protestant pastors; and finally the development of a sophisticated

Church structure. Where the Second Reformation did differ from the original movement was in the social dynamics of the process, for it was imposed from above, often without the support of the Estates or the subject population. And it was possible only because the Protestant prince, by the latter sixteenth century, enjoyed total control over the Church in his lands. This was a consolidation of power with monumental consequences for the German Nation.

The Politics of Religious Change

As soon as the Luther affair became a matter of public concern it was absorbed into the political dynamic. The meeting between Luther and Cajetan in Augsburg, for example, was a concession granted by the papacy in the hope that it would influence Saxony's vote in the pending imperial election. In this instance, the role played by political intrigue was direct and obvious; but even in the wider context of events, it is not possible to understand the development of the Reformation without taking the political dynamic into account. Indeed, one of the reasons why Charles V was unable to stop the spread of the movement was the conflicts and struggles that plagued his reign. Paramount was the ongoing quarrel between Charles, the Habsburg Emperor, and Francis I, the Valois King of France. Both had claims to the lands of northern Italy, and both sovereigns exercised their rights by marching troops into the peninsula. The quarrel was most intense during the decade following the imperial election, and though it seemed at one time that it might end in the emperor's favour after Francis was taken prisoner at Pavia (1525), the campaigns continued until the Peace of Cambrai (1529) and beyond. Meanwhile, as the French king harried the Italian lands, the Turks, under the leadership of Suleiman the Magnificent, advanced into central Europe. Turkish forces moved into areas of Africa, the Mediterranean, the Balkans, ultimately investing Belgrade, Rhodes, and after defeating Lewis II, King of Bohemia and Hungary, at Mohács (1526), most of the territory of Hungary. Here was yet another fragile frontier for the Christian emperor to safeguard, and the threat presented by the Turkish presence in central Europe would occupy Charles for the entirety of his reign. Throughout the 1520s, as the evangelical powers pushed the emperor to grant the movement more liberties, the emperor was forced to make concessions due his need for support against the advancing Turk.

But the most threatening developments were not necessarily those gathering strength at the margins of the realm. Within the Empire itself, as the cities and the princes joined together in support of the evangelical faith, military leagues and political associations started to take shape (Rabe, 1991, pp. 317–35). In 1526 Philipp of Hesse and Johann of Saxony formed the League of Torgau as the first step in a common defence against Catholic aggression (as they perceived it). A few years later Hesse and Saxony entered into an agreement with Strasbourg, Ulm and Nuremberg to assist each other if threatened by Catholic forces. But the culmination of this Protestant entrenchment was the creation of the League of Schmalkalden (1531), a military alliance with the explicit purpose of defending the Reformation in the German lands. The original membership included the Elector of Saxony and the Landgrave of Hesse, effectively the ruling powers of the association, along with two other evangelical princes and ten cities. Within a few years the League would have its own constitution (which included a corps of infantry and cavalry) and regular assemblies, where the Protestant powers could gather to discuss their common purpose. With the formation of the League, the possibility of negotiation was effectively brought to an end, for the Protestant princes (representing a minority) had set themselves against the emperor and his efforts to reestablish unity by way of the imperial diets. The formation of the League was thus a revolutionary turning-point in imperial politics – though it came as no surprise, as the symptons of a political revolution were in evidence many years before.

In 1524 the emperor informed the imperial city of Nuremberg that he was deeply displeased 'that you and the other estates support Luther so much', and he advised the city to renounce the new faith 'since most of the others in the Holy Empire will follow your example' (Brady, 1999, p. 117). Charles wrote this letter in April, a few weeks after the reaffirmation of the Edict of Worms at the third diet of Nuremberg (4 April 1524). The urban representatives had not signed the recess (the final resolution of the imperial diet), however, claiming that the enforcement of the edict would bring about a revolution of the common man and 'damage and ruin' to the Empire. By this stage the faith had already spread to a number of important urban centres and it was no longer possible to suppress the movement without risking revolt. Faced with this dilemma, representatives of the evangelical communes gathered in diets and tried to work out a political solution to the problems posed by the Luther affair. It was the first substantial sign that the evangelical movement had affected traditional relations of power in the Empire. At the urban diet of Speyer (July 1524), the envoys drafted a preaching mandate, spoke loosely of a general defensive policy and reiterated the claim that the Edict of Worms could not be enforced. At the following urban diet of Ulm (December 1524) the city representatives dealt openly with the issues raised by Luther and worked out a strategy. At the close of the sittings the cities drafted a 'Christian letter' in defence of both their politics and their religious convictions, reassuring the emperor 'that in this we seek nothing else and ask for nothing more earnestly from God, than that His divine honor, praise and honor of His holy name, and also brotherly love, to be advanced ... and that the prosperity, welfare, and prestige of the Holy Roman Empire and of Your Imperial Majesty be increased' (Brady, 1999, p. 122). Inspired by this higher vision, the urban envoys began to speak of evangelical solidarity, even as they challenged the very essence of imperial rule.

In the end, however, it would not be the imperial cities that decided the fate of the Reformation but the German princes (Schorn-Schütte, 1996, pp. 72–90). Urban solidarity started showing signs of weakness as early as the Ulm diet, when the edict of Burgos revealed Charles V to be an unlikely ally. The Peasants' War of 1525 did further damage to the standing of the cities, especially as many of the territorial rulers blamed the urban communes for the unrest. By July 1525 the larger cities had started to drift apart. Augsburg was against the idea of a general alliance; Nuremberg continued to hope for an agreement with the emperor; Strasbourg and other south German cities embraced Zwinglianism and thus turned away from the Lutheran north; while the Catholic cities started to treat among themselves. At this stage a general urban league was no longer likely. The largest cities began to go their separate ways and concentrate instead on their own security (Schmidt, 1986, p. 239).

Eventually, the only place of safety for the evangelical cities was the Schmalkaldic League. The problem remained, however, that even though the communes made up the majority, the princes never viewed the cities as equal partners. And while urban wealth remained essential to the maintenance of the League, the important political decisions fell to the territorial rulers. 'It is the intention of the princes to bring and to force the cities to such a point,' warned Strasbourg's Claus Kniebis, 'that each city would surrender itself to the nearest prince in exchange for protection, which would be like escaping the wolf only to fall prey to the lion's claws' (Brady, 1985, p. 212). Ultimately the cities fell prey to both: Emperor Charles held the urban communes to ransom for the Schmalkaldic War, while the Protestant princes emerged as the main beneficiaries of the final peace brokered in Augsburg.

The career of Jacob Sturm, Strasbourg's chief magistrate, provides a window on this development. Sturm stepped onto the imperial stage during the diet of Speyer (1526), the meeting which freed the Estates from the conditions imposed by the Edict of Worms and referred the religious matter to a general council. With this concession, the evangelical princes emerged in force, and both Saxony and Hesse approached Sturm's city of Strasbourg with hopes of an alliance. By 1528 Sturm entered into negotiations with Hesse, and the following year the city decided to pursue a 'Christian alliance' with the Lutheran princes of northern Germany. Strasbourg's public association with Zwinglianism was a stumbling-block for any union with the Lutheran powers; but as Sturm recognized in Speyer (1529), the emperor was starting to take a hard line against the evangelical powers. There was only one solution: 'If Strasbourg is to be deprived of its rights for having worked for the greater glory of God and dethroning idolatry,' he declared, 'then the city can no longer take any regard for the Empire in its affairs' (Brady, 1997, p. 101). Like many of his urban counterparts, Jacob Sturm steered a course which took his city into the orbit of the Protestant princes. Strasbourg turned its back on Zwinglianism and the Swiss association, placing its trust instead in the Schmalkaldic League. With that, a traditional pattern of imperial politics re-emerged: the princes looked to exploit the cities for their wealth, while they marginalized the urban vote at the diets. Martin Bucer, the Strasbourg reformer, picked up on this trend when he remarked how 'the Protestant princes as well as the others have recommended and voted for the suppression of the cities; and many papists mock the cities for having put so much trust in the Protestant princes' (Brady, 1997, p. 171). Sturm feared that the princes were marching the League into a war with the emperor – and he was right. But by mid-century Strasbourg, like all other urban communes in the Empire, had been marginalized. Faith alone had not held the urban front together, especially when faith itself (as between the Lutherans and the Zwinglians) had become a point of division; the emperor had not entered into an agreement with the imperial cities, nor had he weakened in his Catholicism; and any solidarity created by the Schmalkaldic League waned as the cities fell prey to the larger territorial powers. By mid-century, leadership of the Reformation movement, and thus to a large extent its fate as well, was firmly in the hands of the German princes.

History had prepared the princes for this role, but with the Reformation came the added element of religious conviction. Never before in German history had confessional allegiance divided the Estates or created a rift between the emperor and his subjects. And never before had such a powerful sense of destiny informed the act of resistance. For the Protestant rulers, this had a twofold yield. On the one hand, the princes now saw themselves as God's viceroys on earth, placed in office to defend the True Church and ensure the spread of the Reformation. As early as 1526, the princes of Hesse and Saxony were appearing at imperial gatherings with the words *Verbum Dei manet in aeternum* ('the Word of God is eternal') stitched on the sleeves of their livery as testimony to their mission. The Protestant prince did not just think of himself as a champion of earthly reform, but rather as the guardian of the Church and the executor of the divine will. As the *Hohenlohe Church Order* (1533) worded it, the prince was in power 'to protect God's name and his Word' and to make sure that the requirements of the faith were preserved. In Württemberg's *Great Church Order* (1559) the duke proclaimed that he was not only responsible for his own salvation, but the salvation of everyone subject to his rule. This fusion of personal governance and public faith gave rise to a potent form of sovereignty. Not only was the Protestant ruler the final authority in both Church and State, but he had been placed in office to watch over a higher cause. Protestant thought gave rise to a powerful ideology of princely rule, for final justification was always sought in scripture itself, with its range of historical precedent, its Old Testament terminology and its defence of temporal authority. In this age, there was no higher sanction.

On the other hand, religious conviction, and with it the burden of conscience, became a source of conflict in imperial politics. After the publication of the Edict of Worms, it was a crime to support Luther or his teachings. For the evangelicals, faced with the facts of law and history, the central dilemma was how to invest their private conversions with a semblance of public legality. 'The subjective *causa religionis* had to be transformed into an objective *causa iuris*,' is how the historian Eike Wolgast words it, 'so that both the refusal to obey, maintained on religious grounds, and the defence of the consequences brought about by this refusal to obey, could be legally justified and secured' (Wolgast, 1980, p. 9). Resisting the emperor, however, as all parties were aware, was a radical step. A handful of theologians had sounded out the idea in the early 1520s, but it was not until the diets of Speyer (1529) and Augsburg (1530) that the Protestant princes began seriously to consider the notion of a military alliance. Philipp of Hesse now spoke openly of opposing the emperor, an idea he pressed on the rulers of Saxony and Brandenburg-Ansbach as well as the theologians of Wittenberg. At first Luther reacted with suspicion and reserve. In his eyes, the princes derived their powers from the emperor and thus did not have the right to resist. More importantly, the idea of resistance was contrary to his theological principles, which taught that tyranny should be suffered in Christian silence. But tensions continued to build in the Empire, especially after Charles V rejected the Augsburg Confession (1530) and demanded a return to the Catholic fold. Moreover, anti-Lutheran powers, sensing that there would be no quick solution to the religious breach, began to go on the offensive.

Realizing that the faith could not survive long isolated and defenceless, Luther gave way to a theory of Protestant resistance. In truth it was two theories: the Hessians drew on a notion of constitutional resistance, grounded in the belief that the emperor did not rule as a monarch but rather shared sovereignty with the imperial Estates (or rather with the princes). Charles had overstepped his office and thereby violated the agreement between the German Nation and its elected king. Thus it was not just a question of faith, but of German liberty. Even Leonhard von Eck, the Catholic Chancellor of Bavaria, warned the German princes that 'emperor and King share the same mind and the same intention, to suppress the German Nation and reduce it to a monarchy' (Schmidt, 1999, p. 85). The Saxon jurists, in contrast, building on theories of private law, claimed that when an authority went beyond the bounds of his office he was no longer a rightful judge but a private citizen – and thus no longer a lawful magistrate. In this case, the emperor was abusing his office by legislating in matters of belief. Luther tried to steer clear of a theme which, in his opinion, had little to do with theology, but in fact both theories of resistance were closely tied to the Reformation. When speaking of the sovereignty or the *imperium* of the territorial princes, the Hessians thought in terms of the *cura religionis*, the obligation of every ruler to watch over the Church in his lands. This was the principle mandate of territorial reform. Equally, Luther's assurance in his *Warning to his Dear German People* (1531) that he would not reprove anyone for defending themselves against the unwarranted attacks of the 'murderers and bloodthirsty papists' had its roots in the rationale of the Saxon jurists (Skinner, 1996, vol. 2, pp. 189–225). The Catholics had become unlawful magistrates, trying to impose a corrupt faith through force. Taken to its extremes in the early 1550s by the besieged Protestants of Magdeburg, the theory of resistance proved capable of equating the emperor with the Antichrist and labelling all pro-Catholic agitators as servants of the Devil. By this stage Reformation thought had turned the emperor of the German Nation into an enemy of political liberty and religious truth.

No less confirmed in his personal (Catholic) faith, and no less certain of his political cause, was Charles V. The emperor first made this clear at the diet of Worms (1521). One day after Luther had revealed the depth of his own faith, Charles responded in kind:

> You know that I am born of the most Christian Emperors of the noble German Nation, of the Catholic Kings of Spain, the Archdukes of Austria, the Dukes of Burgundy, who were all to the

death true sons of the Roman Church, defenders of the Catholic faith, of the sacred customs, decrees and uses of its worship, who have bequeathed all this to me as my heritage, and according to whose example I have hitherto lived. Thus I am determined to hold fast by all which has happened since the Council of Constance. For it is certain that a single monk must err if he stands against the opinion of all Christendom. Otherwise Christendom itself would have erred for more than a thousand years. Therefore I am determined to set my kingdoms and dominions, my friends, my body, my blood, my life, my soul upon it. (Brandi, 1965, p. 131)

In part this was religious conviction, a defence of Catholicism and its centuries of tradition. In part it was political philosophy, the long-held Habsburg vision of a universal monarchy bound by religion and preserved by the Holy Roman Emperor. There could be no place for confessional division in such an outlook, for the monarchy itself inhered in the divine order. That is why Charles initially sought a policy of conciliation and reunion by treaty, even after most theologians had given up hope of a rapprochement, for he held that order could be restored in an Empire at peace with itself. The invitation to the diet of Augsburg (1530), for instance, was irenic in spirit, calling for a gathering where every 'belief and opinion' might be sounded. In the years that followed, there would be dialogue (Schorn-Schütte, 2000b, pp. 47–61). Charles himself was present at the diet in Regensburg (1541) when a group of Catholic and Protestant theologians tried to bridge the divide between the faiths. Similarly, when threatened by the approach of the Turks or the machinations of the French, the emperor proved willing to enter into agreements with the Protestant powers, the first being the Peace of Nuremberg (1532), then the truces of Frankfurt (1539), Regensburg (1541) and Speyer (1544). For many years Charles thought the Reformation could be kept in check, if not effectively reversed, by way of compromise and concession. It was a political matter; it required a political solution. In the essential articles of the faith, however, there could be no capitulation. For while he occasionally spoke of allowing the Protestants to continue certain practices (such as clerical marriage and communion in both kinds), his Catholic faith remained constant. In the end political compromise, working in the shadow of such strong religious beliefs, proved impossible.

The turning-point came with the failure of the theologians to reach an agreement at the diet of Regensburg (1541). From this point forward, as Geoffrey Elton once observed, 'the emperor conducted affairs with a single eye to the defeat of the Schmalkaldic League' (Elton, 1999, p. 170). Tensions had been building for some time. In 1534 the League, led by Philipp of Hesse and backed by French funds, marched on the duchy of Württemberg and restored the exiled duke. Henceforth Lutheranism had an important stronghold in south-west Germany, the League grew in strength and status (negotiating with French, English and Scandinavian rulers), while the faith itself assumed greater definition with the Wittenberg Concord (1536) and the Schmalkaldic Articles (1537). Recognizing the growing military threat presented by the Protestant alliance, a number of Catholic powers joined together in the League of Nuremberg (1538), but the Catholic union was neither a political reality nor a military force, and it was certainly no match for the Schmalkaldic League. The only effective counterweight to Protestant expansion was the emperor, as Charles V himself realized. But his fortunes were mixed. He could do nothing as the League chased Duke Heinrich out of Braunschweig-Wolfenbüttel (1542), occupied the duchy, and forced through a Lutheran Reformation. But he was able to stave off Protestant expansion into the duchy of Cleves-Jülich (1543), and he put an end to the reform efforts undertaken by Hermann von Wied, the Archbishop of Cologne.

In the end, compromise and negotiation had come to nothing. All that remained was force. The victory in Cleves was especially important, for now the emperor realized, as he wrote in his memoirs, that not only was it possible to push back the Protestants, 'but on the contrary – under the appropriate conditions, using the appropriate means – it was easy to subdue such insolence by way of force' (Kohler, 1999, p. 283). Charles now prepared for war with the Protestants. He secured the 'appropriate conditions' by signing an agreement with the French king and the Turks; he received troops from the papacy and was promised free passage through Bavaria; he entered into agreements with a number of significant German princes; and he waited and watched as the League itself fell into disarray. In the summer of 1546, using the pretence of the imperial ban, the emperor went to war with the Schmalkaldic League. It did not last long. Less than a year later the imperial forces crushed the army of Johann

Friedrich of Saxony at Mühlberg (24 April 1547) and the Schmalkaldic War came to an end. The League had been routed, and Charles took both the Elector of Saxony and the Landgrave of Hesse as his prisoners. His victory was complete.

When the Estates met at the diet of Augsburg (1547/8), the emperor was at the height of his powers. The Schmalkaldic League had been defeated on the field of battle; the two most powerful Protestant princes were under arrest; and the evangelical cities, especially those in Swabia and Alsace, were held to ransom for the war. There was even talk of executing Johann Friedrich of Saxony; though in the end the emperor thought it sufficient to strip him of his lands and electorship (which were conferred on Moritz of Saxony, in accordance with an earlier agreement) and keep him under lock and key. In other matters, however, Charles proved less flexible. Politically, he wanted to set his house in order by establishing a peace-keeping federation in the Empire; religiously, he wanted to win back some of the ground ceded to the Protestants by imposing the Catholic provisions required by the Augsburg Interim (1548) (Kohler, 1999, pp. 295–326). Neither policy was successful, however, for each presented a fundamental threat to the religious and political liberties of the German Nation. Charles realized this to his cost when Moritz of Saxony abandoned the imperial alliance, gathered an army of Protestant princes (backed by the French) and forced the emperor to agree to the Treaty of Passau (1552). It was now clear that the advances made by the Reformation could not be reversed. From this point forward Protestantism became a constitutional force in the German lands.

The final reckoning came three years later, when a series of negotiations between King Ferdinand and the German Estates resulted in the Peace of Augsburg (25 September 1555). Although intended as a provisional solution, the settlement remained imperial law for over two centuries (though with modifications after the Peace of Westphalia). With the peace, the Lutheran confession was placed on the same legal footing as Catholicism (though this equality was not extended to the other evangelical religions, such as Calvinism, Zwinglianism or Anabaptism). It did not enshrine any sense of religious tolerance; it was a legal and political compromise between two forces exhausted by war. The Lutherans were no longer subject to the heresy laws, nor were they subject to ecclesiastical jurisdiction.

Moreover, it was legally observed, and later encapsulated in the Latin tag *cuius regio, eius religio* ('his the rule, his the religion'), that the imperial Estates directly subject to the emperor should have the right to determine the religion of their subjects. Some fine-tuning was needed: Ferdinand appeased the Catholics by including an ecclesiastical reservation stipulating that bishops and abbots had to surrender their offices and territories if they converted to Protestantism. Equally, although it was not included in the official recess, the *Declaratio Ferdinandei* protected Lutheran powers (knights, territorial towns) resident in ecclesiastical lands. Other provisions of note included an article preserving the status quo in those imperial cities where the two religions were already practised, and the *ius immigrandi* ('the right to immigrate'), a provision which allowed for the subjects of any imperial estate to sell their property and emigrate if they did not share the same faith as their sovereign. The Peace soon set its stamp on the realm: Germany became a land where confession was bound up with territorial politics and conscience a matter of public law.

In the final analysis, the peace proved most beneficial to the Protestant princes, for their essential political goal had always been recognition of the *ius reformandi*, the right to reform, and this right was now extended to the adherents of the Lutheran religion. As the Elector of Saxony put it, the settlement guaranteed that the Protestant princes were 'not obliged to tolerate the papal abuses' in their lands (Tüchle, 1971, p. 154). The sovereign now had the right to rule over the Church in his territory and determine the religion of his subjects. And while the peace left many questions unanswered and many problems unresolved, it was a constitutional watershed. Two religions, Lutheranism and Catholicism, now had equal legal status in the German lands of the Empire. The medieval idea of a universal monarchy, united under the papacy and protected by the Holy Roman Emperor, was no longer a possibility. In both politics and religion, the forces of particularism had triumphed at the expense of universalism. Germany would remain a land of territorial rulers and the Reformation, now recognized by imperial law, would not be reversed (Heckel, 1983, p. 114). Thus the Peace of Augsburg, to a considerable extent, brought to a close the political dymamic unleashed by Luther's appearance at Worms. Confessional struggles continued, but the Lutherans

could now defend their interests on equal terms. No one realized this better than the emperor himself, now fragile in health
and broken in spirit. One year after the Peace of Augsburg,
Charles V abdicated the last of his thrones, left the German
lands forever, and lived out the rest of his days, surrounded by
monks, ministers and ticking clocks, near the Spanish monastery
of San Jeronimo de Yuste.

5

The Reformation Legacy

In the sixteenth century religion was central to all aspects of daily experience. It offered the faithful a basic framework for understanding the world, and in its primary role as a source of meaning and consolation, religious belief was the most influential psychological force of the age. The Reformation did nothing to change this. Despite the confusions created by the confessional divide, theology remained the dominant public discourse of the century. Both its language and its concerns were fundamental to the shared sense of intellectual order. Even those who challenged certain features of the official faith, Catholic and Protestant alike, recognized that religion was indispensable for making sense of the world. In a similar manner, religious culture was elemental for the general structures and schemes of daily life. Most people regulated their lives around the annual holidays of the Christian calendar. Important rites of passage were expressed through forms of observance, whether that meant gathering *en masse* for a public ritual or getting together in relative seclusion for an act of personal faith. And more than this: religious principles were at the heart of the culture and society of the time. Even in the secular world, from the relations between sovereigns and subjects to the status of women in society, the place of the poor, the purpose of art, or the nature of public conduct and private conviction, religious belief provided a framework for thought and action.

It follows, therefore, that any fundamental reform of the basic principles of the faith would naturally and necessarily have broader implications for the culture and society of the age. A reformation of religion would, in time, lead to a reformation of both the secular and the spiritual world. For some religious thinkers, Luther in particular, this was not a crucial feature of the movement. For others, such as Zwingli and Calvin, this was an expressed goal. But for all of the people who experienced the Reformation, this is exactly what happened.

The Growth of Confessions

On 25 June 1530 an event occurred at the diet of Augsburg which Georg Spalatin, former secretary to Friedrich the Wise of Saxony, described as 'the most significant act that has ever taken place on earth'. He continued:

> For on the afternoon [of the day after the festival of Saint John the Baptist] my gracious lord, the elector of Saxony [and the other princes and municipal representatives who joined him] gave public confession of their faith and of the whole Christian teaching which they permitted to be proclaimed in their prince-doms, lands, and cities. They had it read in German in a fine, cheerful Christian spirit, not just in front of all the electors, princes, estates, bishops, and councillors who were present, but also in front of the Roman Imperial Majesty himself and his brother. (Kolb, 1991, p. 44)

The public confession Spalatin made reference to came to be known as the *Augsburg Confession* (1530), the first general syn-thesis of the Lutheran faith. Written by Philipp Melanchthon, the confession was drafted in order to delineate the basic prin-ciples of the Lutheran religion and their points of division with Catholicism. It came at a time when the Protestants were in need of doctrinal clarity, and it remained the primal synthesis of Lutheranism throughout the sixteenth century. It was the first in a series of confessions – statements or declarations of the faith – that developed during the age of Reformation, and it proved fundamentally important to the course of German history. From this point forward the Empire was witness to the growth of antagonistic confessional communities, each drawing a sense of purpose, a sense of mission and a sense of identity from the public confessions of the faith.

By the end of the century, all the major religions in Germany had an accepted corpus of belief. For the Lutherans, as mentioned above, the first general confession was the *Augsburg Confession*, and while other syntheses followed in times of necessity or crisis, Melanchthon's draft remained largely inviolate until mid-century. With the rise of internecine quarrels between the Philippists and the Gnesio-Lutherans, however, the status of the *Augsburg Confession* was challenged, to the point where a series of alternative confessions appeared in the second half of the century. It was not until a majority of Lutheran powers accepted the *Formula of Concord* in 1577, and with it the *Book of Concord* in 1580, that any lasting sense of consensus returned. By this stage the public confessions were at the very heart of the Reformation movement, for it was in works such as the *Book of Concord* that 'the majority of German Lutheran churches found their substitute for medieval popes and councils as the authoritative source and guide (later designated *norma normata*) for the interpretation of the scriptures (the *norma normans*)' (Kolb, 1996, p. 120). For the followers of Zwingli and the south German movement, the earliest confessions could also be traced back to the diet at Augsburg, but in general the Reformed communities tended to provide syntheses of the faith in Church orders and catechisms rather than pointing to a single authoritative text. It might be said that the most influential statements emerged in the most influential communities, which is why the *Heidelberg Catechism* (1563) and *The Second Helvetic Confession* (1566), both written for the Palatinate, held such an important place. And finally, while the Protestant communities were constructing a confessional corpus, the Catholic Church was consolidating centuries of doctrine. At the close of the Council of Trent, the Catholic community could look to *The Form of Profession of the Orthodox Catholic Faith* (1564), a synthesis of the conclusions taken at the Church council. In addition, the Catholic faithful could learn the basics from the catechisms, the two most influential being a work by Peter Canisius and the later Tridentine *Roman Catechism*, published in 1566. By the end of the century the Catholics, like the Lutherans and the Reformed, had a clear and uncompromising profile of the faith.

Confessional division was one of the most direct and profound consequences of the Reformation. By the end of the century, the Empire was split up into distinct religious groupings. Any hope of religious unity had passed. This gradual breakdown of relations, and with it the growing dogmatism and inflexibility of the parties involved, came to the fore in the religious colloquies. The first to meet in such a forum were the evangelicals, the followers of Luther and Zwingli, brought together at Marburg (1 October 1529) by Philipp of Hesse in an effort to create a unified Protestant front. But on the question of the Real Presence and the meaning of Christ's words *Hoc est corpus meum* ('this is my body') the reformers could not agree, and the colloquy ended without unity or resolution. More fateful for the progress of the Reformation movement as a whole was the series of colloquies held between the Catholics and the Lutherans. It began in Augsburg (1530), where Charles V, openly declaring that he wanted to hear 'every belief and opinion', invited the Estates to discuss the religious issues raised by the submission of the Augsburg Confession. Despite agreement on some crucial issues, the meeting ended in failure. Further attempts at dialogue were undertaken at Hagenau (1540) and Worms (1540/1), but it was the meeting at Regensburg (1541) which presented the confessional communities with the best chance at reconciliation. At this juncture, with the Turks and the French growing in strength, the emperor was ready to compromise. But once again, despite broad-based consensus on many points, the two confessional parties failed to reach agreement. Moreover, by this stage it was clear that it was no longer just a question of the theological subtleties at stake but the essential meaning of religious reform (*reformatio*), including the purpose, function and authority of the Church (Augustijn, 1993, pp. 64–80). In the colloquies which followed the Catholics were far less willing to compromise, and indeed Ferdinand more or less set the terms for the discussion at Worms (1557). After Regensburg few people held any serious hopes that a colloquy would provide a solution to the confessional divide.

The only other forum for religious dialogue was the Church council, promised by Rome after the Luther affair surfaced and demanded by the imperial Estates at each of the diets. In truth, reference to a pending Church council proved an effective strategy for both parties, for the notion that religious division would be settled at some stage in the *future* was enough to make compromise in the *present* a possibility. But political dissimulation could not conceal the differences between the two confessions (Brockmann, 1998). The Protestants considered the Church council a human institution, capable of error, and subject to the influence of Rome. The council did not speak for the Christian community, it was not guided by the Holy Spirit, and it was not the final authority in matters of faith. Scripture alone was the arbiter of God's will. To add to this, the Protestants refused to countenance a council arbitrated by the pope. As Melanchthon cautioned, the pope would not call a council 'in order to allow for dialogue or to hear anyone out, but for this reason and this reason alone: to determine how best to root out our professed faith, condemned by him in advance as heresy' (Brockmann, 1998, pp. 270–1). The Catholics, in contrast, had completely different ideas about the power and the function of a Church council. For men like Johannes Eck and other champions of the papacy, the council represented the universal Church, it was guided by the Holy Spirit, it realized the will of God, and it was, under certain conditions, infallible. To question the authority of the council was to question the basic truths of the faith. These were completely antagonistic conceptions of truth, faith, authority, jurisdiction and history, all of which were given voice by the contending confessions in the dialogue over the Church council. Little wonder the Protestants refused to attend the sessions in Trent. By mid-century, the traditional ideas and institutions of Catholic Europe could no longer heal the breach.

In place of compromise and reconciliation, the sixteenth century experienced the growth of confessions, the emergence of discrete communities of worship. The result was the existence of three major religious communities in Germany – Catholic, Lutheran, Reformed – along with an associated process of social, cultural and political transformation. The historian Ernst Walter Zeeden first spoke of this phenomenon in terms of 'the formation of confessions' (Zeeden, 1985). According to Zeeden, all of the confessions, Protestants and Catholics alike, developed sophisticated Church structures and syntheses of the faith. This was the age of synods and consistories, marriage courts and inquisitions, published confessions and articles of belief, catechisms, hymnals, new forms of church music, art, rites and impassioned propaganda. Building on this insight, the historians Heinz Schilling and Wolfgang Reinhard have introduced the idea of confessionalization, a concept which broadens the range of analysis to include other aspects of sixteenth-century life. Religion remains the 'heuristic indicator' for fundamental change, but now its effects are considered so far-reaching that the religious reforms of the sixteenth century are placed at the heart of 'a universal social-historical process' of change. In Schilling's words:

> The confessional hypothesis focuses both on the cultural, intellectual, social, and political functions of religion and confession within the early modern social order and on the confessions' roles as spurs and barriers to the emergence of modernity. These are the two sides of the historical paradigm we call 'confessionalization'. It holds that the late sixteenth-century emergence of confessions was one of the key events in early modernization, because the doctrinal and organizational strengthening of the churches became a powerful prelude to political and social reorganization in the following era. (Schilling, 1995, pp. 642–3)

The result of the process was twofold: first, the Church was integrated into the State, with its ministers often performing the same functions as secular officials, presiding over the same organs of governance and concerned with the same aspects of rule (discipline, public welfare, education). Second, the state became quasi-sacral, the interpreter and defender of the faith. Religious identity and secular norms began to merge as the Church, 'in cooperation with the early modern state . . . set about purifying, standardizing, and unifying religious life' (Schilling, 1995, p. 652). This process was common to all the confessions of this period. Indeed, Reinhard considers it an essential part of the early modern phase of state formation, which, despite the clear differences in theology and liturgy, was central to both the Reformation and the Counter-Reformation movements of the sixteenth century (Reinhard, 1999, pp. 164–92).

A credal map of late sixteenth-century Germany provides plenty of evidence for the growth of confessions. The Empire was split up into communities of religious allegiance, gathered as Churches, defined and maintained as political blocs (Stievermann 1997, pp. 45–65; Ziegler, 1997, pp. 67–90). In most of the lay territories in the north the public confession was Lutheran, and these principalities were soon joined by powerful allies further to the south. In the lands at the southern edges of the Empire a process of Catholic reform kept the Reformation movement at bay. Meanwhile, in the second half of the century, the introduction of the Reformed faith made the religious com-

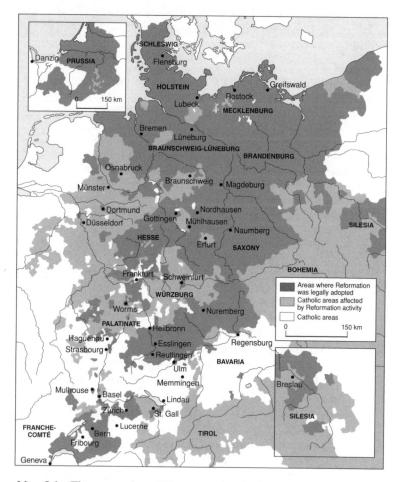

Map 5.1   The expansion of Protestantism in Germany to 1570.

Source: Hans J. Hillerbrand (ed.), *The Oxford Encyclopedia of the Reformation* (Oxford: Oxford University Press, 1996), vol. 4, p. 332.

plexion of the German Nation even more elaborate. The situation was further complicated by the imperial cities, the majority of which had introduced Lutheranism before the Peace of Augsburg and remained powerful representatives of the Reformation. At the same time, those cities that remained Catholic, joined by reinvigorated bishoprics, emerged as important centres of the Counter-Reformation. The setting was thus very complex, and there were many variables at work as the confessional communities took shape, both at the level of imperial politics and in the urban communes and the territories themselves. And yet, for all the complexity, there were certain basic features and key stages common to most of the Catholic and Protestant reform projects. The best way to illustrate this is to look closely at the process, to examine the growth of confessional communities at the level of the territory and the urban commune.

The margravate of Brandenburg-Ansbach-Kulmbach, as we have seen in the discussion of the princely Reformation, was one of the first territories in the Empire to embrace the Reformation. Following events in Saxony, the prince and his theologians drew up confessions of the faith. A Church order along with visitation articles emerged in 1528. These were ultimately replaced by the *Brandenburg-Nuremberg Church Order* of 1533, a comprehensive synthesis of Lutheran belief drafted by Andreas Osiander and Johannes Brenz and approved by the theologians of Wittenberg. Once the Church order was published it was distributed to every parish in the land, 800 copies alone going to the churches of Ansbach. Other confessional statements followed – articles of visitation and marriage, a synodal ordinance, a consistory ordinance and a final corpus of official works (which included the Augsburg Confession, the Formula of Concord, Luther's catechisms and the *corpus doctrinae* of Philipp Melanchthon). The next step was the creation of a state Church with the explicit mission of enforcing the tenets of the faith. As the organs of ecclesiastical governance grew in complexity, the State provided many of the church officials and most of the rationale behind Church rule. Indeed, the primary organ of Church governance, the consistory, was staffed by three theologians and three members of the margravial council, with a secular official assuming the office of president. There was no contradiction here, no abuse of power. As the consistory ordinance proclaimed (1594), all of the members gathered in order to realize the same goal: 'The maintenance of constant unity, discipline, order, and honour among the clergy and their audience, and to punish and make an example of evil in our land and principality in the name of God' (Dixon, 1996a, p. 59).

In the Protestant cities the process was more or less the same. In each instance, the secular powers (and this usually meant the city council) assumed control over the movement. This was done by usurping diocesan jurisdiction and subjecting the clergy to civic laws. Supervision of the Church thus fell to the council, including matters relating to the exercise of religion, the appointment of clergy, and the fate of the religious foundations. Even the public confessions of faith evolved out of political decisions taken by the council members. The ruling elite set a confessional stamp on the city by publishing Church orders, articles of visitation, catechisms, and mandates of religious reform and urban order. In the imperial city of Nuremberg, for instance, the city council intervened as soon as the evangelical movement took hold. The first reaction was a defensive one. As early as 1522 the authorities advised the clergy that they should not do anything 'that serves to encourage general unrest, or disrespects or diminishes our sovereign council . . . but rather [the clergy] should remain true to the gospel and Christian teaching and do nothing to sow discord or give any parties cause for unrest' (Vogler, 1998, p. 397). Once it was clear that the movement could not be suppressed, the urban authorities took up the reins of reform. By degrees, and wholly by secular writ, evangelical pastors were appointed, diocesan jurisdiction was suspended, wayward sects were rooted out and the clergy were made subject to the laws of the city. In March 1525 the council staged a debate between the evangelicals and the Catholic regulars in the city hall and, once the reformer Andreas Osiander had emerged as the victor, the council introduced the Reformation. A temporary Church order was drafted in 1528, which also served as a handbook for the visitation of that year, until a final synthesis of the faith, along with Osiander's catechism, was issued in 1533. From this point forward the council was in effect the bishop of the city.

The emergence of confessional communities, this diffusion of religious ideals through Church *and* State, was not limited to the Protestant realm. There was little to distinguish the process of confessionalization in the Catholic lands from the phenomenon in a Lutheran or a Calvinist territory. Perhaps the best example is offered by the history of Bavaria, one of the largest and most influential Catholic territories in southern Germany. As soon as the evangelical movement emerged in the duchy the authorities worked to root it out. Preachers were arrested, books were confiscated, public lectures were forbidden. The Edict of Worms was enforced to the letter, and soon afterward the dukes published a new religious mandate (1522) confirming Bavaria's

Catholic profile. Later in the century, partly in reaction to Protestant initiatives, further reform measures were introduced. The secular authorities supervised the first territorial Church visitation (1558), published religious mandates, issued a revised school ordinance and introduced censorship laws that made it next to impossible to publish anything other than Catholic texts. Moreover, as in the Protestant lands, Church and State formed an explicit association at the level of rule. In Bavaria, the high point of this alliance was reached with the foundation of the Spiritual Council (1570), an organ of governance which called on the clergy and the secular officials to work together in common cause (Ziegler, 1992, pp. 57–68).

All of this reform was initiated and supervised by the Dukes of Bavaria themselves. For many of them it was a personal crusade, a pious and private hope that the subjects of Bavaria might share the same faith as their rulers. There was no greater example of this than Duke Maximilian (1573–1651). During his time of rule Jesuits, Franciscans and Capuchins moved deeper and deeper into the parishes while the Lutheran communities were rooted out. The clergy fell subject to comprehensive rules of discipline and learning, and even lay subjects had to take a credal oath to the local parish priest once they returned from studies abroad. Strict laws of censorship were imposed, including an index of forbidden books, while Maximilian made sure that every other year two informed Catholics visited the book-stalls in his major cities and checked the shelves. On his death, due to his intense devotion, the cult of the Virgin Mary was flourishing in the land. The last great chapel founded in her honour emerged in 1645, with the charter of consecration signed in Maximilian's own blood (Albrecht, 1998, pp. 285–337). By this stage Bavaria was the premier Catholic power in the German lands, a model of the confessional state.

Of course, the evolution of confessional communities did not occur without evidence of friction. Developments in Brandenburg-Ansbach-Kulmbach, Nuremberg and Bavaria illustrate the essentials of the process, but not all territories could claim the same degree of success. On the contrary, quite often the final settlement was the outcome of bitter and protracted struggles. Confessionalization was a dynamic process, and the religious profile of any city or territory was frequently a hybrid or a compromise – an interim solution between antagonistic communities as they struggled for advantage. This was evident from the very outset of the Reformation movement, as Catholics and Protestants won and lost advantage in diets, debates and colloquies. As a historical phenomenon, however, the confessional dynamic did not really intensify until the period following the Peace of Augsburg (1555). From this point forward religious programmes were translated into social and political reality: not only was the Lutheran faith invested with the legal right to take root in Germany, but the Catholic Church embarked on an inspired campaign of reform and revival. And to add to the tensions, by mid-century the Reformed faith emerged as a third confessional force in the Empire. Claims to religious truth and the right to rule were on the increase, while notions of tolerance and submission were on the wane. The stage was thus set for a collision of religious interests, a struggle for existence between the Catholic, Lutheran and Reformed communities. At the level of the urban commune and the rural parish, this often brought tensions and discord to local religious life.

The Catholic reform movement, for instance, was a campaign to win back the parishioners lost to Protestantism. Any spirit of compromise had ended in 1564 with the final session at Trent. When Cardinal Guise acclaimed the decrees drafted in the council's name, the remaining fathers shouted in reply: 'So be it, Amen! Amen! Anathema to all false teachings, Anathema!' (Hsia, 1998, p. 24). The period of Catholic renewal began, and for the German lands that meant closer ties to Rome, an injection of reforming spirit into the imperial bishoprics, the gradual dissemination of the Tridentine decrees in the diocesan statutes and the emergence of reforming bishops in the major imperial sees. The period also witnessed the arrival of the Jesuits, many of whom had been educated at the German College in Rome, travelling throughout the Empire in an effort to win back souls to the Catholic faith. Jesuit missions were sent into Austria and Bavaria, schools and seminaries were founded in Mainz, Eichstätt, Munich, Würzburg, Dillingen, Cologne and Ingolstadt, while the order worked its way into a number of major German universities. Catholic reform was given a further boost by the reform-minded Habsburgs of the latter decades of the sixteenth century. Protestant estates in Styria and Lower Austria were marginalized; Lutherans were banished from the towns of Inner and Upper Austria, their schools and churches suppressed; Protestant communities in the Tyrol were exiled. And while the evangelicals were rooted out, the Habsburgs promoted the Catholic reform movement in their lands. Jesuits settled in Vienna, Graz, Innsbruck and Linz, while the mendicant orders began to flourish. Traditional forms of Catholic devotion were encouraged, including the local rites and observances, while a host of new shrines and cults sprang up in the parishes. The faith became an essential component of the state. The nobility emerged as the arch-Catholic extension of Habsburg sovereignty, while a 'universal (imperial) ideology and a revived cosmopolitan (Catholic) Church' provided the ideas and the symbols of imperial rule (Evans, 1979, p. xxiii).

But the Counter-Reformation was not without its setbacks, nor was it without its hostilities and open resistance. On occasion, as Marc Forster has pointed out in his study of Catholic reform in the parishes of Speyer, the strength and depth of local religion was enough to deflect the aims of the state (Forster, 1992, pp. 94–116). In a sense, the parish and its traditions were in a struggle for survival with the forces of confessional change. As an example we might look to Marktgraitz and Marktzeuln, two small Lutheran communes in Franconia subject to the bishops of Würzburg and Bamberg. Even in the face of drastic Counter-Reformation measures the parishioners refused to abandon their faith. When the bishops placed new candidates in office, the diocesan officials were greeted with weapons and threats and chased out of the parishes. Better to lose life and limb, the parishioners declared, than to surrender the Church (Dippold, 1996, pp. 148–99). With the election of Johann Gottfried von Aschhausen to the see of Bamberg in 1609, a man with a similar sense of mission as the Würzburg bishop Julius Echter von Mespelbrunn, the re-Catholicization of the parishes became a priority. Various measures to force compliance were adopted: fines were imposed, embargoes on wood were introduced, troops were quartered, locals were sent into exile and on numerous occasions the Lutherans were rounded up and placed under arrest. There was even a term in a Bamberg tower, a stinking hole twelve feet wide full of snakes, toads, worms and other poisoned vermin beyond human tolerance (Dippold, 1996, p. 164). Yet nothing seemed to work. As late as 1619 the Marktzeuln pastor reported that some parishioners still refused to convert to the Catholic faith. Only when Johann Georg Fuchs von Dornheim, Aschhausen's successor in Bamberg, decided to 'plant' Catholicism in 1624 by sending in a small army to force submission and occupy the town was the Catholic religion secure. But until they were at the point of a sword the people of Markt-graitz and Markzeuln refused to abandon the Lutheran religion.

Similar scenes were played out in the territories which experienced the advance of the Reformed faith. Calvinism made inroads after the Peace of Augsburg (even though it was not a legal beneficiary of the settlement). In many ways, perhaps because it evolved in the fractured climate of mid-century Protestantism, it was the most aggressive of the three confessions. German Calvinists not only held the eradication of 'papal superstition' as their essential mission, but the completion and correction, as they saw it, of the Lutheran Reformation. At its most extreme, it did not complement Lutheranism; it sought to supersede it. As a political force in Germany, Calvinism first surfaced in the Electoral Palatinate, where Friedrich III, whose personal conversion inspired the movement, transformed his territory into a Calvinist state in 1563. From there the movement spread to Nassau-Dillenburg, Anhalt, Pfalz-Simmern, Baden-Durlach, Lippe, Hesse-Kassel and, at various stages, the Electorate of Saxony. Throughout, as the pastor Christoph Petzel made clear, the purpose remained the same: to construct a defence against Catholicism and bring the first Reformation to its necessary conclusion – and this meant the elimination of leftover 'papal superstitions' (Nischan, 2000, p. 396).

And yet, despite clarity of purpose and singleness of mind, the Second Reformation frequently experienced opposition once it was introduced. In Saxony, the nobles resisted it and the parishioners avoided the churches; in Anhalt, the townspeople together with the nobles objected to it, claiming that 'it created divisions in our churches and anguish in the hearts of many pious Christians'; in Hesse-Kassel, the subject population presented massive opposition, gathering together in open revolt (Nischan, 1996, pp. 152–6). Perhaps the best-known case of conflict arose in the Electorate of Brandenburg. In 1613, seven years after his own conversion, the Elector Johann Sigismund introduced the Reformed faith into his lands. Reform proposals were presented to the council, as was a personal credal statement (the *Confessio Sigismundi*), a Church council was created in order to enforce the change, and Reformed clergy were appointed at the expense of Lutherans. But Johann Sigismund's efforts were opposed by all levels of society. The Lutheran clergy launched a pamphlet war against the Reformed confession, while the nobility, most of whom saw it as a threat to their political autonomy as well as their religious conscience, refused to cooperate. But the most direct and aggressive opposition was offered by the parishioners themselves. When Berlin cathedral was stripped of its crucifixes, altars and images, the local burghers gathered together and swore an oath of resistance. A riot broke out, crowds shouted down the Margrave Johann Georg, Calvinist preachers were attacked and their houses ransacked. To bring peace back to the city, Johann Sigismund was forced to station a militia in the streets (Nischan, 1994, pp. 81–234). The events illustrated the limitations that might be placed on confessional change, just as they demonstrated how deeply rooted religious identity could be among the subject population. Germany in the age of the Reformation and Counter-Reformation was not a land of tolerance or compromise.

In the imperial cities, the turning-point in the history of confessional relations came with the Peace of Augsburg (1555). At Augsburg, the territorial rulers secured the right to determine religion in their domains (*cuius regio, eius religio*). Histories of tolerance often find a point of origin in this settlement, and it did create the legal framework for two confessions in the Empire (due to mutual exhaustion more than anything else). And yet the same right of reform had not been extended to those imperial cities where both religions were practised at the time of the peace. Article twenty-seven guaranteed the preservation of both Catholicism and Lutheranism wherever 'they have been practised for a number of years' (meaning since the introduction of the Augsburg Interim). For most of the imperial cities, this was not a problem. The Lutheran communes had never introduced the Interim and were thus monoconfessional at the time of the peace. Equally, the Catholic cities had managed to preserve the status quo and there was no need for concessions. In the south, however, there was a clutch of Swabian communes which were confessionally mixed at the time of the peace. In these cities, religious coexistence was legally preserved by suspending the right of reformation. The problem was, however, that this condition ran counter to the nature of urban religion, for it was not possible to maintain coexistence in a commune where there was no closed religious settlement, where both communities had the right and the latitude to compete for space and power within the city walls, and where both communities had a public forum for their claims.

An example of the fragility of biconfessional relations in this type of urban setting is provided by events in Augsburg. Although Augsburg retained a Lutheran majority after the introduction of the Reformation, the conditions of the Interim, however fleeting, made it possible for the Catholic community to recover in strength and numbers. By mid-century, both confessions had the legal right to exist, and both confessions worshipped freely in the city. But this cooperation would not last. Confessional relations broke down in 1583 when the council introduced the Gregorian calendar. The calendar was a reworking of its Julian predecessor, and while many Protestants acknowledged that the recalculation was needed, fears remained that it was primarily a papal scheme to do away with the Lutheran faith. From this point forward coexistence became increasingly difficult in the city (Warmbrunn, 1983, pp. 359–86; Roeck, 1989, vol. 1, pp. 137–89). Questions of sovereignty were at stake, for it was essentially a struggle for the right to determine Augsburg's public time and with it the cycle of trade, harvest, justice, toil, leisure and worship. The Lutherans, including the Tübingen astronomers called on to advise the city, spoke of the pope as the Devil and the calendar as a diabolical plot intended to reintroduce papal sovereignty. The Catholics, in turn, spoke of the Lutherans as arch-heretics and advised the emperor to 'spare no means of punishment, neither sword, nor wheel, nor water, nor fire' to root them out. Ultimately the civic peace was shattered. On 4 June 1584 the authorities visited the Lutheran clergyman Georg Müller (Mylius) and demanded that he stop preaching against the calendar. In time, a crowd gathered in support of the clergyman and took up arms. The result, as Müller described it a few years later in *The Augsburg Affair* (1586), was a street riot, replete with violent crowds, broken windows, gunshots and the siege of the city hall. Only the appearance of the Lutheran clergy restored civic order, and only the intervention of external powers guaranteed peace in the city. The Catholics turned to Bavaria and Habsburg Austria, while the Lutherans called on Württemberg, Hesse, Saxony and a host of sympathetic Protestant cities. From this point forward the city sat at the centre of a web of confessional antagonism. Order was restored, but the tensions remained.

Other cities would suffer similar instability, as would many of the surrounding territories. By this stage, negotiation between the confessions was proving impossible. And in many ways this breakdown of relations, whether in the bishoprics of Franconia, the march of Brandenburg, the city of Augsburg or elsewhere, was inevitable. The Peace of Augsburg, from the very outset thought of as an interim solution, could no longer mediate between the antithetical aims of the emerging confessions. The Empire was fractured by hostile and incompatible religious beliefs. Territory was now divided against territory, city against city. Even at the level of the rural parish or the urban commune, the emergence of antagonistic confessions was making religious coexistence difficult. In part, this was due to the sheer variety of religious culture that developed after the first stages of the movement. But it was also due to the fragmented nature of the political landscape, and in many ways the Reformation could not have survived without a framework of this kind. As Martin Heckel has observed, the pluralistic constitutional structure of the Empire afforded the Protestant princes the security of the imperial liberties against the Catholic emperor, but the end result was that the Reformation movement was split up and absorbed by the territories. And while this domestic phenomenon was taking shape, the framework of relations between the princes and the emperor was completely transformed. As Heckel has noted, the Reformation had strengthened the political independence of the imperial Estates and steeled their resolve against any absolutist tendencies on the part of the emperor. Resistance was doubled, for it was now opposition to the hated suppression of religious beliefs (Heckel, 1983, p. 114). By the end of the century, the formation of state confessions, with their own syntheses of the faith, their own Church constitutions, and their own religious and moral prescriptions, had brought about a transformation of the German lands.

The Protestant State

The evangelical movement, as we have seen, found its earliest support in the urban and rural communes of the Empire. The princes, aware of the issues at stake, were fairly slow to react. With the spread of unrest in the mid-1520s, however, it was no longer feasible to remain on the margins of events, and once the rebels had been defeated on the field of battle the territorial rulers of Germany seized control of the Reformation. The princes made some concessions to the peasants at the diet of Speyer (1526), including a reduction of the death tax and additional rights in marriage and inheritance, but the majority of demands were not addressed and the impetus of the communal Reformation was brought to an end. After Speyer, the rural parishioners were largely excluded from the process of reform and the princes stepped in to direct the Reformation (Blickle, 1982, pp. 149–75). The same development ultimately pushed the urban communes into the background. Once in the vanguard of the movement, the cities found themselves weakened by a lack of common purpose and exposed by theological divisions. The larger imperial cities, virtual city-states such as Nuremberg, Strasbourg, Ulm and Schwäbisch Hall, maintained their hold over the reform movement within their walls, but many other communes were overpowered by the approach of the territorial rulers. As the influence of the communes declined, the princely state stepped in to fill the void.

Once the dust from the peasant revolution had settled, most of the reformers strongly supported the idea of a territorial Church under the guidance of a prince. Two basic principles of Lutheran thought underwrote the notion: first, the idea of the priesthood of all believers, which eliminated the distinctions between the spiritual and the temporal and thus made the Church an earthly institution; second, the idea of Two Kingdoms, the recognition that there were two spheres of rule, the rule of the Church and the rule of the State, each ordained by God and necessary for Christian society (Steinmetz, 1986, pp. 112–25). 'Because the sword is most beneficial and necessary for the whole world in order to preserve peace, punish sin, and restrain the wicked,' explained Luther in his work *On Secular Authority* (1523), 'the Christian submits most willingly to the rule of the sword, pays his taxes, honours those in authority, serves, helps, and does all he can to assist the governing authority, that it may continue to function and be held in honour and fear.' Other reformers would build on this doctrine, though in truth the princes did not need much help or persuasion in grasping the importance of these ideas. As early as Philipp of Hesse's *Church Order of 1526*, the evangelical prince was justifying his intervention in religious affairs with reference to his role as the protector of the common good and the defender of God's honour. In later Lutheran Church orders this would become a commonplace, and it was also a common belief among the Reformed princes of the German lands. When the *Heidelberg Catechism* was published in 1563, the Elector Friedrich prefaced an edition with the assertion that it was his duty to make sure his subjects were led to the proper fear and understanding of God's Word (Münch, 1978, p. 162).

Protestant thought could thus provide ideological support for the emerging state; yet it could just as easily be turned against the ungodly ruler if the reformers felt their religious liberties were under threat. This happened later in the century, after the territorial Church started to take shape in the realm. The principles of Protestant ecclesiology remained the same: the reformers still spoke of a unified order of creation, with the secular order given the commission to watch over the divine ordinance (*custodia utriusque tabulae*). But later clergy, invoking the traditional model of the three Estates (each with its own sphere of sovereignty), and looking to the Word of God as the highest authority in all matters of Church and State, placed limits on the powers that could be claimed by the Protestant prince. A dispute of this kind errupted between the Lutheran faculty at the university of Jena, led by the reformer Matthias Flacius Illyricus, and the territorial prince Duke Johann Friedrich. When the duke placed restrictions on the preaching and publishing activities of the reformers, the theologians ignored the prohibitions and published regardless, insisting that it was their duty to defend God's Word and speak out against ungodly rulers and the dangers of tyranny (Schorn-Schütte, 2000b, pp. 34–5). There was thus an inherent tension at the heart of Protestant notions of Church and State, for while the early reformers invested the prince with the right to rule over the earthly Church, later theologians stressed the distinctions between the different spheres of sovereignty, and with time both Lutherans and Calvinists developed sophisticated theories of resistance against the encroachments of an ungodly ruler. In general, the territorial state in Germany was strengthened by the introduction of the Reformation, especially larger Lutheran principalities such as Saxony, Württemberg and Brandenburg, but Protestant ideas of authority could also undermine systems of rule if they seemed in conflict with the reformers' reading of scripture. The seventeenth century, rather than the sixteenth, would bear witness to the impact of these ideas.

But more than ideology marked this transformation. Not only was there a philosophy of rule in support, a rationale of authority (with checks and balances) derived from evangelical theology; there was also a fusion of purpose as the moral and the spiritual concerns of the age were incorporated in a single programme of reform. Perhaps the best evidence of this union was the actual organs and structures of governance. Of course, many features of modern rule were already in place, including the councils, constitutions, bureacracies, legal codes and trained officials, but with the introduction of the Reformation it became necessary for the rulers to exercise a more direct and informed quality of rule. Religion provided the rationale. The Protestant visitation facilitated this development as the secular officials joined together with the higher clergy to take an inventory of the parishes. Soon afterward the jurisdiction of the dioceses was neutralized and the bishop's officials deposed; the Protestant superintendents appeared, working with the district officials to enforce the will of the prince in regions determined by the contours of secular governance. Later in the century, sophisticated organs of rule would evolve to consolidate the rule of the prince over the Church – the marriage courts, the church treasuries, the chapter synods and the consistories. As an example we might look at developments in the duchy of Zweibrücken, where the Reformation led to the secularization of Church property, the usurpation of diocesan jurisdiction, the assimilation of the local clergy into state rule, the drafting of a Church ordinance which combined the concerns of temporal rule with religious principles in a way, to cite the 1557 Church order, 'that would not be detrimental to the godly laws', and the evolution of new instruments of rule, including the visitation process, marriage courts and a Church council, the latter taking on the role of a consistory soon after its creation (Konersmann, 1996, pp. 140–236).

The Reformation also gave rise to a new member of the ruling elite, the Protestant pastor. No longer distinguished by sacral status or legal privilege, the clergyman in Protestant lands became, to a certain extent, an agent of the developing state. Like any other official, the pastor was appointed to office to honour the will of the sovereign; and while recognized spheres of influence remained in place, many of the tasks facing the parish pastors were similar to those of the other power elites. The clergyman was the final link in a chain of command reach-

ing from the courts and the chanceries down to the churches
and households of the parish. Realizing this, Protestant rulers
were quick to support measures designed to raise the competence of the clergy. On average, the Protestant pastors were
better trained than their medieval predecessors. By mid-century,
the majority had been educated at a university; their grasp of
the theological issues was more profound and their understanding of the faith more explicit. Moreover, if we assume that
the basic demands of the Church orders were observed, the
pastor was also much more involved in parish affairs than the
medieval Catholic priest had been. Above all, it was the concern
with discipline that really set the Protestant clergyman apart.
As Luise Schorn-Schütte has observed, 'the disciplinary role elevated the clerical office above the other functionaries of the
day, not only in terms of daily praxis but in the sense of self-
perception shared by the incumbents themselves. For it turned
the clergy into the arbiters of proper conduct, a judge over all
members of the parish' (Schorn-Schütte, 1996, p. 372).

In this role as the arbiters of parish behaviour the clergy
could work as important adjuncts to the general effort to control
the subject population. There is little doubt that the Protestant
clergy did form one branch of the ruling elite comprising the
early modern state. Having said this, however, we should
remember that the clergy were more than mere servants of the
secular powers. On occasion the pastors fell out with the authorities over matters of discipline. Tilemann Heshusius, for
instance, was a rather famous example of this. Harried out of
Goslar and Rostock for his efforts to increase the disciplinary
powers of the clergy, he made his way to Magdeburg, where he
gave vent to his ideas in a work entitled *On the Office and
Authority of the Clergy* (1561), a tract which gave full expression to his conviction that the clergy, not the secular officials,
should have the right to exercise the small bann (Brecht, 1992,
pp. 406–7). Quarrels of this kind were played out in many cities
and territories in the Empire, and it would be years before the
central issues were settled.

With the elimination of the Catholic Church in his lands the
Protestant ruler became the sole proprietor of Church property.
And as the only setting for public worship was now the church,
all lines of control and allegiance ran from the parish to the
organs of princely governance. The most immediate casualty in

this transformation was the monastic community. The regular clergy were forced to adopt the Protestant faith or go into exile. In some instances the clergy abandoned the cloisters voluntarily; but in most cases the monasteries were not completely dissolved until the final resident had passed away or decided to leave. In general, in accordance with the advice offered by Luther, the regular clergy were not roughly treated, and many left their cloisters with a substantial pension in hand. With one eye on the imperial courts and another on the resident nobility, the Protestants acted with caution. But the rulers were not slow to recognize that the monasteries represented a precious source of wealth and power. Almost overnight a sovereign could increase both the reach of his domain and the number of people subject to his rule. This happened in Albertine Saxony, for instance, where the district of Stolpen, long a possession of the Meissen bishopric, was confiscated by the duke, later followed by a host of monastic territories that were then transformed into units of secular governance (Dixon, 2000, pp. 159–61; Cameron, 1991, pp. 294–5). Many of the princes used the threat of peasant unrest to occupy the monasteries and take an inventory of the available wealth. For some of the Protestant rulers, expecially those who embraced the faith in the early stages of the movement, the Catholic foundations provided the state with huge additional resources. Ulrich of Württemberg was able to increase his annual income threefold; Philipp of Hesse amassed over 75,000 gulden in just over twenty years. But the wealth was not used indiscriminately. In some cases, as in Hesse and Saxony, the income was absorbed by the demands of evolving governance. At other times, as happened in the Palatinate, Württemberg and Baden-Durlach, the assets were used for the construction of new churches, the maintenance of the public welfare or the reform of schools and universities.

Protestantism invested the state with the duty to oversee Christian welfare, including poor relief, public charity and education. A move in this direction was already evident in the medieval period, especially in the urban communes, but the Reformation accelerated the trend. Begging, once a central feature of the medieval community, was prohibited, for the culture of good works had been discredited by the principles of evangelical theology. The Christian community, not the pious individual, determined what served the public welfare and what did not. In Wittenberg, for instance, the first Church order instructed that the funds should be gathered in a common chest and only be given to the deserving poor, parcelled out as loans to workers and artisans, or used in support of the Church as a fabric fund or an increase to clerical salaries. With this as a model, common chests were soon established in a number of evangelical towns, including Nuremberg, Kitzingen, Schwabach, Magdeburg and Windsheim (Lindberg, 1996, pp. 111–34). We should not imagine, however, that it was left to the parishioners themselves to control Church funds. In Strasbourg, for example, the control of public welfare was placed firmly in the hands of a special committee. All gifts and bequests intended for the poor were distributed by the urban authorities. Similarly, the council created a standing school committee (9 February 1526) which drew on the foundation wealth in order to establish schools in the dependent parishes, the aim being 'to habituate the youth to the fear of God and to study' (Chrisman, 1967, p. 268). The urban officials, not the Christian commune, judged what was in the best interests of the public welfare. And this imbalance was even more extreme in the territories, where the Protestant princes controlled the flow of local ecclesiastical wealth through Church orders and visitation mandates. The picture could be quite complex, for there were so many contending lordships in the German territories, but in general the princes drew on the same sources of wealth as the cities – the monasteries, foundations, bequests, parish tithes and local funds – and used it to the same ends: the reform of education, the care of the deserving poor, the ill and the needy, and the upkeep of the church and the maintenance of the clergy. Quite often the management of these concerns was left to local men, elected officials such as the church wardens, but the final authority was always the Protestant sovereign.

In the German lands all aspects of religious life, from right behaviour to right belief, now fell within the purview of the secular authority, for in effect the Protestant faith had turned the ruler into the bishop in his land. As the mandates proclaimed, God had placed him in office to watch over both the belief *and* the morals of his subjects, with the result that there was an increase in the amount of control exercised by the sovereigns. Historians consider this a general phenomenon of the age, part of the increase in the reach of the state and the rise of social disciplining. Certainly it seemed common enough in the Protestant lands of Germany, in both the territories and the larger imperial cities, where the ruling elite, working together with the clergy, became the 'moral police' of the subject population (Hsia, 1989, pp. 122–85). The final objective was the transformation of religious ideals into social reality, and in practical terms this meant a reform of the local customs and traditions of parish life. It was essentially a campaign to regulate public culture at the local level, an attempt to bring the parishioners in line with the type of godly society imagined by the reformers.

As an example of the reform of parish culture, we might look at two districts in the duchy of Württemberg, Tübingen and Tuttlingen, where the Lutheran visitors scoured the parishes for suspect forms of popular belief and folk religion and all other 'magical' aspects of parish life, from folk-healing and soothsaying to witchcraft and divining (Tolley, 1995, pp. 64–86). There was also a sustained attempt to control public behaviour – in the first instance the conduct related to religious observance, such as attendance at the sermons, the Lord's Supper and the catechism sessions, as well as the moral quality of the essential social compacts of marriage and the household. City and village were now scrutinized for their moral character: dances were forbidden, spinning bees were flushed out, usury and blasphemy were policed. The issue was even more urgent in the Reformed territories, for the Calvinists considered the reform of public life more than just a corollary of proper faith: it was necessary for the sanctification of both the individual and the community. As the Calvinist Wilhelm Zepper wrote in *On Christian Discipline* (1596), the reform of doctrine had started with Luther, but the time had come for a reform of life as well, 'that is, also in the other main part of Christian living and behavior . . . so that public sins, blasphemies, and transgressions among us Christians . . . may be turned and done away with . . . either by separation from the Lord's Table until visible betterment, or in extreme, special, and unrepentant cases . . . by excommunication' (Hsia, 1989, p. 28).

There is little doubt that the Reformation strengthened the hand of the secular rulers in the German lands. Having said this, however, we should not imagine that the prince simply enforced his will and his subjects simply obeyed. Historians have begun to examine the process of reform at the local level and it now seems clear that the authorities encountered considerable resistance as they worked to translate Protestant norms into social reality.

Despite the emergence of increasingly sophisticated systems of governance, the sixteenth-century state did not always have the reach or the competence to enforce its will at the level of the parish. Villagers often resisted the encroachments of state officials in order to preserve their customs and traditions. Studies of parish life in the final decades of the sixteenth century have suggested that many of the traditional forms of conduct and belief survived (Strauss, 1978, pp. 249–308; Scribner, 1990, pp. 317–43; Dixon, 1996a, pp. 102–207). In spite of the efforts of the authorities, the Reformation could not easily penetrate a culture which had been in place for centuries. Indeed, local culture often had a sense of identity and force of practice that could, to a certain extent, manipulate the reform movement. In the parishes surrounding the Swiss city of Bern, for instance, the attempt to reform local morality turned into a dialogue between the injunctions of the state and the norms of the commune. The result, as Heinrich Richard Schmidt has observed, was a compromise: 'Moral discipline only functioned because it formed coalitions with Christian believers and the interests of the whole community or with groups in the village' (Schmidt, 1995, p. 398). A similar process was at work in the ordering of marriage or the attempted transformation of popular pastimes. The outcome was a synthesis of norms. Of course, in the long term the local communities could not hope to preserve outlawed customs and traditions in the face of the advancing state, but the initial encounter between the Protestant Church and local culture was more of a dialogue or an exchange than a straightforward conquest of the rulers over the ruled.

All of this domestic upheaval was possible because the Catholic emperor was unable to impose his political will. Throughout the course of its evolution, the Protestant state in Germany was able to benefit by the relative weakness of imperial rule and the fragmented nature of the Empire. In many of the territories the most intense period of political activity came in the decades following the Peace of Augsburg (1555), when these two features of the German Nation were most in evidence. Although it created the conditions for one of the longest periods of peace in German history, the Augsburg settlement, due to its vague wording and its secret clauses and provisions, was unable to serve as the basis for a lasting agreement. With substantial theological dialogue at an end, the antagonists could only turn to the political and judicial institutions of the realm in an effort to gain the upper hand. What began as a reform of religion ended as a legal dispute before the imperial courts, and as there was no common ground in the fundamental issues of faith, there was no hope for reconciliation. 'Any reference to the confession of the faith was stipulated and developed with a diametrically opposed preconception and aim,' observes Martin Heckel; 'it was simply a matter of time before this led to open dissension' (Heckel, 1983, p. 82).

The main points of division were derived from the clauses and provisos granted by Ferdinand during the negotiations. Paramount were the problems associated with the ecclesiastical reservation, the clause which stipulated that a spiritual lord had to surrender his office if he converted to Protestantism. This was a dead letter. By 1566, with the exception of Hildesheim, all of the north German bishoprics beyond the River Weser were in Protestant hands (Wolgast, 1995, pp. 255–85). When called to account by the Catholics, the Protestants turned to the Word of God in their defence. At the same time they dismissed the reservation as illegal, for it had not been supported by the Estates and no emperor had the power to enforce it. In a similar fashion, the declaration of Ferdinand, by which the right of worship was preserved for evangelical Estates subject to a spiritual lord, proved unworkable once the Catholic reform movement had gathered momentum. It was a provision that relied on the grace of the emperor for its enforcement, but once the devout Catholic Rudolf II had replaced the more temperate Maximilian II in 1576, the Protestants could no longer be guaranteed security. Central too were the problems associated with the ownership of ecclesiastical property and the right of immigration, both of which were soon elevated by the Protestants to fundamental issues of religious freedom. In time mutual suspicion and lack of dialogue crippled the Empire. The Imperial Chamber Court became ineffective after the Peace, the Imperial Aulic Council (*Reichshofrat*) with its Catholic constituency was held as biased and untrustworthy by the Protestants, the *Reichstag* was paralysed, and the emperor Rudolf, a pious Catholic slowly declining into a state of madness, was no longer considered capable of rule. The German Empire, which had provided the setting for the rise of the Reformation, could not accommodate the repercussions of the movement, and ultimately it would collapse in on itself.

Thus the final years of the sixteenth century were marked by an atmosphere of unease, a growing sense that warfare between the Catholic and the Protestant powers was inevitable. At one stage it seemed that the Protestant princes might go to war with the emperor over the see of Cologne, when the archbishop Gebhard Truchseß von Waldburg converted to Lutheranism and granted the diocese the freedom to practise the faith. Similar conflicts arose in Aachen, Magdeburg and Strasbourg, while numerous other localized disputes, all of which revolved around the issues left unresolved by the Augsburg peace, simmered just below the surface.

As an illustration of the fragile condition of imperial politics we might look at the dispute which errupted in the Swabian city of Donauwörth, one of the biconfessional communes in Swabia (Stieve, 1875, pp. 1–107). On a wet St Martin's Day (25 April 1606), as a Catholic procession wound its way through the city streets, the two religious communities finally came to blows. The Lutherans attacked the procession and chased the monks back to the monastery of the Holy Cross. On hearing the news, the neighbouring Bishop of Augsburg sent an appeal to the imperial court in Prague. After considerable hedging by Emperor Rudolf, the city was placed under ban and Duke Maximilian of Bavaria was commissioned with its execution. Tensions now came to the surface. A number of Protestant powers, including the Palatinate, Württemberg, Brandenburg-Ansbach, Baden, and the cities of Ulm and Nuremberg gathered together in defence of the Donauwörth Lutherans, claiming that the process was illegal and a violation of the Peace of Augsburg. Using similar arguments, the Bavarians condemned the Lutheran community for their repeated attacks on the Donauwörth Catholics and, by implication, the spirit of the peace. As the imperial diet gathered after the incident (12 January 1608) there was little hope that a solution could be found. The Protestants repeated their objections to the process, while the Catholics answered with objections of their own, including the familiar refrain relating to the violation of ecclesiastical property. In the end the diet was disbanded without publishing a recess, and the Protestant powers, Lutherans and Calvinists together, began discussing a military defence, an initiative which ultimately led to the formation of the Protestant Union (14 May 1608). The following year the Catholics, directed by Maximilian of Bavaria, responded in kind with the creation of the Catholic League. War would consume the German lands in the decades that followed.

Protestant Culture

Scholars have long considered the Reformation a major turning-point in western history. Quite often this is described as the turn towards modernity. The confessional age is seen as the point of division between the stagnant world of medieval Europe and the dynamism of the modern age (Dülmen, 1999, pp. 193–219). In part, this is fictionalization, the projection of the virtues and values of modern society onto a reading of the past. We value the Reformation because we live in an age which has been shaped by it, and we think of the Reformation as the turn towards modernity, rather than a continuation of the medieval condition, because that is where we find the first signs of ourselves. Yet there are also basic historical truths in the claim. The process of reform, as we have seen, did contribute to the rise of the modern state. During the century of confessional division the methods and organs of governance grew in sophistication, while the strong association between the secular and the spiritual realms gave shape to new ideologies of rule. But the transformation did not end there. In essence the Reformation began as an attempt to change the way people thought about religion. It was a mission to modify public and private beliefs, and while its language was theological and its forms ecclesiastical, the final design was always the creation of the ideal parishioner. Thus the Reformation has also been associated with the emergence of the type of individual valued by the modern age, and it has not proven difficult to trace a line of descent from the principles of evangelical theology to the virtues of modern times. There is truth in this as well, but quite a lot of fiction besides.

But history is always a balance of fiction and fact, and there is no better testimony to this compact than the making of Protestant history and identity in the sixteenth century. For a religious community, in order to have a sense of association and a sense of destiny, must have a common past. The problem facing the Protestants, however, as their Catholic opponents pointed out with regularity, was the lack of tradition, the absence of an established historical continuum. Recognizing this, the Protestants had to write their own history, using the principles of their faith (*sola scriptura, sola fide*, the providence of God) and relying on the testimony of scripture. Indeed, as Bruce Gordon has pointed out, 'the uncovering of history was a constituent part of establishing the Word of God as authoritative in the world: the true church, so the evangelical reformers argued, would find its history and identity in the study of the scriptures' (Gordon, 1996, p. 3). The Gospel helped to fashion a sense of self, providing communities with the logic and the language for a new identity – the paradigms, the metaphors, the stories and the imagery, the characters and plot. Throughout the century, the reformers thought of themselves as Old Testament prophets, princes and city councillors compared themselves to godly rulers, while the entire movement, in its struggle against Rome, was likened to the suffering of the Israelites. Protestants believed that their own history was revealed in the Bible. This conviction became a cultural commonplace, broadcast in the media of the day, from the chronicles and martyrologies of the first-hand participants, through the pamphlets, the plays and the *memoria*. But even more explicit were the historians themselves, deeply religious men such as Friedrich Myconius, Johannes Mathesius, Cyriakus Spangenberg, Matthias Flacius Illyricus, all of whom imagined the history of the Protestant Church in terms of a battle between the defenders of the Word of God and the powers of the Antichrist. Scripture provided historians with a powerful sense of meaning and a rich field of reference for the making of a Protestant past.

But the evolution of confessional identities was not a phenomenon created by later commentators and historians. As early as the publication of *The Babylonian Captivity* (1520) Luther had labelled the pope the Antichrist and condemned the Catholic faith as false, fabricated and contrary to the Word of God. This was the basis for a Protestant sense of identity. In essence, at least in the beginning, the evangelicals saw themselves as the antithesis of the Catholic Church. They projected a struggle between the Word of God, which stood for the evangelical faith, and the wiles of the Antichrist, which stood for Catholicism. It was essentially the juxtaposition of opposites, a strategy at work, for instance, in the series of woodcuts published by Lucas Cranach the Elder entitled *Passional Christi et Antichristi* (1522) which compared the presumed workings of the papacy with the parables of Christ (Scribner, 1994, pp.

149–63). For Cranach, the evangelical Church was based on the Word of God, while the papacy was a fabrication, a monkish con-game, in total violation of the truths of scripture; the evangelical faith was centred on Christ, while the Catholic faith was built on sin, wealth and deception; the evangelical faithful were the persecuted minority, while the Catholic Church was the persecutor and oppressor. The polarities were basic – true versus false, free versus enslaved, virtuous versus corrupt. Distinctions of this kind made it possible for the reformers to distance themselves from the Catholic inheritance. Moreover, as early Protestant identity was so closely tied to the first principles of its theology, believing in the truth of the projected contrast was to believe in the truths of the religion. As the Lutheran reformer Johannes Aepinus warned in his *Three Fine Sermons* (1558), identifying the nature of the two religions was no small matter, but rather a question which touched on salvation. 'For if the papal religion and faith is correct,' he wrote, 'then all the Lutherans are lost. And equally, if the Lutheran religion is the right one, then no Catholic believer who dies in the faith can hope for salvation. This is a certainty, as certain as fire and water are opposites, or that God is in his Heaven and we are on this earth.'

Later in the century the issue of identity was further complicated by the rise of the Reformed faith. It was no longer just a basic opposition between Lutherans and Catholics. Now the Protestant community had the added element of the resurgent Helvetic tradition. 'We live in a time of great religious division,' wrote the Wittenberg professor Aegidius Hunnius in 1592. 'Papists oppose Lutherans . . . Lutherans fight against Papists and Calvinists, and all three are against the Schwenkfelders and Anabaptists . . . No wonder people get discouraged and know no longer what to believe' (Nischan, 1997, p. 199). One way of identifying the differences between the two religions was public ritual, and it was at the level of liturgy and ceremony that the distinctions were most manifest. For instance, Lutherans and Calvinists did not share the same understanding of the Lord's Supper. The Calvinists were much less flexible when it came to the externals of the faith. There was no place for candles, vestments, pictures, altars or the other 'vain papal relics' tolerated by the Lutherans. And more to the point, there was no place for the Lutheran doctrine of the Real Presence in the Lord's Supper, for this was considered a Catholic superstition and a degradation of the sacrament. The Lutherans, in turn, thought that the Reformed aversion to images and altars was proof that they lacked in faith, while their rejection of the Real Presence was clear evidence, in the words of the clergyman Christoph Fischer, that they 'are inspired by Satan and misled by blind reason when they claim that Christ cannot be truly present with his body and blood in the holy Eucharist' (Nischan, 1997, p. 209). At the end of the century, the most bitter hostilities were not those between the Catholics and the Protestants, but those between the Lutherans and the Reformed.

In order to distance themselves from the Catholic inheritance, Protestants developed new traditions of Christian art. At root this revaluation was theological, for the evangelical faith had done away with the intermediaries between man and God. There was no need for representations of saints – the paintings, the statues, the crafted altars. Andreas Karlstadt believed the use of icons and images was false worship, idolatry, and led to damnation, but more common was the position established by Luther (partly in reaction to radicals such as Karlstadt and Müntzer, and partly a natural extension of his maturing theology) that tolerated representational art as long as it did not lead the parishioners away from Christ. Luther did not believe, as Karlstadt did, that the externals of worship were natural barriers to true faith. But he did recommend the removal of representational art when it was too Catholic in inspiration (such as the portraits of saints) and he advised the pastors of Saxony to remove images from public view once they had become objects of worship rather than aids to understanding (Eire, 1989, pp. 54–73). Other Lutheran territories followed the example set by Saxony. When the faith was introduced into the duchy of Mecklenburg, for instance, the visitors were quite willing to leave much of the medieval art in place, even recommending that it be nailed to the walls and placed in areas where the greatest number could see it; but if the image seemed too close in kind to a Catholic icon, or if it were viewed as an object of devotion rather than a spur to reflection, it was removed. As the visitation instructions made clear, 'where it is discovered that there is an idol or an image on hand that is an object of devotion, then it should be removed immediately, destroyed and reduced to ashes' (Wolgast, 1997, pp. 63–4). Most Lutheran territories, including Saxony, Württemberg, Brandenburg and Hesse, followed a similar strategy. The south German and Swiss reformers, however, were much less flexible when it came to images. For men like Zwingli and Calvin, pictures and

icons were contrary to the teaching of scripture. They trans-
gressed the commandment not to worship false idols and were
thus detrimental to faith. As a consequence, in the areas touched
by the Zwinglian or the Reformed faith, the churches were often
shorn of all art. The walls were bare, whitewashed, the pictures
and statues removed.

But the Reformation did not just overthrow medieval art; it
created a tradition of its own (Pettegree, 2000, pp. 461–90).
From the very outset imagery and illustration were central to
the spread of the message. With time other styles and genres of
iconography evolved, including Bible illustrations, altar friezes,
epitaph memorials and panel paintings, and Protestant artists
would prove as inspirational as any in Europe. Lucas Cranach
the Elder, for instance, whose Wittenberg workshop provided
Luther with many of his early book illustrations, was an artist
of profound skill. In his early woodcut portraits of Luther, he
placed him in various guises (teacher, prophet, nobleman) to
relate the basic features of his personality and, by association,
the basic features of the Reform movement inspired by him.
In his composition *Law and Gospel* (1529), finished once the
movement was in full swing, Cranach used biblical imagery to
juxtapose the teaching of the Catholic Church with the message
of the reformers (Christensen, 1979, pp. 123–51). Protestant art
usually served a pedagogical function of this sort. It did not distinguish itself from Catholic art in its quality or form, or even
in its themes, but rather in its content and its underlying theological design. Protestant art used icons and imagery to relate
the basic principles of the faith. The Church was portrayed as
the community of the faithful; pictures were composed, using
traditional icons such as the Lamb of God or the dove as the
holy spirit, to convey the notion of justification through faith
alone; pictures placed stress on the figure of Christ or on the
saving power of his Word. Even as image, the Word of God was
paramount. In mid-century the Lutheran city of Regensburg
replaced a depiction of the coronation of Mary (already covered
so that it would not deceive or mislead the faithful) with a paint-
ing of words summarizing the meaning of the Old and New Tes-
taments (Karant-Nunn, 1997, p. 123). This was an extreme case,
but all Protestant art drew its inspiration from the Word.

The Protestant reading of scripture transformed the church
itself. By the end of the century many Lutheran and Reformed

communities gathered in church buildings with distinct aspects of form and design. Both the inner and outer fabric had been modified by evangelical theology. In the early days of the movement many of the Protestant communities made their faith public by defacing parish churches. It happened in Wittenberg, where Karlstadt orchestrated a removal of icons and images from the churches, but it was much more common in the south, in the lands influenced by the ideas of Zwingli and Calvin, where the interiors were often completely transformed. In the churches that embraced the Zwinglian Reformation statues and images were removed, murals were chipped away, costly vessels were confiscated and the walls were whitewashed (Wandel, 1995, pp. 53–189). In the Lutheran lands the transformation was less dramatic, but nevertheless the church was different from its Catholic predecessor. Unsuitable images had been taken down, the side altars removed, while the high altar, now sharing space with a simple communion table, no longer commanded the attention of the congregation. The pulpit, the site of the sermon, was the focal point of the Lutheran church. The first building constructed specifically for Lutheran worship was a chapel in Hartenfels, Torgau. It was a basic rectangle with four bays and a stone gallery with very little embellishment, save for the elaborate carvings on the elevated pulpit. Similar chapels were built after the middle of the century in Dresden, Schwerin, Stuttgart and Rotenburg, while the first churches emerged in Joachimstal, Marienberg, Freudenstadt and Wolfenbüttel – all designed with the same evangelical principles in mind (Spicer, 2000, pp. 505–20). The pulpit, rather than the high altar, became the focal point of the service, much of the Catholic ornamentation and equipage was removed, and the congregation sat in fairly bare naves full of light, watching the pastor perform the communion service and preach the Word of God.

The Reformation also transformed the sights and sounds of worship. In Protestant lands, evangelical theology had removed much of the sensate and visual from public worship. Art had been displaced, the church interior had been simplified, and the rites and liturgy had been reduced to a modest and essential core. Instead, the Protestants dressed up the printed word. The flood of pamphlets, broadsheets, printed sermons, devotional works and theological tracts was without precedent in German history. The appearance of Luther's New Testament in 1522, for instance, was a publishing phenomenon, with the work, despite its cost, going through forty-three editions in three years (Pettegree, 2000, pp. 109–26). The faith and the text became inseparable, and with the Gospel captured on the printed page and written in the vernacular, the laity could worship on their own terms and in their own time – alone, if they desired, and in silence. In the churches themselves, however, the Reformation introduced some new sounds to the service. Luther was a talented musician (he was a lute-player as well as a flautist) and he wrote a number of hymns for the Lutheran church service. Together with Johann Walther he published a collection of compositions in 1524, all with his lyrics and some with his score, which was designed for the participation of the congregation. The most famous hymn was perhaps Luther's *A Mighty Fortress is our God* ('Ein feste Burg ist unser Gott'), but there were well over 4,000 works of this kind in circulation by the end of the century. After the death of the reformer the tradition would continue in the work of such renowned Lutheran composers as Hans Leo Hassler, Michael Praetorius, Heinrich Schütz, and ultimately Johann Sebastian Bach (Higman, 2000, pp. 494–5).

But the transformation did not end there. Most of the major reformers recognized that the faith had to be planted at the most basic level of social organization – the household. The Protestants imagined the household in terms of a church, a domestic community of the faithful, with the father assuming the role of the pastor, the mother working as a faithful adjunct, and the children and dependants thought of as catechumens. To a large extent this notion derived from the evangelical reworking of marriage: no longer a sacrament, marriage replaced the Catholic notion of celibacy as the highest spiritual ideal obtainable by Fallen Man. The very point of wedlock was to pay witness to the Word of God and strengthen faith through a life of probity, piety, harmony, fruitfulness and love. As Cyriakus Spangenberg wrote in *The Marriage Mirror* (1570): 'The estate of marriage is a bringing together or union of a man and a woman, through God's word, with the consent of both, who are to congenially and honourably live with one another until death, avoid sin, and bear fruit' (Harrington, 1995, pp. 74–8). As witness to this ideal, many of the Protestant pastors entered marriages of their own. This was one of the most emphatic ways to declare a conversion to evangelical principles (as it was, of course, an emphatic declaration of love), and it was viewed as the perfect setting for the creation of the godly family. 'Marriage,' as Steven Ozment has noted, 'created the conditions for a new awareness of human community' (Ozment, 1980, p. 392). Little wonder that so many clergymen, fresh out of the cloisters and emboldened by evangelical theology, rushed to the altar.

The domestic setting became a miniature church (*Hauskirche*) and its inhabitants became model figures of the faith. To speed this vision, the Protestant clergy offered their parishioners advice on how to maintain a godly household. In addition to the sermons, the catechisms and the daily admonitions, the clergy wrote prescriptive literature for the household, homiletic tracts, printed sermons and devotional publications. In essence, as the works spelled out, the model Protestant household paid witness to God by avoiding sin, begetting children, demonstrating domestic love, lasting piety and good faith. Moreover, each member of the household had to live up to specific moral and spiritual expectations. The Protestants had much more exact notions of what constituted a household. It was no longer thought of in terms of the diffuse family structures of the medieval period – the imprecise kinship networks, the spiritual confraternities, the links between the quick and the dead. Among other things, the Reformation 'revised the context of the family, unconsciously paring it down to its core, scraping away what leaders of the church and state saw as a surfeit of allegiances, occasions, and gratifications' (Karant-Nunn, 2000, p. 436). When the Protestant clergy spoke of the household they meant the husband, the wife, the children and the remaining dependants, and each had specific responsibilities before God in the domestic church. This did not mean, however, that the Reformation brought with it a radical reworking of the nuclear family. The master of the Protestant household was the husband, the patriarch, and wives were resigned to the role of obedient adjuncts. The early Reformation may have created some opportunities for women, especially among the Anabaptists, but the Protestant household preserved the theory and practice of male dominance. The reformers encouraged women to attend sermons and sacraments, pray with regularity, and teach children the basics of the faith, but there was no suggestion of gender equality. Notions of sovereignty, whether in the home, city council or state, remained patriarchal (Wiesner, 1993, pp. 186–95; Roper, 1989).

The ideal of the Protestant household reveals an important feature of the Reformation movement. Unlike medieval Catholic theology, which tended to project the parishioners as voiceless agents in an economy of salvation, evangelical thought, especially in the early years, imagined the laity as active participants in a religious compact. Luther provided the theological groundwork for this notion, in particular his idea of the priesthood of all believers and the principle of *sola scriptura*. But in part it was a natural corollary of the belief that Catholicism had fallen away from the Word. As the pamphleteer Heinrich von Kettenbach put it, the Pope and his clergy had built a religion based on falsehoods and deceit, pieced together out of 'human fables, papal bulls, spiritless laws, and Imperial mandates' (Ozment, 1993, p. 47). It was inevitable that truth would be embodied in its opposite, a faith built on the pure Word of God embraced by the layman. Indeed, for many of the evangelicals, the fact that the common man was now so versed in Holy Writ was proof that God's Word was at work. The reformers made use of this image, contrasting the deceptions of the twisted minds in the monasteries and universities with the revelations of scripture as voiced by the laity. In part this was pure hyperbole, at times brutal in its simple contrasts; and yet there was some truth in the claims. Many supporters openly professed that the Reformation movement made it possible for them to read the Gospels and think independently about religion for the first time. As Menno Simons testified, before the Reformation he had never read the scriptures. 'I had never touched them,' he wrote, 'for I feared if I should read them, I would be misled.' But with time he mustered the courage to work through the text, and soon came up with his own ideas in the Lord's Supper. 'I had not gone very far when I discovered that we were deceived, and my conscience, troubled on account of the aforementioned bread, was quickly relieved, even without any instruction' (Scribner, 1994b, p. 255). Empowered by the evangelical emphasis on scripture as the sole authority, and legitimized by the removal of clerical privilege, the laity came forward with their own reading of the sacred texts.

The emergence of the autonomous believer, independent of thought, versed in scripture and alone before God, has long been held as one of the legacies of the Reformation. Protestant theology did away with religious intermediaries and referred believers to scripture. Salvation was no longer dependent upon the rites and rituals of the medieval Church, and there was no need for the clergyman to stand in for the faithful. With the Reformation, the essence of belief became 'verbal, non-sensual communication'. Protestants were responsible for their own salvation, and that meant coming to terms with the meaning of scripture. The consequences, according to a long historiographical tradition, were manifold. In time, Protestant culture gave rise to a new religious plurality, not just the creation of lasting confessions, but a deluge of revolutionary ideas. Some remained at the heart of theological discourse, others would be translated in the centuries to follow into social and political utopias. And at the centre of the rethinking was the individual, for with the Reformation 'a man's subjective faith, his "internal" religious attitude, came to occupy the centre of religious and ecclesiastical life for the first time' (Dülmen, 1999, p. 203). As a result, if by degrees, there was a rise in religious tolerance as the burden of individual reflection made the faithful more aware of other beliefs. There was an increasing sense of responsibility, as each man and woman had to answer for his or her individual conduct before God. There was even a revaluation of the secular world and the standing of lay pursuits, for the religious ideal was no longer monasticism but an active and engaged life of labour spent in assurance of God's grace. But the fundamental transformation came with the evangelical conviction that faith alone, faith granted through the Word of God, was the only means to salvation. From this point forward the individual believer inherited the responsibility, and the burden, of coming to terms with the essentials of the faith.

It should not be imagined, however, that the Protestant authorities left it to the parishioners to determine the truths of their religion. The evangelical believer may have inherited the responsibility of coming to terms with the faith, but the clergy were quick to explain exactly how this was done and exactly what this meant. The reform movement did not just unleash a flood of religious ideas; it also inspired a massive campaign of indoctrination, a sustained attempt, common to all three of the main confessions, to fashion a uniform and orthodox community of believers (Rublack, 1995, pp. 585–605). This was a difficult mission, though one well-suited to the Protestant pastor. With the elimination of the apparatus of the Catholic Church, including the monasteries and nunneries, the confraternities, the foundations, the wayside chapels and the sites of pilgrimage, religion had become an intensely localized activity: it was more or less reduced to the relationship between the pastor, now divested of the sacral standing enjoyed by the Catholic clergy, and the local parishioners. Moreover, with the elimination (or at least the reduction) of the medieval rites, rituals, feasts and festivals, the relic displays and annual cultic processions, parish religion in Protestant Germany had lost much of its broader horizons of time and space. Instead, the parishioners faced the attentions of the local clergyman, supervised and sustained by the state, who set about to create the pious community. In essence, this involved the translation of complex religious ideas into a living church, and in order to facilitate the teaching process the Protestants developed a number of aids to learning – the schools, the sermons, the catechisms, the pamphlets and works of piety. The message remained consistent throughout the century: the only means of salvation was through faith alone, and the only sure path to faith was by way of God's Word. The old convictions had to be cast off, not just the Catholic 'superstitions' such as the reliance on good works or the trust in sacramentals, but the entire arsenal of popular beliefs, including the spells and the blessings and the forms of local magic.

The process of religious reform at the parish level began apace soon after the first visitation in Saxony (1528). The results convinced Luther that the preaching of the Word alone had not been enough to fashion a pious congregation. As he recognized in the preface to his *Shorter Catechism* (1529), 'the common man, especially in the villages, knows absolutely nothing about Christian doctrine, and unfortunately, many pastors are practically unfit and incompetent to teach ... They live just like animals and unreasoning sows.' In response the reformers of Saxony, with the rest of Lutheran Germany following suit, launched a programme of reform and indoctrination. In the words of Gerald Strauss, the Lutheran authorities

embarked on a conscious and, for the first time, remarkably systematic endeavour to develop in the young new and better impulses, to implant inclinations in consonance with the reformers' religious and civic ideals, to fashion dispositions in which Christian ideas of right thought and action could take root, and

to shape personalities capable of turning young into new men –
into the human elements of a Christian society that would live
by evangelical principles. (Strauss, 1978, p. 2)

The object of reform was the parishioner (in particular the
young parishioner), the aim was the translation of Reformation
ideas into social and cultural reality, and the methods included
the reform of educational institutions, the publication of catechisms, the drafting of church and visitation orders, and the
enforcement of reform measures. All of the Protestant powers,
to a greater or lesser extent, launched a campaign of this kind.
It arose out of the conviction that their culture was not Christian enough, but rather mired in superstition and paganism. The
parishioners had to be taught the very basics of Christianity.
This is the note Luther struck in his work *The Freedom of a
Christian* (1522), writing of how the 'the riches and the glory of
the Christian life' are all that a man needs on this earth. 'But
alas in our day this life is unknown throughout the world; it is
neither preached about nor sought after; we are altogether ignorant of our own name and do not know why we are Christians
or bear the name of Christians.'

In order to remedy the perceived lack of faith, charity, and
understanding the authorities looked for ways to implant the
faith in the minds of the parishioners. It began with a reform of
education. The Protestant state assumed responsibility for
public schooling, from the drafting and publication of new cur-
ricula and school ordinances to the examination and appointment of pastors, schoolmasters and village sextons. In addition
to the schoolroom, the Protestant powers looked to the catechism as a tool of indoctrination. Conceived as a supplement to
the weekly sermons, the catechism was a cheap and readable
guide to the principal teachings of the Protestant religion. In
essence, to borrow a phrase from the reformer Johannes Brenz,
the catechism was a small Bible; most of the cardinal points of
the religion were found somewhere in the text. The text was ele-
mentary, composed in very basic prose, with the major points of
the religion listed in a question-and-answer format to aid mem-
orization. All of the parishioners were expected to familiarize
themselves with the contents of these booklets, for the reformers realized that the Reformation would not effect a change in
thought and conduct until (to cite the words of the Lutheran

officials in Leipzig) 'our doctrines have been implanted and rooted among the people and have won them over to a common and peaceful understanding' (Strauss, 1999, p. 236, no. 56). And in order to assure that this 'common and peaceful understanding', once taught, was preserved, the Protestant authorities published wave after wave of Church and visitation orders in the latter half of the sixteenth century. Each was designed, as a Württemberg ordinance worded it, to safeguard 'the imposition of good government and discipline, but first and foremost the planting among our people of God's saving Word' (Strauss, 1999, p. 240). The result, in many cases, was an exhaustive inventory of parish religion, from the varieties of popular belief to the outward character of public worship. It was the final stage in a campaign of indoctrination that began with the school texts and catechisms and ended with the visitors' interrogations in the village church.

In essence, the Reformation was a campaign to make the parishioners more Christian than they had been before. In the eyes of the reformers, the Catholic Church had fallen away from the teachings of Christ. The evangelical clergy saw themselves as missionaries, planting the true seeds of the faith and uprooting the superstitions, idolatry and human inventions of the medieval Church. Many of them drew parallels between their own age and the age of the apostles, couching their published sermons in terms that reminded the reader of the Epistles of Paul. But the mission was not merely to call to mind the customs of ancient Christian worship. The reformers wanted to effect a fundamental change of religious understanding at the level of the parish. All of the reforms in Church and State, all of the mandates and orders published by the Protestant authorities, were ultimately directed to this end: the transformation of religious belief at the parish level. The main target was the Catholic notion of a sacramental religion (often conflated with ideas of popular magic). Instead of a world infused by sacred power as in the medieval Church, where the dividing lines between magic and religion had become blurred, the Protestant Church launched an assault on all forms of 'superstitious' beliefs, including the medieval Catholic notion that the universe was charged with sacramental power. The evangelical reformers set about their task 'by taking the "magical" elements out of Christian religion, eliminating the ideas that religious rituals had any automatic efficacy, that material objects could be endowed with any sort of sacred power, and that human actions could have a supernatural effect' (Scribner, 1999, p. 262). In Protestant lands, parish religion was cleansed of the Catholic sacramentals (the blessed water and salt, the psalms, altars and images), while the parishioners were told that it was impossible for them to tempt the favour of God through created means. The belief in magic, in equal measure, was damned as contrary to proper faith in Christ, for the only alternative to the divine was the diabolic. By decree, the world was robbed of its charms. Pastors and visitors probed deeper and deeper into parish life, preaching and teaching the faith, labouring to eradicate the beliefs and customs at the heart of popular culture (Dixon, 1996a, pp. 162–202). For many of the faithful, this is how the Reformation movement was actually experienced: far from a liberation of the religious mind, it had evolved into a campaign of acculturation without precedent in history.

As with the reform of conduct, historians have just begun to evaluate the effect of the Reform movement on the parish mind. It is a complex task, for the history of the Reformation is a tale written from the perspective of the reformers, the Protestant rulers and the educated elite. Little remains of the thoughts or the sentiments of the common man. Granted, there was a surge of lay participation in the early years of the movement; but once the reform endeavour was absorbed by the state the parishioners left the stage. Thus much of what we identify as Protestant culture and associate with the subject population has been abstracted from general trends or derived from the principles of the faith. Very little is known about the actual encounter between the process of reform and the German parishioners of the sixteenth century. To date, what historians have been able to learn by sifting through the visitation returns and the parish documentation suggests that the Reformation movement encountered considerable resistance. In the words of Gerald Strauss, whose *Luther's House of Learning* was the pioneering work on this theme, 'a century of Protestantism had brought about little or no change in the common religious conscience and the ways in which ordinary men and women conducted their lives' (Strauss, 1978, p. 299). Others historians have challenged this conclusion, specialists on the urban Reformation in particular, identifying a substantial correlation between the declared aims of the reformers and religious culture in the parishes. But the debate has only just begun (Parker, 1992, pp. 43–82). No doubt the degree of 'success and failure' varied from place to place, though it does appear that a general picture of the Protestant parish at the end of the century is beginning to emerge and it was far removed from the ideals of the evangelical reformers. Much of what the early Protestant authorities wanted to accomplish remained unfulfilled, many of the basic features of the religion had not taken root (Strauss, 1978, pp. 249–308; Vogler, 1981, pp. 158–96; Scribner, 1993b, pp. 221–41). No one realized this better than the Protestant clergy themselves, in particular the Lutheran clergy, who withdrew deeper and deeper into a sense of pessimism, failure and impending doom as the century counted down.

But perhaps the Protestant clergy were wrong, as we would be wrong, to judge the movement by the standards established by men of such systematic and inspired thought as Martin Luther, Huldyrich Zwingli and Jean Calvin. Perhaps the true legacy of the Reformation lies less in its faithfulness to an original vision than the complex, if unforeseen, change of perspective it inspired. 'Perhaps,' writes Peter Matheson, 'what happened in the Reformation was that one imaginative architecture was replaced by another' (Matheson, 2000, p. 7). For this much seems certain: once the Reformation movement had spread beyond the culture of the clergy and the schoolmen, it had the ability to inspire people to think differently about things, all things, from the world of the spirit to the matters of the mind to the constituents of earthly welfare. Few episodes in European history have embraced so many aspects of the human condition.

6

Reformation Histories

In the sixteenth century, public understanding of the German Reformation was first expressed through figurations of Martin Luther. The reformer was portrayed in a number of symbolic guises, each of which served to explain and legitimize the movement. First and foremost was the notion of Luther as prophet, God's chosen vessel sent to preach the Gospel and overthrow idolatry (by which the Protestants meant the papacy). Most of the leading reformers thought of Luther as God's messenger on earth, and by mid-century this idea was rooted in the evangelical histories of the day. Cyriakus Spangenberg, for instance, spoke of him as 'the great prophet and third Elijah', while Michael Coelius testified that 'he was truly for our time a true Elijah and Jeremiah, a John the forerunner before the day of the Lord, or an apostle' (Kolb, 1999, p. 35). Associating Luther with Elijah, Daniel or the Angel of Revelation invested the Reformation with historical meaning. The cycle of prophets and prophecies could account for origins, while the narrative of sacred history could place the event in a historical continuum. Similarly, emphasizing Luther's qualities as a teacher of Holy Writ or an interpreter of scripture helped to legitimize the break with the Catholic Church. For this reason early woodcut images portrayed the reformer as a monk inspired by the Holy Spirit, a learned doctor of the Church, or a teacher of the Gospel standing with scripture in hand (Warnke, 1984, pp. 5–68). Depicting Luther as 'the superior man of God and enlightened teacher', as Spangenberg did, or suggesting that he was 'the first to expound the pure, true, godly doctrine aright, as it is contained in Holy Scripture, and bring it into the light of day', as Georg Gloccer did, gave sanction to the movement, for it implied it was not the work of a single man but rather the unfolding of God's Word (Zeeden, 1954, p. 30). Later depictions continued in the same vein, emphasizing, as Johannes Mathesius did in a series of biographical sermons, that Luther was 'the worthy German prophet' come to do battle with the Latin Antichrist. In this figuration both Luther and the Reformation movement were understood in secular terms, as expressions of the revolutionary spirit of the German peoples in the face of Roman oppression. Luther as hero, in the same manner as Luther as prophet and teacher, worked as a symbol for the understanding of Reformation.

The first substantial historical narratives also emerged in the mid-sixteenth century. Figurations of Luther abounded still, but published accounts of the Reformation assumed a broader perspective (Dickens and Tonkin, 1985, pp. 7–38). The context of analysis was extended to include social and cultural forces, the notion of historical causation looked beyond the biblical prophecies and identified crucial secular events, and the historians began to rely on new standards of proof to support their analyses, above all, the weight of primary documentation. One of the earliest and most influential histories in this cast was *Commentaries on Religion and the State in the Reign of Emperor Charles V* (1555) by Johannes Sleidan, historiographer to the Schmalkaldic League. Sleidan wrote his account of the Reformation from the vantage point of high politics. The narrative revolved around the relations between the princes and the emperor, the crucial events being the diets, the colloquies, the publication of decrees and the wars. God still informed human destiny, but the *Commentaries* went to great lengths to take a range of secular concerns into account. Moreover, as Sleidan himself emphasized, the work was trustworthy because it was based upon primary sources. Histories of the German Reformation now looked to the proofs of the past, the primary documentation, to fashion a narrative. In his *Annales Reformationis* Georg Spalatin took a somewhat similar approach, identifying the turning-points in the saga and speaking of the broader tensions and politics in the realm, while Friedrich Myconius, in a work that remained in manuscript form until the eighteenth century, began his analysis with a short (biased) study of the medieval Church in an attempt to explain Reformation developments. Biblical prophecy still played a role, but no more than references to important (and contingent) events and primary source materials. Even when Reformation history was little more than an exercise in confessional propaganda, as in the works of the Lutherans Johann Pappus or Lucas Osiander the Elder, or in the biography of Luther written by the Catholic polemicist Johannes Cochlaeus, there was primary documentation cited in the text to lend truth to claims. Equally, there was a clear historical narrative in place, relatively fixed in its basic framework of characters and events but growing in analytical complexity.

For two centuries after the posting of the *Ninety-Five Theses* Reformation history balanced the need to preserve the memory of the original reformers with the obligations of a self-critical, source-based narrative. Scholars moved between the accepted truths of the faith and the testimony of first-hand, archival evidence. In the German context, the most influential texts tended to feature both strands of the historiographical tradition. Heinrich Bullinger, for instance, wrote a comprehensive history of the Swiss Reformation in an effort to reveal the hand of God in the affair. Yet at the same time he boasted how his efforts to accumulate primary evidence had taken him over thirty years. Johannes Cochlaeus wrote a year-by-year account of the early Reformation rich in primary documentation, all of which was meant to discredit Luther and his faith. In response to this and other Catholic works, Matthias Flacius Illyricus oversaw the publication of the *Magdeburg Centuries* (1559), a Church history based on massive documentation conceived primarily as a defence of the Lutheran inheritance. Confessionally biased history remained the norm throughout this period, from the early works by Viktorin Strigel, a Melanchthon student, the Lutherans David Chytreaus and Christoph Petzel, to Abraham Scultetus, who wrote a Church history in mid-century from the perspective of the Reformed confession (Dickens and Tonkin, 1985, pp. 19–29; Cameron, 1996, pp. 116–27).

Perhaps the most impressive work of the following period was Veit Ludwig von Seckendorff's *History of Lutheranism* (1692). Seckendorff, as he explained in the preface, had been inspired to write the work after coming across Louis Maimbourg's *Histoire du Lutheranisme* (1680). Maimbourg was a French Jesuit, critical and suspicious of the Lutheran legacy. Seckendorff was a Saxon official, a Lutheran, and a politician experienced in the intrigues of confessional dialogue. Thus in essence Seckendorff wrote a defence of Reformation history, a dismantling of Maimbourg's censures and a confirmation of the principles of Lutheran orthodoxy. But more than this, the *History of Lutheranism* was the most substantial source-based history of the German Reformation since the age of Sleidan. Seckendorff went to great lengths to assure his readers that his history was rooted in the primary materials, the diplomatic letters, documents, mandates and judgements sent to him by princes, councillors, consistory presidents and members of the imperial courts. He believed that the only true history was history *ad fontes*, knowledge tied to the textual evidence of the past. And he believed just as strongly that ultimately the aim of historical dialogue was the revelation of religious truth.

On the eve of the Enlightenment histories of the German Reformation generally began to move away from the controversies and concerns of the early narratives. As one scholar put it, 'the controversial writings of the late seventeenth century show signs of increasing distance from the heat of the original battles' (Dickens and Tonkin, 1985, p. 109). Many of the initial articles of dispute were now foreign to a general readership, a point Seckendorff made in the preface to his *History of Lutheranism* when he advised against 'laughing over the enthusiasm of our forefathers'. Moreover, the confessional landscape was no longer as straightforward as it had been when Catholics, Lutherans and Calvinists flung diatribes at each other. For instance, one of the most influential works of Church history during this period, the *Non-partisan History of Churches and Heresies* (1699), was written by Gottfried Arnold, a man of pronounced Pietist sympathies, and yet a man who could also claim to the end of his life that he was a good Lutheran. Arnold's most dogged opponent was not a Catholic or a Calvinist, but the orthodox Lutheran Ernst Salomon Cyprian, a Helmstedt professor convinced that Arnold was a liar, a freethinker, an enthusiast, an anarchist and an atheist. Traditional confessional identities were polarizing and the historical narratives were following suit. Faced with the growing complexity, men like Cyprian called on the rules of scholarship to hold the religious freethinkers in check. 'For the historian must not look in his own mind in his quest for the truth,' wrote Cyprian in the preface to *A Necessary Defence of the Evangelical Church against Arnold's History of Heretics* (1745), 'nor should he search for it in his own ideas of what is good and bad in history or what is good and bad in mankind; rather he should seek it out solely and singularly where it resides, beyond himself, in the nature and the properties of the thing he wants to describe.'

In this age, religious sympathy was no longer so easy to fit into established narratives. Knowledge of the past had grown far too complex for the parameters of traditional Church history. Instead, scholars tended to write broader-based surveys of the evolution of Christianity or sweeping exegetical studies of scripture. New concerns entered the profession as the tools of scholarship forced a more critical approach. Source analysis replaced mimesis, footnotes and marginal citations replaced tradition and hearsay, while authors revealed the scientific nature of their studies in cross-references and double narratives. Reformation history was still a form of religious polemic, but most historians of this age were more interested in uncovering the facts or piecing together an explanatory pattern than being bogged down in religious debate. Johann Georg Walch, for instance, a practising Lutheran, wrote a study of the Reformation informed by the themes of the Enlightenment. Walch was more inclined to credit historical circumstance with the outbreak of the movement than Luther's notions of justification. Johann Lorenz von Mosheim, chancellor of Göttingen University, wrote the most comprehensive survey of the age, and in the end he concluded it was not dogma or spiritual destiny that accounted for the rise of the Protestant Church but the political struggle against Rome. Similarly, Johann Salomo Semler, a Halle theologian, worked through mountains of documentation before coming to the conclusion that the evangelical movement was as much about liberty as it was about faith. In the end, he believed that the Reformation would have occurred 'even if Luther had died on the spot' (Zeeden, 1958, p. 125). A new conception of the Reformation had emerged, less biblical in inspiration, less polemical in conception, and more inclined to look beyond religious factors in explaining the historical event.

Most scholars would agree that the summit of these historiographical advancements was reached in the nineteenth century in the person and work of Leopold von Ranke, professor of history at the University of Berlin. Ranke did not limit his interests to the German Reformation; he finished multi-volume works on the Renaissance and the papacy, published a study in source criticism, and polished off major histories of England and France. But he also wrote a work entitled *German History in the Age of the Reformation* (1838–47) and this multi-volume opus would shape and inform scholarship for more than a century. The publication was influential for two reasons. In the first place, it was a showpiece for the new 'scientific' approach to the past. In no other work on Reformation history was the documentation, and the appeal to the documentation, such a central feature of the narrative. Previous authors had drawn on documentary evidence before, but no other historian had been able '[to] anticipate Ranke's ability to bring the flavor and texture of the documents into his own text' (Grafton, 1997, p. 57). Moreover, Ranke went beyond his Lutheran predecessors in being highly critical of the traditional sources, and he was the first of the Reformation historians to subject the conventional narratives to systematic analysis. The other reason Ranke has been so influential is the sheer range of his analytical vision. Ranke's main interest was in the Reformation as a national event, as an expression of the evolving German spirit and its role in the making of the German state, but *German History in the Age of the Reformation* views the movement from a number of different vantage points. The survey of the early evangelical movement, for instance, looked in detail at events in the towns and the universities, traced reform ideas from scholastic beginnings to later Humanist coloration, and provided a detailed reconstruction of political developments in the Empire, from the level of the *Reichstag* down to the smaller diets and colloquies. He even researched at the local level, drawing on popular pamphlet materials to re-create the early movement and emphasizing regional differences in his survey of the Peasants' War. It was history on the grandest scale, written with 'a fine sense of history's multilateral dimensions', and constantly aware that social, political and religious forces were intertwined (Dickens, 1980, p. 7). After Ranke, it was no longer defensible to write a general history of the German Reformation without having similar aspirations.

Reformation history in the modern age has grown in its variety and complexity. The range of consideration has broadened, the language has become less polemical, and most of the major interpreters, from Catholics to Protestants to the practitioners of scientific history, have honoured the hermeneutical principles made famous by Ranke. Even when there is a fairly obvious religious agenda, the depth and quality of scholarship have often overwhelmed personal bias. The Catholic historian Ignaz von Döllinger's three-volume study *The Reformation* (1846–8) was very critical of Luther, as his predecessors had been, yet Döllinger was just as willing to criticize the medieval Catholic Church or look beyond religious concerns in order to interpret the age. Even more nuanced was the work by the Catholic Johannes Janssen, whose *History of the German People since the Close of the Middle Ages* (1876–94) set out, in Janssen's own words, 'to depict the German national life in all its varying conditions and stages and phases of destiny' (Dickens and Tonkin, 1985, p. 183). The result was a multilayered study of German culture on the eve of the Reformation. By the time of Joseph Lortz, whose *The Reformation in Germany* (1939/40) was perhaps the last grand synthesis in the Catholic tradition, the wealth of detail and the density of argument were leaving little room for explicit religious polemic. Lortz thought of Luther as a profound religious thinker, a man whose intense religiosity could not come to terms with the failings of the late medieval Church. The tragedy, as Lortz saw it, was that Luther lost sight of the Catholic faith and fell into a dialogue with its earthly imperfections. The Reformation, in this view, can only be understood in its relation to the social, cultural and political forces of the age.

Even Protestant historians, inspired by Ranke and legitimized by archival evidence, began to turn their backs on established interpretations. In his *History of Dogma* (1886) Adolf von Harnack related Luther's ideas to centuries of Christian thought and ended by criticizing the reformer for being unfair to some central Catholic ideas. Still more revisionist was the work of Ernst Troeltsch, like Harnack a Protestant scholar, who extended his critique to the movement as a whole. In contrast to the many scholars who thought of the Reformation as the point of division between the medieval and the modern age,

Troeltsch held that the movement should be understood as a continuation of medieval culture, for the century of Reform, no less than the age which preceded it, tied Church to State, devalued the secular world and delayed the arrival of modernity in its search for religious truth. Of course, not all Protestants agreed with Troeltsch, and indeed one corollary of this revisionism was a return to, and a confirmation of, the themes that had long been at the heart of Reformation scholarship. Karl Holl, professor of theology at Berlin, was perhaps the most influential voice in this 'Luther Renaissance', a scholarly campaign to reassess Luther's theological legacy in the context of its age (Wohlfeil, 1982, pp. 52–6). But by the age of Holl there was too much depth and variety in Reformation scholarship to return to the previous narratives. No greater evidence of the transformation exists than the rediscovery of the radical tradition. Thinkers throughout Europe and North America began to reassess the place of the radical Reformation in the traditional histories. Marginalized figures such as Hans Denck, Thomas Müntzer and Sebastian Franck now surfaced as central characters in the movement; the Peasants' War, the affair in Münster and the spread of Anabaptism now emerged as crucial developments. The grand synthesis of this tradition came with the publication of George Huntston Williams' *The Radical Reformation* (1962), a work which has had a lasting influence on the academic community, even if the act of reinterpretation was the work of many hands (Dickens and Tonkin, 1985, pp. 213–33).

By the dawn of the twentieth century the sheer volume of work on the German Reformation had become overwhelming. No single scholar could hope to master it all. Historians thus turned to theory, models and paradigms to cut through the details and speak in terms of cause and effect. Among the earliest to apply theory to the study of the Reformation were the Marxists, the first being Friedrich Engels, Karl Marx's longtime friend and collaborator. In his work *The Peasant War in Germany* (1850), Engels surveyed the early evangelical movement from a Marxist perspective. The result was a work which tied the event to the social, political and economic conditions of the day. He also introduced new categories to the debate, including questions relating to class, revolutionary groupings and the different levels of reception. The Marxist interpretation remained influential throughout the twentieth century, with fundamental contributions to the field coming from the Russian scholar M. M. Smirin's study of Thomas Müntzer and the East German historian Max Steinmetz, who claimed that Luther's ideas were 'the theological expression of the economic and political struggle between the bourgeoisie and the masses of people against the Church of the Pope which was governed by Rome and which hampered any social progress' (Dickens and Tonkin, 1985, p. 256; Wohlfeil, 1982, pp. 63–7). Other models emerged in the works of social scientists, the most famous and influential being Max Weber's extended essay *The Protestant Ethic and the Spirit of Capitalism* (1904/5). Weber identified features of the Protestant faith (in particular, what he termed its 'worldly asceticism') that had a direct affinity with features of modern capitalism. This model, much like the Marxist model, tied religious ideas to the social and political conditions of the day (though Weber granted faith a causal role). In a similar spirit, Ernst Troeltsch developed an approach in *The Social Teaching of the Christian Churches* (1911) which sought to synthesize religious ideas with formal social structures. Other models, too numerous to detail, have followed from these initial efforts. Sociologists, anthropologists, political scientists, historians of culture and ideas, even psychoanalysts – all have tried their hand at explaining the essence of the movement by way of a specialized approach.

These days it is common for historians to speak of *Reformations* in Germany rather than think in terms of a single or unique historical event. Aspects once peripheral to the traditional narratives (the radical movements, for instance, or the contributions of the common man) have become basic features of the general surveys, while the meaning of the term *Reformation* has grown in such scope and complexity that scholars use it in a very general sense as a shorthand for describing the age instead of investing it with any precise historical meaning. Even the theological essence of the Reformation movement is subject to conflicting opinions, as a recent discussion of Church historians in Germany made clear (Hamm et al., 1995). For some the evangelical doctrine of justification was fundamental to the event; its sum and substance was theological in nature. For others, the Reformation was too fluid and disparate a movement to speak of a theological core. Any idea of unity, whether projected in this century or a previous age, is a construct of the historian.

Thus the question remains in dispute, and there is no sign of general consensus. Nor do the trends in recent Reformation historiography suggest a ready conflux of perspectives. Modern scholarship tends to focus on specific features of the movement, such as the urban dimension of reform or the relationship between the religious message and the media of the day, rather than try to capture the essence of the event in a grand synthesis. Of course, this does not mean that a general history of the Reformation is no longer possible, but it does mean that the surveys will grow in depth and consideration as historians continue to broaden their perspectives and extend the range of their analyses. Recent work has added important insights to the historiographical tradition, and there is certainly no reason to assume that the innovation is at an end. The theme grows with time. Future studies of the German Reformation, in order to comprehend the significance of the event, will read more and more like general histories of the age.

Bibliography

Abray, Lorna Jane 1985: *The People's Reformation*. Oxford: Clarendon Press.

Albrecht, Dieter 1998: *Maximilian I von Bayern 1573–1651*. Munich: R. Oldenbourg.

Augustijn, Cornelis 1993: 'The Quest of *Reformatio*: The Diet of Regensburg as Turning Point.' In Hans R. Guggisberg & Gottfried G. Krodel (eds), *Die Reformation in Deutschland und Europa: Interpretationen und Debatten*. Gütersloh: Gütersloher Verlagshaus, 64–80.

Bagchi, David V. N. 1991: *Luther's Earliest Opponents. Catholic Controversialists, 1518–1525*. Minneapolis: Fortress Press.

Bast, Robert James 1997: *Honor Your Fathers. Catechisms and the Emergence of a Patriarchal Ideology in Germany*. Leiden: E. J. Brill.

Baylor, Michael G. 1991: *The Radical Reformation*. Cambridge: Cambridge University Press.

Bierbrauer, Peter 1993: *Die unterdrückte Reformation. Der Kampf der Tiroler um eine neue Kirche (1521–1527)*. Zurich: Chronos.

Blickle, Peter 1981: *The Revolution of 1525*, trans. Thomas A. Brady, Jr. and H. C. Erik Midelfort. Baltimore, MD: Johns Hopkins University Press.

Blickle, Peter 1992a: *Communal Reformation. The Quest for Salvation in Sixteenth-Century Germany*, trans. Thomas Dunlap. London: Humanities Press.

Blickle, Peter 1992b: *Die Reformation im Reich*. 2nd edn. Stuttgart: Eugen Ulmer.

Blickle, Peter 1997: *Obedient Germans? A Rebuttal. A New View of German History*, trans. Thomas A. Brady, Jr. Charlottesville: Virginia University Press.

Blickle, Peter 1998: *Der Bauernkrieg. Die Revolution des Gemeinen Mannes.* Munich: C. H. Beck.

Blickle, Peter 1999a: 'Reformation and Communal Spirit: The Reply of the Theologians to Constitutional Change in the Late Middle Ages.' In C. Scott Dixon (ed.), *The German Reformation.* Oxford: Blackwell, 133–68.

Blickle, Peter 1999b: *From the Communal Reformation to the Revolution of the Common Man,* trans. Beat Kümin. Leiden: Brill.

Bossy, John 1987: *Christianity in the West 1400–1700.* Oxford: Oxford University Press.

Bouwsma, William J. 1988: *John Calvin. A Sixteenth Century Portrait.* Oxford: Oxford University Press.

Brady, Thomas A. 1985: *Turning Swiss. Cities and Empire, 1450–1550.* Cambridge: Cambridge University Press.

Brady, Thomas A. 1988: 'In Search of the Godly City: The Domestication of Religion in the German Urban Reformation.' In R. Po-Chia Hsia (ed.), *The German People and the Reformation.* Ithaca, NY: Cornell University Press, 14–31.

Brady, Thomas A. 1997: *The Politics of the Reformation in Germany: Jacob Sturm of Strasbourg (1489–1553).* Atlantic Highlands, NJ: Humanities Press.

Brady, Thomas A. 1999: 'The Reformation of the Common Man.' In C. Scott Dixon (ed.), *The German Reformation.* Oxford: Blackwell, 91–132.

Brady, Thomas A. and Dilcher, Gerhard 1997b: 'The urban belt and the emerging modern state.' In Peter Blickle (ed.), *Resistance, Representation and Community.* Oxford: Clarendon Press, 217–55.

Brandi, Karl 1965: *The Emperor Charles V,* trans. C. V. Wedgwood. London: Jonathan Cape.

Brecht, Martin 1992: 'Lutherische Kirchenzucht bis in die Anfänge des 17. Jahrhunderts im Spannungsfeld von Pfarramt und Gesellschaft.' In Hans-Christoph Rublack (ed.), *Die lutherische Konfessionalisierung in Deutschland.* Gütersloh: Gütersloher Verlagshaus, 400–20.

Brecht, Martin 1993: *Martin Luther. His Road to Reformation 1483–1521,* trans. James L. Schaaf. Minneapolis: Fortress Press.

Brecht, Martin 1994: *Martin Luther. Shaping and Defining the Reformation, 1521–1532,* trans. James L. Schaaf. Minneapolis: Fortress Press.

Brecht, Martin and Ehmer, Hermann 1984: *Südwestdeutsche Reformationsgeschichte. Zur Einführung der Reformation im Herzogtum Württemberg 1534.* Stuttgart: Calwer.

Brockmann, Thomas 1998: *Die Konzilsfrage in den Flug- und Streitschriften des deutschen Sprachraumes 1518–1563.* Göttingen: Vandenhoeck & Ruprecht.

Bubenheimer, Ulrich 1985: 'Luthers Stellung zum Aufruhr in Wittenberg 1520–1522 und die frühreformatorischen Wurzeln des landesherrlichen Kirchenregiments,' *Zeitschrift der Savigny-Stiftung für Rechtsgeschichte*, 102, 147–214.

Cameron, Euan 1991: *The European Reformation*. Oxford: Clarendon Press.

Cameron, Euan 1996: 'One Reformation or Many? Protestant Identities in the Later Reformation in Germany.' In Ole Peter Grell & Bob Scribner (eds), *Tolerance and Intolerance in the European Reformation*. Cambridge: Cambridge University Press, 108–27.

Chrisman, Mirian Usher 1967: *Strasbourg and the Reform*. London: Yale University Press.

Chrisman, Miriam Usher 1996: *Conflicting Visions of Reform. German Lay Propaganda Pamphlets, 1519–1530*. Atlantic Highlands, NJ: Humanities Press.

Christensen Carl C. 1979: *Art and the Reformation in Germany*. Athens: Ohio University Press.

Clasen, Claus-Peter 1972: *Anabaptism. A Social History*. Ithaca, NY: Cornell University Press.

Conrad, Franziska 1984: *Reformation in der bäuerlichen Gesellschaft. Zur Rezeption reformatorischer Theologie im Elsass*. Stuttgart: Franz Steiner.

Dickens, A. Geoffrey 1974: *The German Nation and Martin Luther*. London: Edward Arnold.

Dickens, A. Geoffrey 1980: *Ranke as Reformation Historian*. Reading: Reading University Press.

Dickens, A. G. and Tonkin, John M. 1985: *The Reformation in Historical Thought*. Oxford: Blackwell.

Dipple, Geoffrey 1996: *Antifraternalism and Anticlericalism in the German Reformation*. Aldershot: Scolar.

Dippold, Günther 1996: *Konfessionalisierung am Obermain. Reformation und Gegenreformation in den Pfarrsprengeln von Baunach bis Marktgraitz*. Staffelstein: Obermain Buch- und Bildverlag.

Dixon, C. Scott 1996a: *The Reformation and Rural Society. The Parishes of Brandenburg-Ansbach-Kulmbach, 1528–1603*. Cambridge: Cambridge University Press.

Dixon, C. Scott 1996b: 'The German Reformation and the Territorial City: Reform Initiatives in Schwabach, 1523–1527,' *German History*, 14, 123–40.

Dixon, C. Scott 2000: 'The Princely Reformation in Germany.' In Andrew Pettegree (ed.), *The Reformation World*. London: Routledge, 146–75.

Du Boulay, F. R. H. 1983: *Germany in the Later Middle Ages*. London: Athlone Press.

Dülmen, Richard van 1982: *Entstehung des frühneuzeitlichen Europa 1550–1648.* Frankfurt: Fischer Verlag.

Dülmen, Richard van 1987: *Reformation als Revolution. Soziale Bewegung und religiöser Radikalismus in der deutschen Reformation.* Frankfurt: Fischer Verlag.

Dülmen, Richard van 1999: 'The Reformation and the Modern Age.' In C. Scott Dixon (ed.), *The German Reformation.* Oxford: Blackwell, 193–220.

Dykema, Peter 1996: 'The Reforms of Count Eberhard of Württemberg.' In Beat Kümin (ed.), *Reformations Old and New. Essays on the Socio-Economic Impact of Religious Change c.1470–1630.* Aldershot: Scolar Press, 39–56.

Edwards, Mark 1994: *Printing, Propaganda, and Martin Luther.* University of California Press.

Elton, Geoffrey 1999: *Reformation Europe 1517–1559.* 2nd edn. Oxford: Blackwell.

Enderle, Wilfried 1993a: 'Ulm und die evangelischen Reichsstädte im Südwesten.' In Anton Schindling and Walter Ziegler (eds), *Die Territorien des Reichs im Zeitalter der Reformation und Konfessionalisierung,* vol. 5. Münster: Aschendorff, 194–212.

Enderle, Wilfried 1993b: 'Rottweil und die katholischen Reichsstädte im Südwesten.' In Anton Schindling & Walter Ziegler (eds), *Die Territorien des Reichs im Zeitalter der Reformation und Konfessionalisierung,* vol. 5. Münster: Aschendorff, 214–30.

Estes, James Martin 1982: *Christian Magistrate and State Church: The Reforming Career of Johannes Brenz.* Toronto: University of Toronto Press.

Evans, G. R. 1992: *Problems of Authority in the Reformation Debates.* Cambridge: Cambridge University Press.

Evans, R. J. W. 1979: *The Making of the Habsburg Monarchy 1550–1700.* Oxford: Oxford University Press.

Fife, Robert Herndon 1957: *The Revolt of Martin Luther.* New York: Columbia University Press.

Forster, Marc 1992: *The Counter-Reformation in the Villages.* Ithaca, NY: Cornell University Press.

Fuhrmann, Rosi 1995: *Kirche und Dorf. Religiöse Bedürfnisse und kirchliche Stiftung auf dem Lande vor der Reformation.* Stuttgart: Gustav Fischer Verlag.

Goertz, Hans-Jürgen 1987: *Pfaffenhaß und groß geschrei. Die Reformatorischen Bewegungen in Deutschland 1517–1529.* Munich: C. H. Beck.

Goertz, Hans-Jürgen 1993: 'Eine "bewegte" Epoche. Zur Heterogenität reformatorischer Bewegungen.' In Heiko Oberman et al. (eds), *Reformiertes Erbe: Festschrift für Gottfried W. Locher zu seinem 80. Geburtstag.* Zurich: Theologischer Verlag, 103–25.

Goertz, Hans-Jürgen 1995: *Antiklerikalismus und Reformation. Sozialgeschichtliche Untersuchungen.* Göttingen: Vandenhoeck & Ruprecht.

Goertz, Hans-Jürgen 1996: *The Anabaptists*, trans. Trevor Johnston. London: Routledge.

Gordon, Bruce 1996: 'The Changing Face of Protestant History and Identity in the Sixteenth Century,' In Bruce Gordon (ed.), *Protestant History and Identity in Sixteenth-Century Europe*, vol. 2. Aldershot: Scolar Press, 1–22.

Grafton, Anthony 1997: *The Footnote: A Curious History*. London: Faber & Faber.

Grane, Leif 1994: *Martinus Noster: Luther in the German Reform Movement 1518–1521*. Mainz: Zabern.

Greengrass, Mark 1998: *The European Reformation c.1500–1618*. London: Longman.

Greyerz, Kaspar von 1985: 'Stadt und Reformation: Stand und Aufgaben der Forschung,' *Archiv für Reformationsgeschichte*, 76, 1–63.

Grossmann, Maria 1975: *Humanism in Wittenberg 1485–1517*. Nieuwkoop: de Graaf.

Guggisberg, Hans. R. and Krodel, Gottfried G. (eds) 1993: *Die Reformation in Deutschland und Europa: Interpretationen und Debatten*. Gütersloh: Gütersloher Verlagshaus.

Hamm, Berndt 1988: *Zwinglis Reformation der Freiheit*. Neukirchen-Vluyn: Neukirchener Verlag.

Hamm, Berndt 1995a: 'Einheit und Vielfalt der Reformation – oder; was die Reformation zur Reformation machte.' In Berndt Hamm, Bernd Moeller and Dorothea Wendebourg (eds), *Reformationstheorien. Ein kirchenhistorischer Disput über Einheit und Vielfalt der Reformation*. Göttinger: Vandenhoeck & Ruprecht, 57–127.

Hamm, Berndt 1995b: 'The Urban Reformation in the Holy Roman Empire.' In Thomas A. Brady, Jr, Heiko A. Oberman and James D. Tracy (eds), *Handbook of European History, 1400–1600: Late Middle Ages, Renaissance and Reformation*, vol. 2. Leiden: E. J. Brill, 193–220.

Hamm, Berndt 1996a: *Bürgertum und Glaube. Konturen der städtischen Reformation*. Göttingen: Vandenhoeck & Ruprecht.

Hamm, Berndt 1996b: 'Die Reformation als Medienereignis,' *Jahrbuch für biblische Theologie*, 11, 137–66.

Hamm, Berndt 1999a: 'Normative Centering in the Fifteenth and Sixteenth Centuries: Observations on Religiosity, Theology, and Iconology,' *Journal of Early Modern History*, 3/4 (1999), 307–54.

Hamm, Berndt 1999b: 'What was the Reformation Doctrine of Justification?' In C. Scott Dixon (ed.), *The German Reformation*. Oxford: Blackwell, 53–90.

Harrington, Joel F. 1995: *Reordering Marriage and Society in Reformation Germany*. Cambridge: Cambridge University Press.

Heckel, Martin 1983: *Deutschland im konfessionellen Zeitalter*. Göttingen: Vandenhoeck & Ruprecht.

Heer, Friedrich 1995: *The Holy Roman Empire*, trans. Janet Sondheimer. London: Phoenix.

Higman, Francis 2000: 'Music.' In Andrew Pettegree (ed.), *The Reformation World*. London: Routledge, 491–504.

Hohenberger, Thomas 1996: *Lutherische Rechtfertigungslehre in den reformatorischen Flugschriften der Jahre 1521–1522*. Tübingen: Mohr.

Höpfl, Harro 1991: *Luther and Calvin. On Secular Authority*. Cambridge: Cambridge University Press.

Hsia, R. Po-Chia 1989: *Social Discipline in the Reformation: Central Europe 1550–1750*. London: Routledge.

Hsia, R. Po-Chia 1998: *The World of Catholic Renewal 1540–1770*. Cambridge: Cambridge University Press.

Hughes, Michael 1992: *Early Modern Germany, 1477–1806*. London: Macmillan.

Huizinga, Johan 1996: *The Autumn of the Middle Ages*, trans. Rodney J. Payton and Ulrich Mammitzsch. Chicago: Chicago University Press.

Isenmann, Eberhard 1988: *Die deutsche Stadt im Spätmittelalter 1250–1500. Stadtgestalt, Recht, Stadtregiment, Kirche, Gesellschaft, Wirtschaft*. Stuttgart: Ulmer.

Johnston, Pamela and Scribner, Bob 1993: *The Reformation in Germany and Switzerland*. Cambridge: Cambridge University Press.

Karant-Nunn, Susan 1988: 'What was preached in the German Cities in the Early Years of the Reformation? *Wildwuchs* versus Lutheran Unity.' In Phillip N. Bebb & Sherrin Marshall (eds), *The Process of Change in Early Modern Europe*. Athens: Ohio University Press, 81–96.

Karant-Nunn, Susan 1997: *The Reformation of Ritual*. London: Routledge.

Karant-Nunn, Susan 2000: 'Reformation Society, Women and the Family.' In Andrew Pettegree (ed.), *The Reformation World*. London: Routledge, 433–60.

Kießling, Rolf 1996: 'Markets and Marketing. Town and Country.' In Bob Scribner (ed.), *Germany. A New Social and Economic History*, vol. 1. London: Arnold, 145–79.

Klueting, Harm 1989: *Das konfessionelle Zeitalter 1525–1648*. Stuttgart: Ulmer.

Knecht, R. J. 1994: *Renaissance Warrior and Patron. The Reign of Francis I*. Cambridge: Cambridge University Press.

Kohler, Alfred 1999: *Karl V, 1500–1558. Eine Biographie*. Munich: C. H. Beck.

Kolb, Robert 1991: *Confessing the Faith. Reformers Define the Church, 1530–1580*. St Louis, MS: Concordia.

Kolb, Robert 1996: 'Formula of Concord,' In Hans Hillerbrand (ed.), *The Oxford Encyclopedia of the Reformation*. Oxford: Oxford University Press, 117–21.

Kolb, Robert 1999: *Martin Luther as Prophet, Teacher, Hero. Images of the Reformer 1520–1620*. Grand Rapids, MI: Baker Books.

Konersmann, Frank 1996: *Kirchenregiment und Kirchenzucht im frühneuzeitlichen Kleinstaat. Studien zu den herrschaftlichen und gesellschaftlichen Grundlagen des Kirchenregiments der Herzöge von Pfalz-Zweibrücken 1410–1793*. Cologne: Rheinland Verlag.

Krodel, Gottfried G. 1968: 'State and Church in Brandenburg-Ansbach-Kulmbach 1524–1526,' *Studies in Medieval and Renaissance History*, 5, 141–213.

Krumwiede, Hans-Walter 1967: *Zur Entstehung des landesherrlichen Kirchenregiments in Kursachsen und Braunschweig-Wolfenbüttel*. Göttingen: Vandenhoeck & Ruprecht.

Lindberg, Carter 1992: *The European Reformations*. Oxford: Blackwell.

Locher, Gottfried W. 1979: *Die Zwinglische Reformation im Rahmen der europäischen Kirchengeschichte*. Göttingen: Vandenhoeck & Ruprecht.

Locher, Gottfried W. 1981: *Zwingli's Thought. New Perspectives*. Leiden: E. J. Brill.

Lohse, Bernhard 1987: *Martin Luther: An Introduction to his Life and Work*, trans. Robert C. Schultz. Edinburgh: T. & T. Clark.

Lortz, Joseph 1949: 'Zur Problematik der kirchlichen Mißstände am Spätmittelalter,' *Trierer Theologische Zeitschrift*, 58, 1–26, 112–27, 257–79, 347–57.

Lortz, Joseph 1968: *The Reformation in Germany*, trans. Ronald Walls. vol. 2. London: Danton, Longman & Todd.

Lottes, Günther and Greschat, Martin (eds) 1997: *Luther in seiner Zeit*. Stuttgart: Kohlhammer.

Lutz, Heinrich 1983: *Das Ringen um deutsche Einheit und kirchliche Erneuerung. Von Maximilian I. bis zum Westfälischen Frieden 1490 bis 1648*. Berlin: Propyläen Verlag.

Lutz, Heinrich 1991: *Reformation und Gegenreformation*. Munich: Oldenbourg.

Matheson, Peter 1998: *The Rhetoric of the Reformation*: Edinburgh: T. & T. Clark.

Matheson, Peter 2000: *The Imaginative World of the Reformation*. Edinburgh: T. & T. Clark.

McGrath, Alister E. 1986: *Iustitia Dei. A History of the Christian Doctrine of Justification*, vol. 1. Cambridge: Cambridge University Press.

McGrath, Alister 1987: *The Intellectual Origins of the European Reformation*. Oxford: Blackwell.

McGrath, Alister E. 1993: *Reformation Thought. An Introduction.* Oxford: Blackwell.

Moeller, Bernd 1972a: *Imperial Cities and the Reformation*, trans. H. C. Erik Midelfort and Mark U. Edwards. Durham: Labyrinth Press.

Moeller, Bernd 1972b: 'Religious Life in Germany on the Eve of the Reformation.' In Gerald Strauss (ed.), *Pre-Reformation Germany.* London: Macmillan, 13–42.

Moeller, Bernd 1981: *Deutschland im Zeitalter der Reformation.* Göttingen: Vandenhoeck & Ruprecht.

Moeller, Bernd 1983: 'Das Berühmtwerden Luthers,' *Zeitschrift für Historische Forschung*, 15, 65–92.

Moeller, Bernd (ed.) 1998: *Die frühe Reformation in Deutschland als Umbruch.* Gütersloh: Gütersloher Verlagshaus.

Moeller, Bernd 1999: 'What was Preached in German Towns in the Early Reformation?' In C. Scott Dixon (ed.), *The German Reformation.* Oxford: Blackwell, 33–52.

Moeller, Bernd and Stackmann, Karl 1996: *Städtische Predigt in der Frühzeit der Reformation. Eine Untersuchung deutscher Flugschriften der Jahre 1522 bis 1529.* Göttingen: Vandenhoeck & Ruprecht.

Münch, Paul 1978: *Zucht und Ordnung. Reformierte Kirchenverfassungen im 16. und 17. Jahrhundert (Nassau-Dillenburg, Kurpfalz, Hessen-Kassel).* Stuttgart: Klett-Cotta.

Nischan, Bodo 1994: *Prince, People, and Confession. The Second Reformation in Brandenburg.* Philadelphia: University of Pennsylvania Press.

Nischan, Bodo 1996: 'Ritual and Protestant Identity in Late Reformation Germany.' In Bruce Gordon (ed.), *Protestant History and Identity in Sixteenth-Century Europe*, vol. 2. Aldershot: Scolar Press, 142–58.

Nischan, Bodo 1997: 'Demarcating Boundaries: Lutheran Pericopic Sermons in the Age of Confessionalization,' *Archiv für Reformationsgeschichte*, 88, 199–216.

Nischan, Bodo 2000: 'Germany after 1550.' In Andrew Pettegree (ed.), *The Reformation World.* London: Routledge, 387–409.

Oberman, Heiko A. 1992: *The Dawn of the Reformation.* Edinburgh: T. & T. Clark.

Oberman, Heiko A. 1993: *Luther. Man Between God and the Devil.* London: Fontana Press.

Oberman, Heiko A. 1994: *The Impact of the Reformation.* Edinburgh: T. & T. Clark.

Ozment, Steven 1975: *The Reformation in the Cities.* London: Yale University Press.

Ozment, Steven 1980: *The Age of Reform 1250–1550.* London: Yale University Press.

Ozment, Steven 1993: *Protestants. The Birth of a Revolution*. London: Fontana Press.

Packull, Werner 1995: *Hutterite Beginnings. Communitarian Experiments during the Reformation*. Baltimore, MD: Johns Hopkins University Press.

Parker, Geoffrey 1992: 'Success and Failure during the First Century of Reformation,' *Past and Present*, 139, 43–82.

Pelikan, Jaroslav 1978: *The Growth of Medieval Theology (600–1300)*. Chicago: University of Chicago Press.

Pelikan, Jaroslav 1984: *The Reformation of Church and Dogma (1300–1700)*. Chicago: University of Chicago Press.

Pettegree, Andrew 2000a: 'Art.' In Andrew Pettegree (ed.), *The Reformation World*. London: Routledge, 461–90.

Pettegree, Andrew 2000b: 'Books, pamphlets and polemic.' In Andrew Pettegree (ed.), *The Reformation World*. London: Routledge, 109–26.

Press, Volker 1979: 'Adel, Reich und Reformation.' In W. J. Mommsen et al. (eds), *Stadtbürgertum und Adel in der Reformation*. Stuttgart: Klett-Cotta, 330–83.

Press, Volker 1990: 'Constitutional Development and Political Thought.' In G. R. Elton (ed.), *The New Cambridge Modern History*, vol. 2. Cambridge: Cambridge University Press, 505–25.

Preus, Robert D. 1970: *The Theology of Post-Reformation Lutheranism*, vol. 1. London: Concordia Publishing House.

Rabe, Horst 1989: *Reich und Glaubensspaltung: Deutschland 1500–1600*. Munich: C. H. Beck.

Rabe, Horst 1991: *Deutsche Geschichte 1500–1600*. Munich: C. H. Beck.

Rapp, Francis 1971: *L'église et la vie religieuse en l' occident à la fin du moyen âge*. Paris: Presses Universitaires de France.

Reardon, M. G. Bernard 1995: *Religious Thought in the Reformation*. London: Longman.

Reinhard, Wolfgang 1995: 'Was ist katholische Konfessionalisierung?' In Wolfgang Reinhard and Heinz Schilling (eds), *Die katholische Konfessionalisierung*. Gütersloh: Gütersloher Verlagshaus, 419–52.

Reinhard, Wolfgang 1999: 'Presures Towards Confessionalization? Prolegomena to a Theory of the Confessional Age.' In C. Scott Dixon (ed.), *The German Reformation*. Oxford: Blackwell, 169–92.

Roeck, Bernd 1989: *Eine Stadt in Krieg und Frieden. Studien zur Geschichte der Reichsstadt Augsburg zwischen Kalenderstreit und Parität*, vol. 1: Göttingen: Vandenhoeck & Ruprecht.

Roper, Lyndal 1989: *The Holy Household: Women and Morals in Reformation Augsburg*. Oxford: Oxford University Press.

Rösener, Werner 1996: 'The Agrarian Economy, 1300–1600.' In Bob Scribner (ed.), *Germany. A New Social and Economic History*, vol. 1. London: Arnold, 63–84.

Rubin, Miri 1992: *Corpus Christi. The Eucharist in Late Medieval Culture*. Cambridge: Cambridge University Press.

Rublack, Hans-Christoph 1978: *Gescheiterte Reformation. Frühreformatorische und protestantische Bewegungen in süd- und westdeutschen geistlichen Residenzen*. Stuttgart: Klett-Cotta.

Rublack, Hans-Christoph 1984: 'Political and Social Norms in Urban Communities.' In Kaspar von Greyerz (ed.), *Religion, Politics and Social Protest. Three Studies on Early Modern Germany*. London: George Allen and Unwin, 24–60.

Rublack, Hans-Christian 1995: 'New Patterns of Christian Life.' In Thomas A. Brady, Jr, Heiko A. Oberman and James D. Tracy (eds), *Handbook of European History, 1400–1600: Late Middle Ages, Renaissance and Reformation*, vol. 2. Leiden: E. J. Brill, 585–605.

Rublack, Hans-Christoph and Demandt, Dieter 1978: *Stadt und Kirche in Kitzingen* Stuttgart: Klett-Cotta.

Rummel, Erika 1995: *The Humanist-Scholastic Debate*. Cambridge, MA: Harvard University Press.

Rupp, Gordon 1969: *Patterns of Reformation*. Philadelphia: Fortress Press.

Russel, Paul 1986: *Lay Theology in the Reformation. Popular Pamphleteers in Southwest Germany 1521–1525*. Cambridge: Cambridge University Press.

Schilling, Heinz 1992a: 'The Second Reformation – Problems and Issues.' In Heinz Schilling, *Religion, Political Culture, and the Emergence of Early Modern Society*. Leiden: Brill, 247–301.

Schilling, Heinz 1992b: 'Alternatives to the Lutheran Reformation and the Rise of Lutheran Identity.' In Andrew C. Fix and Susan C. Karant-Nunn (eds), *Germania Illustrata. Essays on Early Modern Germany Presented to Gerald Strauss*. Kirksville, MS: Sixteenth Century Essays and Studies, 99–120.

Schilling, Heinz 1993: *Die Stadt in der frühen Neuzeit*. Munich: R. Oldenbourg.

Schilling, Heinz 1995a: 'Confessional Europe.' In Thomas A. Brady, Jr, Heiko A. Oberman and James D. Tracy (eds), *Handbook of European history, 1400–1600: Late Middle Ages, Renaissance and Reformation*, vol. 2. Leiden: E. J. Brill. 641–81.

Schilling, Heinz 1995b: 'Die Konfessionalisierung von Kirche, Staat und Gesellschaft – Profil, Leistung, Defizite und Perspektiven eines geschichts-wissenschaftlichen Paradigmas.' In Wolfgang Reinhard and Heinz Schilling (eds), *Die katholische Konfessionalisierung*. Gütersloh: Gütersloher Verlagshaus, 1–49.

Schilling, Heinz 1998: *Aufbruch und Krise. Deutschland 1517–1648*. Berlin: Siedler.

Schindling, Anton 1989: 'Nürnberg.' In Anton Schindling and Walter Ziegler (eds), *Die Territorien des Reichs im Zeitalter der Refor-*

mation und Konfessionalisierung, vol. 1. Münster: Aschendorff, 32–42.

Schlemmer, Karl 1975: 'Gottesdienst und Frömmigkeit in Nürnberg vor der Reformation,' *Zeitschrift für bayerische Kirchengeschichte*, 44 (1975), 1–27.

Schmidt, Georg 1999: *Geschichte des Alten Reiches. Staat und Nation in der Frühen Neuzeit*. Munich: C. H. Beck.

Schmidt, Heinrich Richard 1986: *Reichsstädte, Reich und Reformation*. Stuttgart: Franz Steiner.

Schmidt, Heinrich Richard 1995: *Dorf und Religion. Reformierte Sittenzucht in Berner Landgemeinden der Frühen Neuzeit*. Stuttgart, Jena, New York: Gustav Fischer.

Schorn-Shütte, Luise 1992: 'Lutherische Konfessionalisierung? Das Beispiel Braunschweig-Wolfenbüttel (1589–1613).' In Hans-Christoph Rublack (ed.), *Die lutherische Konfessionalisierung in Deutschland*. Gütersloh: Gütersloher Verlagshaus, 163–94.

Schorn-Schütte, Luise 1996a: *Evangelische Geistlichkeit in der Frühneuzeit. Deren Anteil an der Entfaltung frühmoderner Staatlichkeit und Gesellschaft*. Gütersloh: Gütersloher Verlagshaus.

Schorn-Schütte, Luise 1996b: *Die Reformation. Vorgeschichte-Verlauf-Wirkung*. Munich: C. H. Beck.

Schorn-Schütte, Luise 2000a: 'Priest, Preacher, Pastor: Research on Clerical Office in Early Modern Europe,' *Central European History*, 33, 1–39.

Schorn-Schütte, Luise 2000b: *Karl V. Kaiser Zwischen Mittelalter und Neuzeit*. Munich: C. H. Beck.

Schulze, Manfred 1991: *Fürsten und Reformation. Geistliche Reformpolitik weltlicher Fürsten vor der Reformation*. Tübingen: J. C. B. Mohr.

Schulze, Winfried 1987: *Deutsche Geschichte im 16. Jahrhundert 1500–1618*. Frankfurt: Suhrkamp.

Schwarz Lausten, Martin 1983: 'Lutherus: Luther and the Princes.' In Peter Newman Brookes (ed.), *Seven-Headed Luther*. Oxford: Clarendon Press, 51–76.

Scott, Tom 1989: *Thomas Müntzer. Theology and Revolution in the German Reformation*. London: Macmillan.

Scott, Tom 1991: 'The Common People in the German Reformation,' *Historical Journal*, 34, 183–92.

Scott, Tom 1993: 'The Communal Reformation between Town and Country.' In Hans R. Guggisberg and Gottfried G. Krodel (eds), *Die Reformation in Deutschland und Europa: Interpretationen und Debatten*. Gütersloh: Gütersloher Verlagshaus, 175–93.

Scott, Tom 1996: 'Economic Landscapes.' In Bob Scribner (ed.), *Germany. A New Social and Economic History*, vol. 1. London: Arnold, 1–25.

Scott, Tom 1998: 'Germany and the Empire.' In Christopher Allmand (ed.), *The New Cambridge Medieval History*. Cambridge: Cambridge University Press, 337–66.

Scott, Tom and Scribner, Bob 1991: *The German Peasants' War. A History in Documents*. London: Humanities Press.

Scott, Tom and Scribner, Bob 1996: 'Urban Networks.' In Bob Scribner (ed.), *Germany. A New Social and Economic History*, vol. 1. London: Arnold, 113–43.

Scribner, Bob 1986: *The German Reformation*. London: Macmillan.

Scribner, R. W. 1987: *Popular Culture and Popular Movements in Reformation Germany*. London: Hambledon Press.

Scribner, Bob 1990a: 'The Reformation Movements in Germany.' In G. R. Elton (ed.), *The New Cambridge Modern History*, vol. 2. Cambridge: Cambridge University Press, 69–93.

Scribner, Bob 1990b: 'The Impact of the Reformation on Daily Life.' In *Mensch und Objekt im Mittelalter und in der frühen Neuzeit. Leben-Alltag-Kultur*. Vienna: Österreichische Akademie der Wissenschaften, 315–43.

Scribner, Bob 1993a: *Varieties of Reformation*. London: Historical Association.

Scribner, Bob 1993b: 'The Reformation and the Religion of the Common People.' In Hans R. Guggisberg and Gottfried G. Krodel (eds), *Die Reformation in Deutschland und Europa: Interpretationen und Debatten*. Gütersloh: Gütersloher Verlagshaus, 221–41.

Scribner, Bob 1994a: *For the Sake of Simple Folk. Popular Propaganda for the German Reformation*. Oxford: Oxford University Press.

Scribner, Bob 1994b: 'Heterodoxy, literacy and print in the early German Reformation.' In Peter Biller and Anne Hudson (eds), *Heresy and Literacy, 1000–1530*. Cambridge: Cambridge University Press, 279–93.

Scribner, Bob 1999: 'The Reformation, Popular Magic, and the "Disenchantment" of the World.' In C. Scott Dixon (ed.), *The German Reformation*. Oxford: Blackwell, 259–80.

Skinner, Quentin 1996: *The Foundations of Modern Political Thought: The Age of Reformation*, vol. 2. Cambridge: Cambridge University Press.

Spicer, Andrew 2000: 'Architecture.' In Andrew Pettegree (ed.), *The Reformation World*. London: Routledge, 505–20.

Spitz, Lewis W. 1996: *Luther and German Humanism*. Aldershot: Variorum.

Stayer, James 1994: *The German Peasants' War and Anabaptist Community of Goods*. Montreal: McGill-Queen's University Press.

Stayer, James 1995: 'The Radical Reformation.' In Thomas A. Brady, Jr, James D. Tracy and Heiko A. Oberman (eds), *Handbook of Euro-*

pean History 1400–1600. Late Middle Ages, Renaissance, and Reformation, vol. 2. Leiden: E. J. Brill, 251–78.

Steinmetz, David C. 1986: *Luther in Context*. Bloomington: Indiana University Press.

Stevens, W. P. 1986: *The Theology of Huldrych Zwingli*. Oxford: Clarendon Press.

Stieve, Felix 1875: *Der Ursprung des dreissigjährigen Krieges 1607–1619: Der Kampf um Donauwörth*. Munich: Rieger.

Sievermann, Dieter 1997: 'Evangelische Territorien im Konfessionalisierungsprozess.' In Anton Schindling and Walter Ziegler (eds), *Die Territorien des Reichs im Zeitalter der Reformation und Konfessionalisierung*, vol. 7. Münster: Aschendorff, 45–65.

Strauss, Gerald 1966: *Nuremberg in the Sixteenth Century: City Politics and Life between Middle Ages and Modern Times*. Bloomington: Indiana University Press.

Strauss, Gerald 1971: *Manifestations of Discontent in Germany on the Eve of the Reformation*. Bloomington: Indiana University Press.

Strauss, Gerald 1978: *Luther's House of Learning. Indoctrination of the Young in the German Reformation*. Baltimore, MD: Johns Hopkins University Press.

Strauss, Gerald 1995: 'Ideas of *Reformatio* and *Renovatio* from the Middle Ages to the Reformation.' In Thomas A. Brady, Jr, James D. Tracy and Heiko A. Oberman (eds), *Handbook of European History 1400–1600. Late Middle Ages, Renaissance, and Reformation*, vol. 1. Leiden: E. J. Brill, 1–30.

Strauss, Gerald 1999: 'Success and Failure in the German Reformation.' In C. Scott Dixon (ed.), *The German Reformation*. Oxford: Blackwell, 221–58.

Swanson, R. N. 1995: *Religion and Devotion in Europe c.1215–c.1515*. Cambridge: Cambridge University Press.

Tolley, Bruce 1995: *Pastors and Parishioners in Württemberg during the Late Reformation 1581–1626*. Stanford, CA: Stanford University Press.

Tracy, James D. 1999: *Europe's Reformations, 1450–1650*. Lanham, MD: Rowman & Littlefield.

Tüchle, Hermann 1971: 'The Peace of Augsburg: New Order or Lull in the Fighting.' In Henry J. Cohn (ed.), *Government in Reformation Europe 1520–1560*. London: Macmillan, 145–65.

Vogler, Bernard 1981a: 'Die Entstehung der protestantischen Volksfrömmigkeit in der rheinischen Pfalz zwischen 1555 und 1619,' *Archiv für Reformationsgeschichte*, 72, 158–96.

Vogler, Bernard 1981b: *Le monde germanique et helvétique à l'époque des réformes 1517–1618*, vol. 2. Paris: Société d'édition d'enseignement supérieur.

Volger, Günther 1988: 'Imperial City Nuremberg 1524–1525: The Reform Movement in Transition.' In R. Po-Chia Hsia (ed.), *The German People and the Reformation*. Ithaca, NY: Cornell University Press, 33–50.

Vogler, Günther 1998: 'Erwartung – Enttäuschung – Befriedigung. Reformatorischer Umbruch in der Reichsstadt Nürnberg.' In Stephen E. Buckwalter and Bernd Moeller (eds), *Die frühe Reformation in Deutschland als Umbruch*. Gütersloh: Gütersloher Verlagshaus, 381–406.

Wallmann, Johannes 1992: 'Lutherische Konfessionalisierung – ein Überblick.' In Hans-Christoph Rublack (ed.), *Die lutherische Konfessionalisierung in Deutschland*. Gütersloh: Güterloher Verlagshaus, 33–53.

Wandel, Palmer Lee 1995: *Voracious Idols and Violent Hands. Iconoclasm in Zurich, Strasbourg, and Basel*. Cambridge: Cambridge University Press.

Warmbrunn, Paul 1983: *Zwei Konfessionen in einer Stadt. Das Zusammenleben von Katholiken und Protestanten in den paritätischen Reichsstädten Augsburg, Biberach, Ravensburg und Dinkelsbühl von 1548 bis 1648*. Wiesbaden: Franz Steiner.

Wartenberg, Günther 1988: *Landesherrschaft und Reformation. Moritz von Sachsen und die albertinische Kirchenpolitik bis 1546*. Weimar: Hermann Böhlaus.

Wiesner, Mary 1993: *Women and Gender in Early Modern Europe*. Cambridge: Cambridge University Press.

Williams, George Huntston 1962: *The Radical Reformation*. Philadelphia: Westminster Press.

Wilson, Peter 1999: *The Holy Roman Empire 1495–1806*. London: Macmillan Press.

Wittmann, Reinhard 1999: *Geschichte des deutschen Buchhandels*, 2nd edn. Munich: C. H. Beck.

Wohlfeil, Rainer 1982: *Einführung in die Geschichte der deutschen Reformation*. Munich: C. H. Beck.

Wolgast, Eike 1980: *Die Religionsfrage als Problem des Widerstandsrecht im 16. Jahrhundert*. Heidelberg: Carl Winter.

Wolgast, Eike 1990: 'Formen landesfürstlicher Reformation in Deutschland. Kursachsen-Württemberg/Brandenburg – Kurpfalz.' In Leif Grane and Kai Horby (eds), *Die dänische Reformation vor ihrem internationalen Hintergrund*. Göttingen: Vandenhoeck & Ruprecht, 57–90.

Wolgast, Eike 1995: *Hochstift und Reformation. Studien zur Geschichte der Reichskirche zwischen 1517 und 1648*. Stuttgart: Franz Steiner.

Wolgast, Eike 1997: 'Die Reformation im Herzogtum Mecklenburg und das Schicksal der Kirchenausstattungen.' In Johann Michael

Fritz (ed.), *Die bewahrende Kraft des Luthertums*. Regensburg: Schnell & Steiner, 54–70.

Wolgast, Eike 1998: 'Die deutschen Territorialfürsten und die frühe Reformation.' In Stephen E. Buckwalter and Bernd Moeller (eds), *Die frühe Reformation in Deutschland als Umbruch*. Gütersloh: Gütersloher Verlagshaus, 407–34.

Zeeden, Ernst Walter 1954: *The Legacy of Luther*, trans. Ruth Mary Bethell. London: Hollis and Carter.

Zeeden, Ernst Walter 1985: *Konfessionsbildung: Studien zur Reformation, Gegenreformation und katholischen Reform*. Stuttgart: Klett-Cotta.

Ziegler, Walter 1992: 'Bayern.' In Anton Schindling and Walter Ziegler (eds), *Die Territorien des Reichs im Zeitalter der Reformation und Konfessionalisierung*, vol. 1. Münster: Aschendorff, 56–71.

Ziegler, Walter 1997: 'Altgläubige Territorien im Konfessionalisierungsprozess.' In Anton Schindling and Walter Ziegler (eds), *Die Territorien des Reichs im Zeitalter der Reformation und Konfessionalisierung*, vol. 7. Münster: Aschendorff, 67–90.

Zimmermann, Günther 1985: 'Die Einführung des landesherrlichen Kirchenregiments,' *Archiv für Reformationsgeschichte*, 76, 146–68.

Index